The PALEOASTRONOMY SERIES: Volume 2

I0454796

ROAR OF THE TEMPESTS

A Dialogue

TIMOTHY J. STEPHANY

ISBN-13: 978-1475231908
ISBN-10: 1475231903

Printed in the United States of America by Createspace

http://www.timothyjstephany.com

To the memory of my father

books by TIMOTHY J. STEPHANY

The Paleoastronomy Series:

    The Eden Enigma: A Dialogue

    Roar of the Tempests: A Dialogue

    The Death of King David: A Dialogue

    The Zodiac Mysteries

    Blood & Incest: The Unholy Beginning of the Universe

The Gilgamesh Cycle

Enuma Elish: The Babylonian Creation Epic

The Holy Bible Revealed I: Genesis through Kings with Sources

The Holy Bible Revealed II: Compositional History

The Yahweh Document: The Holy Bible's First Edition

The Levi Document: The Earliest Biblical Source

The Sources Bible: Genesis through Kings (ASV)

Preface

A successful work of philosophical discourse speaks for itself. *Roar of the Tempests: A Dialogue* is at first glance a study of comparative mythology, but this comes to be merely a mechanism for explaining the fundamental origins of religious ideas. The dialogue is specifically concerned with heroic demon slayer, yet its scope is far more broad and profound. It explicates matters that have thus far remained hidden from the awareness of modern people and escaped the notice of modern scholarship, and both the subject and contents have never before been published.

A great deal has been done to make this work accessible to someone little familiar with the terms of astronomy or the characters of mythology, while providing a sufficient amount of information to create for itself a sufficient scientific context.

An esoteric work is in need, at times, of a system of conventions so as to clarify statements, impart additional information, and provide translations for names which arise from a diversity of languages. Thus as an aid to the reader the contents have been supplemented throughout with parenthetical comments: in instances where a translation is given it is shown in single quotes, while italics is used for an original foreign word or a non-word (such as a syllable or prefix). When a technical or unfamiliar foreign word is given within the text it is also italicized, at least when it first appears.

In other instances there are provided hypothesized names, which do not emerge from any source but are derived from a blend of two or more other names. Within the text these are represented in bold-capitals. The following table summarizes each of these notations with examples.

Additional information	(ocean god)
Translation	('little bear')
Original foreign word or non-word	(*'hvit'*)
Technical word or foreign word	*equinox*
Hypothesized god or goddess name	**EUROPE**

Heavenly objects are given in lower-case, such as 'sun' and 'moon' when such a reference is to them as they appear from the earth. This applies, for example, in instances of the body's apparent motion, such as the perception of a 'sunset' or the sun being in 'decline' during the year (for clearly our Sun does not ever go beneath the Earth, nor does the Sun circle about the Earth). This usage is applied even when a god represents the body in question. In addition, every formally recognized constellation, star name, and planet is given in italics throughout the text, with all other star patterns being referred to as *asterisms*.

As for the dialogue itself, it takes place at an unspecified time and place at the end of the mid-summer festival, after the victuals have been downed, where the final participants of the pursuit games have lately abandoned their sport, and the varied activities of the day have come to an end. Thaeo has met up with the youth Epitheus and together they have settled at the house of Stephanos, until it grows late and all the rest have gone. The remaining three have gathered upon the porch in view of the sea's inlet to take in the still night air and begin to consider what might be a worthy way to take advantage of the time yet left to them upon such a dreamy evening.

ROAR OF THE TEMPESTS

Persons of the Dialogue: *Thaeo* & *Epitheus*

CHAPTER 1

Thaeo: One could believe that nothing is wanting upon an evening such as this, imparting a peaceful repose fit for musing. Now that the wind has changed a gentle breeze off the water has cooled the temper of the air, while wafting in the fragrance of blossoms from the trees which line the river bank. And waters, placidly rippling in reflected moonlight, seek out the mist-enshrouded headland, before passing from here into the sea's enchanted inlet. It makes a fine location if we were to choose to spend it in idle conversation; or we might well do better by weaving from its inspiration some inventive incantation, or do you have something better in mind, Epitheus?

Epitheus: If we might occupy ourselves at this time however we wished my own preference would be to pick up from where we left off when we were having our previous discussion.[*] I mean the one we had a few months back in the sanctuary garden, when Soleos concluded by telling us he had come up with something which had made the discussion suddenly clear to him. And I have been so eager since then to learn of what he might have meant.

Thaeo: So I too, Epitheus. And though I was very much expecting that Soleos would remain with us this evening, while being present for the regal repast, the lure of tranquil slumber, sad to say, caught up with him. And having seen his friends escorting him back to his abode so that he might find his bed before the setting of the sun, you and I, friend, seem to be distinctly out of luck in that regard.

But the evening's festive ambiance seems to have claimed a healthy number of victims, so that only the three of us now remain. And although it appears that we have just breached the midnight hour, I see no reason to retire as of yet, provided Stephanos is willing to bear our company for a bit longer.

Epitheus: Then I would like to ask you Thaeo if at any time since then you might have been privy to what Soleos had discovered?

---

[*] See *The Eden Enigma: A Dialogue*

Thaeo: We have conversed since then on several occasions, and a few at great length which lasted well into the night, since once the conversation begins he is so characteristically inclined to pursue it unto its absolute completion. Though he rather wished to recall for us the many accounts of the voyages of Abrantius, for Soleos had learned much about his travels through the in-laws of his brother Manaos, who are a family descended from that illustrious adventurer.

Thus having occupied our conversations he never once diverged so as to divulge to us anything about the matter relating to our prior conversation. But the reason for this, as I understand it, is that he has done so to give himself ample time to mull the matter over, and collect what he might need in order to understand it more fully before bringing it to our attention. For I believe that this question has sparked a bit of a fever in the old boy, as though he thought he was truly on to something.

Yet despite this regret, I did have a chance to speak with the famed Phaedo concerning it, and he did have something to say. And this since has stirred my thinking and perhaps it is now appropriate to bring the matter to your attention, being that we have here access to the numerous volumes of Stephanos at hand. So I can briefly recall some of the discussion I had with Phaedo that led to my further thoughts concerning the matter, and then we might see if we cannot expound upon them in order to feed our residual curiosity.

Epitheus: Please do, Thaeo, I would be glad to hear it.

Thaeo: Then I will begin by saying that Phaedo at the time proved to be very eager to relate something, which he had recently recollected after the conclusion of our previous conversation. And this tale I will attempt to recount as fully as I am able, although I have it only as it has transfixed itself into my memory, since he told it to me a few months back, and shortly after our previous discourse. And although the composition with its stirring refrains have long since abandoned me, I am sure that I might still relate the basics of it, having mulled it over in my mind from time to time since then, so that I imagine it will not prove too difficult to tell it without incurring abundant anomalies.

So I must begin by going back to what we had been discussing at that time, in our prior discussion, when Soleos was present with us.

4

Since, at that time by his guidance, we found that the 'Great Square' of (the constellation) *Pegasus* was also a figure known (in Mesopotamia) as the 'Great One', and associated with the (Mesopotamian) god of water Enki (Ea). And the story told by Phaedo pertains to this very god's dealings with a particular goddess named Ninhursag ('lady grassland'), who in this tale acts the role of the mother goddess.* It was at a time when that god (Enki), given an opportunity, came to her and, hiding his intentions for a time, first attempted to woo her. But when she resisted him violently, he was encouraged to grab and hold her fast, and then to overpower her, ravishing the lady there in her own place; the outcome of which is that she became pregnant through this and in due course gave birth to a pair of daughters who were named Ninsar ('lady of green') and Ninkurra ('lady of plenty').

Yet Enki remained far from satisfied with Ninhursag and once his daughters were of a ripe age, he being so bountifully lustful, could not resist the nubile allure of his teenage daughters. With Ninhursag nowhere to be found he went to where they were cavorting and raped both girls with great enthusiasm. The result of this was that Ninkurra became pregnant and in due course gave birth to a daughter named Uttu ('spinner').

True to his character Enki was unable to withhold his desires for his own young granddaughter and when again the opportunity arose he went into this modest virgin, forcing his fertility within the ruptured teen. Yet Uttu did not become pregnant from this because, soon after, she went to her grandmother (Ninhursag) who instead saved the precious girl by bringing forth Enki's semen from her womb, which she then disposed of by discarding it over the surface of the earth.

And from the fertility of Enki's rejected semen,† seven fruitful plants grew up from the ground. While Ninhursag and her girls carefully avoided them, they proved to be so succulent and appealing to the eye that Enki himself, who did not know their origin, consumed every one of them, and thus as a consequence impregnated himself by his own semen. This proved itself to be a bit of bad

---

* Ninhursag is also known as Nintu ('lady of birth') and Ki ('earth'), who is the same as the mother goddess Mami.

† The word for semen (*'ab'*) also means 'father' and 'serpent'.

5

business for him, for he lacked a womb and thus had no place in which to grow his children.

So it was after he had experienced much trauma from this that Ninhursag took pity upon him and gathered Enki's semen out from him and into herself, from which in course of time she gave birth to eight gods, each being responsible for healing a different part of the body. The youngest to be born from her was a girl named Ninti, whose name means 'lady rib' (or 'lady life'),[1] and who also received the title of 'mother of all living' which as you know is a title she shares with the first woman Eve, who is likewise known as 'the rib'.

Epitheus: Yes.

Thaeo: And Ninhursag is goddess of the steppes or grasslands which is called (in Sumerian) *edin*. Thus we find doppelgangers for both Eve the 'mother of all' and **EDEN**, the goddess of the garden.

Epitheus: Truly.

Thaeo: This similarity is what made him eager to bring it to our attention, and after I looked into the matter further I found that the epithet 'mother of all living' was also shared by a Hurrian mother goddess by the name of Kheba (Heba), which is clearly of the same form as the (Hebrew) name for Eve ('*Khavvah*').[*]

Epitheus: Indeed.

Thaeo: And too it seemed to me that the name of Kheba was also not far from that of Sheba or Shiva, whom we had reckoned before was likewise the 'Great Square' of *Pegasus*.[†]

Epitheus: Splendidly put.

Thaeo: Thus we may have found enough to cause us to associate Kheba with Eve, both through the name 'Khavvah' and also because both were granted the epithet of 'mother of all living', which was

---

[*] The Hurrians were a people of the Ancient Near East who lived in Northern Mesopotamia and adjacent regions during the Bronze Age.
[†] See *The Eden Enigma: A Dialogue*

6

also shared by Ninti from the Mesopotamian myth that Phaedo told of.

Epitheus: Well done.

Thaeo: And further, this Hurrian goddess (Kheba) might herself be related to the Mesopotamian goddess Kubaba, who is depicted as either holding a mirror or pomegranate within her hand, and was known to be a tavern keeper like the goddess Siduri.[2]

This goddess (Kheba) was known among the Romans as Cybebe, whom the Greeks called Cybele, the 'Great Mother' or 'Mountain Mother' born from the holy springs on Mount Ida. Thus she is, for this reason, similar to (the Greek goddess of birth) Eileithyia. And we might regard that this goddess (Kubaba or Cybele) could also be identified with precisely the same asterism of '*Gula*' ('Great Square' of *Pegasus*).[*]

Epitheus: It would appear so.

Thaeo: And yet Cybele is merely another name for the goddess Rhea, the wife of Cronos, who is equivalent to the Roman goddess Ops, the mother of Jupiter, and also known as 'great mother' ('*magna mater*') and 'mother of the gods'. Thus the lion, as supreme beast of earth, was not surprisingly her sacred animal; two of whom crouched beneath her throne and were to be seen pulling her chariot.[†]

Moreover, Cybele is to have been born from out of the ground with both male and female organs. As the story goes, it was the sky god (Zeus) who during a fitful sleep allowed some of his seed to fall upon the ground which then grew into a being who possessed both sex organs. This being was Cybele, also known as Agdistis. And the gods were so overcome by the sheer power of Agdistis that they severed the male organ and it is said that from it grew an almond tree in full ripeness.

Epitheus: Intriguing.

---

[*] Khumba ('water jar') is the Hindu name for the Zodiacal constellation of *Aquarius*. (Olcott 2004: 32)
[†] She likewise shares some connection to the goddess Demeter, who sometimes went by the name of Cybele.

7

Thaeo: Though more so we might consider that Kubaba was also known to be the protectress of the Hittite city of Carchemish (on the upper Euphrates). And it seems to me that the name of this city truly bears a resemblance to the name of the Mesopotamian hero-king Gilgamesh, just as the name of the goddess Kubaba is like that of the principal adversary Gilgamesh faces upon his quest, the demon Humbaba, the dreaded guardian of the Pine Forest.

Epitheus: Truly, it does.

Thaeo: This is like the Idaean mother goddess (Cybele), who ruled over the forests and mountains, being as she was the mistress of wild animals, especially lions. And there is far more to tell about this particular hero-king, for there is a great deal said about him in the scrolls which constitute what is known as the 'Gilgamesh Cycle' ('The Epic of Gilgamesh'), if you would wish to hear of it I would gladly relate it this evening.

Epitheus: Certainly, as I have never heard it before.

Thaeo: Then I will tell you something of him first, but as the epic is of great length, so that recounting the entirety of it would alone occupy us for the remainder of the night, though undoubtedly time agreeably spent, I will confine myself merely to what relates to the matter at hand. By which I mean to only tell those parts which speak of the confrontation between Gilgamesh and the demon Humbaba. As the epic begins, it says,

> Of him who gazed upon the Abyss, which underlies the world,
> Who came to know all things, and gained wisdom in everything,
> Of Gilgamesh who gazed upon the Deep underlying the world,
> Who came to know all things, and gained wisdom in everything,
> When he set out and explored the many lands of the vast world
> He who experienced everything and came to gain high wisdom,
> He found what had been kept secret, he uncovered the obscured
> And returned with stories even of the era before the Great Flood
> After travelling long distances, in the end he tired and refrained
> And chiseled all of his hard-won deeds upon a memorial stone [3]

> It reveals the story of a man who endured, Gilgamesh by name
> He was a far better king than any, a warlord of huge proportion

He was of mighty form born in Uruk, a raging wild bull of a man
When he marched he walked before his people to lead the way
And stood behind them, lending support and encouragement
Like the firm meshing of a net, he provided security to his men
Like the wild flood-waters, strong enough to topple stone walls,

He was the ideal strong man, Gilgamesh, son of Lugalbanda
Also being the child of the high and untamed wild cow Ninsun
Gilgamesh is the name of him who was second to none in deeds
Who made passes through mountains and into them dug pits
He made his way across the ocean until he reached the dawn
He set eyes upon the edge of the world, looking for eternal life
By his strength he went distances to find faraway Utnapishtim
He restored the flood-spoiled holy places to their former glory
Establishing for the people the holy rituals of the mystic order
Not one among the kings of the world could compare to him
Who can rightfully avow himself as high king but Gilgamesh!
For he was marked at birth to acquire for himself great fame[4]

Then when we reach the section where the confrontation is about to take place, Gilgamesh and his friend Enkidu are debating the perils involved in seeking out the demon Humbaba. But Gilgamesh is intent on continuing and so they outfit themselves with bronze axes and swords strapped on with leather belts. Then it continues,

Gilgamesh spoke to the young men of Uruk, the elders listened,
"Hear me, you young men of Uruk, who know the lure of fame
I remain firm in my purpose, on the road to Humbaba will I go
I am willing to face an unknown danger, to ride a forsaken path
As I have settled upon my course, rather give me your blessings
That I might yet see your faces again when all perils are past
When I return in glorious triumph through the gates of Uruk
That at some future time I might again see the New Year's fair
And I might join with you in the celebration of the New Year
Let the festival procession commence, may it spread joy to all
Let loud cries of 'Halleluiah' resound before the son of Ninsun."

Then Enkidu advised the elders and heroic young men of Uruk,
"Tell Gilgamesh that he must not make his way to the Pine Forest
The journey is far too dangerous for a mortal man, he would die
The one who guards the Pine Forest, Ellil made terrible to man
His voice roars like the storm-surge, his speech is a baleful fire,
His breath is death to man, he can hear as far as sixty leagues,

9

Through the depths of the wood, who could trespass his forest?
For surely Humbaba is second in power only to Adad himself
Who even among the gods would be able to stand against him?
The one who guards the Pine Forest, Ellil made terrible to man
Anyone who found his way through would surely meet his end!"

After listening, the wise men of Uruk rose to advise Gilgamesh,
"Gilgamesh, you are still young and although you are now eager,
You have no idea what adversities you will find upon your quest
Humbaba's voice roars like the storm-surge, his speech is fire,
His breath is death to man, he can hear as far as sixty leagues,
Through the depths of the wood, who could trespass his forest?
For surely Humbaba is second in power only to Adad himself,
Who even among the gods would be able to stand against him?
Ellil has made his sentinel Humbaba to be a terror to mankind
Anyone who found his way through would surely meet his end!"

Gilgamesh listened to every word the wise men of Uruk spoke,
Then he looked over at his friend, making a wide smile at him
"So do you think that this is how I should be making speeches
Is it right that I too ought to be so fearful that I step backward?"
Then Gilgamesh spoke to the wise men of Uruk, to the elders,
"Hear me, you wise men of Uruk, who know the way of things,
I remain firm in my purpose, on the road to Humbaba will I go
I am willing to face an unknown danger, to ride a forsaken path
As I have settled upon my course, rather give me your blessings
That I might return, once again riding through the gates of Uruk."

Steadfast in his resolve the elders now determined to advise him,
"Heed us that you might come back to the safe haven of Uruk!
Gilgamesh, be not so bold to trust only in your physical might
After giving your eyes time to judge, trust in your first stroke
He who leads on the path will be the one who saves his friend
The one well familiar with the ways will be his brother's savior
Thus allow Enkidu to lead the way, he's familiar with the routes
He knows how to fight and can provide you good battle advice
So let Enkidu be a guardian to his friend and preserve your life
That you might come back safely, to return and satisfy brides,
So that we who advise might rely upon you to remain our king,
So that when you return to be king we might be your advisors."

Gilgamesh spoke to Enkidu, so that his voice might be heard,
"My friend, let us go to the grand palace of the queen Ninsun,

10

She is one who is filled with wisdom, all-seeing, all-knowing,
She will set the strong foundation of insight beneath our feet."
Thus they took hands and went off to Ninsun's grand palace
Gilgamesh rose and went into the presence of his wise mother,
"Mother, I am firm that I will travel upon the road to Humbaba
I am willing to face an unknown danger, to ride a forsaken path
Until the day comes when, after a long and perilous journey,
I will enter the Pine Forest and vanquish Humbaba, the terrible,
To wipe out from the world forever a demon Shamash despises."[5]

Ninsun then prays to Shamash (the sun) and provides a burnt offering to him, making appeals to the god's wife Aya that Shamash might strike at Humbaba with his mighty tempests, the thirteen winds, so as to permit the weapons of Gilgamesh to bite. Then afterwards Ninsun takes Enkidu as her foster son, thus making him a brother to Gilgamesh. The two brothers prepare by making oblations and promising to make out of wood from the Pine Forest a door for the temple of Shamash, if they prove victorious. After completing their preparations they set out on their journey to the Pine Forest.

After going a distance of 20 leagues they ate what food they had
After going for 30 leagues they stopped to camp for the night
Then during the day they went on until they had gone 50 leagues
In the duration of new moon to full moon and three days more,
Arrived in Lebanon, digging a hole in the ground before the sun
They refilled their water-skins and poured out a libation to him
Gilgamesh went by himself up the mountain with an offering,
Leaving flour for the spirits of the mountain, then prayed to it,
"O mountain, send to me a dream and one full of good fortune!"

Enkidu took care of things for Gilgamesh, erecting a dream tent
Such that when a wind-devil entered, he covered over the door
And forced it to lie flat within a circle he'd scored on the ground
Setting it down like wild barley, he hacked it, spilling its blood
Gilgamesh himself sat there resting his chin upon his knees,
Until sleep, which spreads itself over humanity, overcame him
In the middle of the watch he awoke and told his companion,
"My brother, if you did not call me then why am I now awake?
If you did not touch me, then why is it I am in such distress?
If a divinity did not go past, then why is my flesh quivering?
Friend, I had a dream and it was a dream that was disturbing
We were standing at the foot of a mountain, looming over us,

11

Then the mountain peak came crashing down, and buried us
In relationship to its size we were like flies compared to a bull."
He who understood, the one who was born in the wilderness,
Enkidu heard and then interpreted the dream for Gilgamesh,
"My friend your dream is a propitious one, of great importance,
For the mountain that you saw falling on us was not Humbaba,
Rather we will strike him down and cast his body into a cesspit
When dawn rises we will hear the favorable words of Shamash."[6]

Enkidu interprets more dreams for Gilgamesh, likewise interpreted to
mean that they will be triumphant against Humbaba. But Enkidu has
a dream of his own which forebodes evil and doom, and thus doubts
that they might now prevail without coming to their deaths. And the
implications of this dream sap Enkidu's desire for further adventure
and combat.

"How could I now enter the Pine Forest and cut through a trail,
How could I open a way when my arms are now so weakened?"
Gilgamesh spoke to Enkidu so that his voice might be heard,
"Why friend do we now speak of hesitation like the cowardly?
We still might first cross over all the mountains, then we'll see
Before we face the Pine Forest and need to start felling trees,
My brother, you know conflict and have learned to fight well
You have protected your skin with herbs that you might not fall
You will shine like the sun in a double-thick Mantle of Brilliance
You will give out a war cry akin to the crash of kettle drums
You will find weakness will no longer be lingering in your limbs
You will find weakness will no longer be lingering at your loins
Come with me, take my hand, friend, and we shall go together
Your heart and soul will soon be eager for the fever of battle,
Do not think at a time like this of death, but think only of life
Man is both worthy and able in battle, looking out for his friend
For if he moves ahead of him and defends him, he will be safe
And by doing such will have secured fame for all of eternity."

So encouraged now by these words, the two arrived together
Merely looking out from where they stood, at a loss for words
They remained there at the forest's edge, just gazing upon it
They regarded the sheer height of the pines and the approach
The trail that Humbaba had made when he went to and fro
The ways were well worn and the road was exceptionally good
From there they could see Pine Mountain, home of the gods
The trees were abundant right up the sides of the mountain

Casting a fine shade which filled their spirits with serene joy
And with rampant undergrowth twining through the wood[7]

They enter the forest, and after they confront a band of lions together at the mountain pass a newfound courage arises after defeating them. Gilgamesh assures Enkidu that not one or the other but both of them working together will surely defeat the demon Humbaba. They begin felling trees, and Humbaba first becomes aware of their presence by the sound of the crashing timber as it resonates through the depths of the wood all the way to his lair. The two heroes continue on through until they reach his dwelling and there confront the demon face to face.

"This fool should ask himself why he brought this brute to me,
His friend is a shrimp who does not even know his own father!
So small, in fact, that to me he is nothing more than a turtle
Who did not even take his mother's milk, thus why take notice
Even if I devoured him I think it would hardly satisfy my hunger
Why then, Gilgamesh, did you bring him within my reach?
While Enkidu stands there watching and waiting like a bandit
I would tear my teeth through his neck and sever his windpipe
Leaving his trunk for lions to gorge upon and birds to peck at."[8]

Then Gilgamesh attacks, but is at first unsuccessful against Humbaba, and so he turns in appeal to his guardian Shamash (the sun) who appears and wages war against the demon, conjuring the force of the thirteen winds so as to weaken the demon that the weapons of Gilgamesh and Enkidu might prevail against him. Now recognizing that his life is at risk Humbaba appeals to Gilgamesh's own greed, with promises of fine woody treasures. Then Enkidu in turn appeals to the hero that he not listen to anything the monster might say or promise him. In return Humbaba turns his attention to Enkidu.

"You now know the character of my forest and of my environs
You now know all its secrets, but here's what I should have done
Apprehended and killed you as soon as you came into my forest
Leaving your trunk for lions to gorge upon and birds to peck at
Yet Enkidu, it is now within your power to save me from death
So will you not plea to Gilgamesh so that he might spare me?"
Enkidu spoke to Gilgamesh so that his voice might be heard,

13

"Friend, bring him to his final end, pulverize him, save my life
Be slayer of Humbaba, the demon guardian of the Pine Forest!
Secure your victory before supreme Ellil hears what's going on,
In case the gods, in retribution, unleash their fury against us:
Ellil in Nippur and Shamash in Sippar; but build a memorial
That eternally recalls the slaying of Humbaba by Gilgamesh!"[9]

Humbaba raised his voice to be heard, to speak a curse to them,
"Neither of you two will live long, nor experience hoary old age,
And Gilgamesh is the one who must bury his friend, Enkidu!"
Enkidu spoke to Gilgamesh so that his voice might be heard,
"Friend, I speak words to you which you do not appear to hear,
Even while the curses he flings are still echoing through the air
Try now to force those curses of his back into his own mouth!"
Gilgamesh listened to the words that were spoken by his friend
Then at once pulled from his belt the dagger he kept at his side
And Gilgamesh gave him a severe stroke, penetrating his neck
Enkidu struck him deep in the gut until his entrails gushed out
From the wound of his severed head, a spring came surging up
Gilgamesh then collected the head, and took its teeth as a prize
A flood of gory blood cascaded down the side of the mountain
A rush of red spilled streaming down the side of the mountain[10]

This marked the end of the demon's life, then Enkidu and Gilgamesh
set out to fulfill their promise to Shamash, to find a tree fit for a vast
door to decorate his temple. So Gilgamesh then cuts down a number
of trees while Enkidu begins the process of selecting the perfect one.

"My friend, I have found and downed a fully-grown pine tree
The crown of the tree being so lofty that it even touched the sky
From it I will fashion a door that is six poles high and two wide
Its post will be a cubit thick, its hinges carved from a single stem
It will go upon the Euphrates to Nippur, and Nippur to Sippar,
Then once in Sippar it will be taken to the temple of Shamash."
Then they bound together a raft, carrying it down to the water
Enkidu boarded carrying the tree he had chosen for Shamash
Gilgamesh embarked hauling the head of the demon Humbaba[11]

The cycle continues as a now ardent Ishtar offers herself to the
victorious Gilgamesh, but when he rejects her she appeals to her
mighty father Anu (god of heaven) to send down the Bull of Heaven
against them, whom the two heroes then destroy. As a consequence

14

of their defeating this foe the gods claim Enkidu's life in return, who soon dies of a wasting disease. Gilgamesh, overcome by grief and hopelessness, and girded only in a lion's skin, wanders hopelessly the far-reaches of the earth searching for the land of Dilmun to find Utnapishtim, the man who escaped the Great Flood and who was the only mortal to have ever attained eternal life. Thus these events all lead Gilgamesh towards his ultimate quest for everlasting life.

Epitheus: Well done, Thaeo.

Thaeo: I must say that this hero's confrontation with the demon Humbaba is also quite similar to another tale that I am well familiar with, being that told by the Greeks of the Gorgon named Medusa. Thus, if you would like me to proceed and relate the exploits of the hero Perseus I would be glad to do so.

Epitheus: Please, I would love to hear it.

CHAPTER 2

Thaeo: Very well, then let me begin by recalling what had befallen Medusa prior to her encounter with Perseus, for at an earlier time she had fallen afoul of the virgin goddess Athena. This had happened because Poseidon in the form of a horse had met secretly with Medusa and made love to the flaxen beauty in the goddess's own sacred garden.[*] Then catching them in the act the bright-eyed goddess could hardly help but eavesdrop upon the passionate lovers and overheard the woman blatantly declaring herself superior in beauty to the garden's goddess herself. This was more than the virgin divinity could stand and blooming with vain rage she punished the lovely woman by bestowing upon her the hideous visage of a Gorgon, so that she would henceforth be deemed hideous both to mortals and immortals alike, but even more so that like them her appearance was so grotesque that it turned any that might look upon her into stone.[†] So I will tell you what a Gorgon's appearance is: they had hands of bronze and wings of gold, their heads were topped by a coil of snakes, while a pair of them too hung from their belts, and they displayed within their mouths two great tusks like a boar's.[‡]

This Athena, in her bitter bid for vengeance, deemed an appropriate punishment for Medusa and thus cut her off from all humanity. In doing so she was driven to madness by her misfortune and went to live in the only place she could, the cave beyond the western Ocean where the two immortal Gorgons lived, whose names were Stheno and Euryale. Although they had the same grotesque appearance as she did, at least among them she found companionship, and they did not turn their own kind to stone as was the fate of any mortal who might gaze upon them.

---

[*] Poseidon in the form of a horse or bird consorted with Medusa.

[†] Serpents were believed to have the power to mesmerize their victims, thus turning them to stone (see Howey 1955: 194, who dedicates an entire chapter to this phenomenon). And we still use the word 'petrify' to signify becoming motionless like a stone.

[‡] The description of the Armenian demons known as Als, who inhabited wet and shadowy places, is quite similar to the Gorgon. (Ananikian 2010: 92)

Gorgon image taken from Attic vase, where upon the original it is shown in the process of being beheaded.

Chavin god of the staffs, from Peru.[12]*

And so I will begin now telling of Perseus by going back to mention the son of Oceanus and Tethys who was the river Inachos in the land of Argos, and he by Oceanus' daughter Melia had two sons Phoroneus and Aigialeus. Aigialeus had no children but his brother Phoroneus by the nymph Teledice had two children, Apis and Niobe. Apis was also the god named Serapis while Niobe had a son by Zeus named Argos. Argos himself had four sons by Evadne named Ecbasos, Peiras, Epidauros, and Criasos. Ecbasos had a son Agenor, who himself had a son also named Argos who was known as the 'all-seeing' Argos because he had more than two eyes and could thus remain awake at all times. Argos by Ismene had a son Iasos who himself had a child named Io.

When Io was still very youthful and quite charming the girl was sought by mighty Zeus, and though having gone to the young girl, as he wished to seduce her, it did not escape the notice of his wife Hera that he had been often and cheerfully leaving home, and so upon one occasion she followed after him. Only Zeus recognized Hera's

---

* Similar to an Andean god of thunder depicted in Tiwanakan, whose two staffs represent thunderbolts. (see Krupp (1991), p. 115, Ill.)

presence soon enough to transform the lovely girl into a white cow. Yet despite Zeus's denials Hera remained suspicious and took the cow away from him, having it tied to an olive tree in the sacred grove of the Mycenaeans under the watchful eyes of the eternally awake Argos.

It was Hermes who went at the request of Zeus to steal the cow back, but his intentions were made known when they were betrayed to Argos by the hawk Hierax. Yet Hermes, after lulling all of Argos' eyes to sleep with his flute playing, killed him there with a stone, and thus the cow went free. After much wandering it ended up in the land of Egypt, which was called the land of Melampodes ('black feet'), where Io regained her prior form of a sweet enchantress and there on the banks of the Nile gave birth to a son named Epaphos.[*] But Hera, now bent on revenge, had the child stolen away from her and so Io went off in search of him into the land of Syria, after she divined that he was being cared for there by the wife of the king of Byblos. So having recovered her son she then returned to Egypt where she married the Egyptian pharaoh Telegonos.

Apollodorus tells us that after she returned to Egypt Io set up a shrine in honor of the goddess Demeter, who was known there as Isis; while Io herself was reckoned to be the identical goddess. And considering the story concerning Demeter's search for her daughter Persephone and Isis' search for her husband Osiris, they seem to be quite similar to Io's search for her son Epaphos.

Epitheus: Indeed, they do.

Thaeo: This is everything there is to say concerning the maiden Io, but after Telegonos ruled in Egypt then Epaphos became pharaoh in his place and he married Memphis, who was a daughter of the Nile. And they had a child Libya who by Poseidon had twin sons named Agenor and Belos. Agenor left Egypt for Phoenicia but Belos remained in Egypt where he married Anchinoe, who was also a daughter of the Nile, and he had twin sons named Aigyptos and Danaos along with two other sons named Cepheus and Phineus. These latter two will become relevant later in relation to the story of

---

[*] This transformation from young woman to cow might be the transition from the 'woman in the moon', visible when the moon is full, to the 'horns' visible when in its crescent phase. (Staal 1988: 273)

Perseus, while we will follow for now the lines of Aigyptos and Danaos. It was Aigyptos who named the land of the Melampodes, which he had conquered, 'Egypt' after himself; while Danaos, after a conflict arose over the Egyptian throne, escaped to the land of Argos where he acquired the throne there and renamed the people of that country the 'Danaans'.

Aigyptos had fifty sons by many wives and Danaos had fifty daughters by numerous wives, so Aigyptos sent his sons to Argos to marry the daughters of Danaos and all were paired up so that there was one daughter for every son. Yet after each had gotten his bride, and they had held the celebratory feast, when they went to bed that night each of the girls brought out from her robe a concealed dagger, which had been furnished for them by Danaos, and thus with it struck her husband dead within his bed, and used it then to cut off his head. Every one of them was killed by his new bride but for one son of Aigyptos named Lynceus who was spared by his wife Hypermnestra because he had not taken her to bed on their wedding night. The heads of the forty-nine sons were then collected and buried at Lerna.

Lynceus succeeded Danaos as king of Argos and himself had twin sons named Acrisios and Proitos, who were at war with one another even while they were yet within the womb of their mother Aglaia. Acrisios had a daughter by Eurydice named Danae. And it was Acrisios who consulted an oracle concerning his male lineage and from the god he received word that his daughter would bear a son who would one day bring about his own death; but that he, as the Fates had decreed, mustn't do anything to cause her any bodily harm. Accepting this he lost no time in having a room constructed beneath the ground with walls, floor, and roof made of bronze, in which to keep the lovely Danae away from any man. Nevertheless it is said that almighty Zeus was yet able to penetrate through the roof as a shower of gold that fell upon her lap and by which means he impregnated her, and she in time gave birth to a son named Perseus.

When Acrisios learned of this he immediately had a wooden chest brought forth and both she and her child were forced to climb into it and he sealed them both within. Then he ordered that it be cast into the sea, which it was; but Poseidon calmed the raging waters at the request of great Zeus and so the chest drifted safely upon the waves until soon thereafter it washed ashore in the kingdom of Seriphos.

The brother of the king of these lands, a fisherman by the name of Dictys, saw the chest and pulled it out from the surf, and prying open the cover beheld the girl with her child and brought them back to his home to live with him, which is where they remained until Perseus had grown into manhood.

King Polydectes had seen Danae with his brother Dictys and became mad with desire for her. Since even now with her son fully grown she was yet in the best ripeness of her years and flourished with a divine splendor that was intoxicating even to the most cold-hearted of men. Considering her to be a fit queen for himself, he sought her out with much ardor, yet found Perseus vehemently opposed to the engagement; as by this time he had already reached the age of majority and now oversaw the affairs and care of his mother. Thus, while hiding both his burning desire for Danae and a new burning hatred for Perseus, he assembled a collection of friends under the pretence of announcing his engagement to Hippodameia, a daughter of Oinomaos. Perseus was pleased by this announcement and was so encouraged by it that, when he was given to produce a worthy crown to sanctify this union, boasted that no less than the very crown of the Gorgon's head would be a fit present to celebrate the occasion.

So soon thereafter, when all the king's men came with offerings to the girl's father in return for her hand, each brought a fine selection from among their horses. Polydectes accepted with gratitude the offerings made by each, however when Perseus came to present his own steeds the king refused them without deference and declared instead that by his very words only the Gorgon's head would provide a fitting emblem for the celebration. Perseus could not deny that these had been his own words, but he was nonetheless stricken with great grief as to how he might possibly manage to carry out the task, which all deemed not only to be extremely dangerous but also impossible for any mortal man to perform.

Yet Perseus through his father Zeus received the assistance of both Athena and Hermes, who advised him to seek out the Nymphs, who held in their possession three objects that would prove indispensible in aiding his endeavor against the dreaded Gorgons. The only ones who knew the whereabouts of these Nymphs were the Graiae ('gray ones'), the three daughters of Phorcos and Ceto, who had been old women from the day they were born, and who shared among them but one eye and one tooth. They were named Enyo, Pephredo, and Deino.

In visiting them Perseus found hospitality, but did not receive a ready answer to his question and so he quickly devised a plan that was accomplished by pulling three apples out of his bag, which he then began to juggle before them. Each was so eager to see this unusual spectacle that they all sought after the eye at once, and as they vied for it among themselves, when it was passing between them, he was able to take it into his hand. Each of the Graiae, however, thought that the other must still have it and thus they cried out for it, blaming the other for keeping it to herself. Then while they were yet embittered with each other he then offered them the apples to eat and they quickly forgot about the eye and now contended over the one tooth. So then Perseus was able to get this too into his hands, as it was being passed between them, and all the while each old woman thought one of her sisters possessed it.

So, now blind and toothless, they were unaware that Perseus had snatched both from them until he made it known that they should not fight amongst themselves since the eye and tooth were in his safe keeping, and that he would quickly return them if they would but offer to him the answer to his question and tell him the location of the Nymphs and of what items they held within their possession. The daughters of Phorcos told him that the Nymphs possessed three items that he must ask for: a pair of winged sandals, a special leather satchel called a *kibisis*, and a hat of invisibility. Thus having found out what he wished to know he duly returned the eye and tooth to them and went upon their advice to the place of the Nymphs.[*]

These Nymphs were required by Fate to surrender what they possessed to him who found them, but only if he asked plainly for the article, and being able to ask each of them only one question. If he failed to ask properly they could then claim anything of him that he then must grant, and often this meant to stay with them forever. Having located their glade, Perseus asked the first if she might give him a pair of winged sandals, which she was then forced to surrender to him; the second he asked for the *kibisis*, which was soon given to him—and they waited in anticipation of his third question, being their

---

[*] Aeschylus says that the Graiae were guardians of the Gorgons. (Pseudo-Hyginus, *Astronomica* 2.12; see Condos 1997: 158)

last opportunity to ensnare him–and of the third he asked for a hat of invisibility. Thus he attained all three prizes and, having saved his own head, outfitted himself for his contest with the Gorgons.

Using the fleet sandals Perseus flew away to the very edge of the western Ocean to the nook where the sun refused to shine; for there lived the three Gorgons. And when he arrived there he waited until he could hear that all of them were sleeping. So at this time, armed with an adamantine sickle provided to him by fleet Hermes, he entered their cave and approached them cautiously. Being aware of their ability to turn anyone who looked upon them to stone, he stepped in only looking into the polished reflection of the bronze shield given to him by the goddess Athena, until he came to be standing among them.

Searching for the one who was Medusa, the only of the three who was mortal, he took the adamantine sickle and, guided by the hand of gracious Athena, struck down at her neck and severed her head from her trunk with one stroke. At this moment there sprung from the bloody wound the winged stallion Pegasus and the golden giant Chrysaor; who were her children by the god Poseidon, and already fully grown the moment they were born. Then Perseus took the head of Medusa and stashed it within the leather satchel, and then began to make his way quietly out of their cavern. Yet the two immortal Gorgons were stirred by his trespassing and rose up; recognizing that Medusa had been struck down they sought after her murderer, but were unable to see him because he had quickly donned the cap of invisibility before making his way forth. Exiting from the mouth of their subterranean cavern, still hearing the wailing cries of distress that the Gorgons produced when beholding their fallen companion, he took flight to make his way back to his home in Seriphos.

Yet while he was flying above the ocean, he passed near the land of Ethiopia (North Africa) and on approaching its shore spied a beautiful girl chained to the coastal rocks. This had arisen from the actions of her mother Cassiopeia, wife of Cepheus the king of Ethiopia, who had boasted of her looks to the point where she claimed to possess a beauty even greater than that of the lovely Nereids (Doris and Panope) and the queen of the gods herself (Hera). Such a boast carried to the golden Nereids who upon hearing it were stricken by a fury and who thus encouraged their father Poseidon to act on their behalf. So the lord of the sea caused a great flood to rise

23

up upon the land while Ammon (Zeus), at the beckoning of Hera, sent a great sea monster to torment the city and its harbors.

The people there were suffering greatly as a result of this plague and were being starved and ruined by these assaults from the gods. And they cried out for appeasements and cast offerings into the sea, but all to no avail, until a seer was called upon to divine the suitable recompense. He prophesied from the oracle of Ammon that the offering that would deliver their city would be that of Cepheus' own daughter, the lovely Andromeda, as a sacrifice to the sea dragon. The people cried out to their king to give up his child, so he had no choice but to sacrifice his only daughter to that monster. Thus the ravishing teen Andromeda had been left there for him, bare and bound, and available for the beast's hungry cravings.

The situation had progressed thus far when Perseus had arrived upon the scene. Flying high above her he could not believe his eyes, nor did he know what land would make such a spectacle of one of their own virgin daughters. Yet perceiving such a charming maiden so stricken and helpless made his heart leap within his breast. Descending then and there to the land he inquired among the people concerning her and found that she was the daughter of King Cepheus. Perseus at once sought out the king and offered to confront the sea monster if only he would promise to present the fair girl to him as a wife. Pleased with this offer, and feeling that he had little to lose by such a bargain, the king agreed at once and each swore oaths to the other to that effect.

The outcome of this was that one could then see the young Perseus streaking to the seashore with his muscles thirsting for battle and with a heart aburst with romantic longings. Still recognizing he must yet deliver the maiden, he contrived to hide himself within a crevasse there among the tortured rocks. So when the wretched monster rose out of the turbid sea, as it passed over him he slit up the full length of its belly with the adamantine blade; though the beast progressed so far that it came within reach of the terrified girl. So Perseus leapt into the air aiming his blade at the serpent's right shoulder and struck a fearful blow that drew back its neck, before it spilled out its guts and expired upon that craggy scree. With the beast now dead Perseus emerged to free the girl from the cords that bound her to the rocks and embraced her for the first time; then leaping up flew with her back to the shore.

Now not only had Perseus been promised Andromeda's hand but the entire affair was likewise extremely pleasing to the bashful girl, who was immediately taken with her newfound hero and thus sudden plans were announced for their nuptials. However, some time before these events had taken place, Andromeda's hand had already been promised by the king to his own brother Phineus who, now that the girl was safe and sound, claimed that she was rightfully his and that the oath made to Perseus was thereby invalid. Cepheus would not heed his assertions, for in his view Phineus had left the girl to her fate upon the rocks, and thus there would be no question of her marrying him now. By divine right she was snapped from the jaws of death and thus Fate had thereby envoided all prior agreements.

As it was, this did not sit well with Phineus, who above all could not bear to see the sweetest lady in the land held within another man's arms and capture the fascination of his eyes, and so he formed a plot directed against Perseus. Yet being made aware by those loyal to the king that they were coming to attack him, Perseus quickly donned the hat of invisibility and lay that night on the floor in Andromeda's room. So when Phineus and his cohorts came to the bed of Perseus and flung off the sheets, they found themselves gazing upon the Gorgon's head, so that every one of them was instantly turned to stone.

This is not the end of the story, however, since Perseus still had to continue on his way back to Seriphos with the prize of the Gorgon's head. And when he arrived there he found the land in a state of civil war, with his mother and Dictys now seeking refuge among the altars of the gods, making their final stand against King Polydectes. So as the soldiers advanced upon that spot led by their king, Perseus emerged before them holding the Gorgon's head aloft; thus the entire company was immediately turned to stone, including Polydectes. And one might still see the ranks of soldiers turned to stone at the temple garden at Seriphos among the altars to the gods.[*]

After the defeat of Polydectes, Perseus crowned Dictys as the new king of Seriphos. Then after his exploits were completed Perseus was quick to return the sandals, satchel, and hat of invisibility to Hermes who duly returned them to the Nymphs for

---

[*] It is also said that Perseus went to the land of the Hyperboreans to slay the Gorgon, and then turned all the people upon the island (Seriphos) to stone. (Pindar, 'Pythian Ode 10'; see Verity 2008: 82)

safe-keeping. Perseus gave the Gorgon's head into the keeping of Athena, who affixed it to her *aegis*-shield or wore it upon her breastplate.

And that marks the end of matters pertaining to Perseus and the Gorgon, although it is otherwise said that the Gorgon in appearance resembled rather more that of a goat and that Athena received this goatskin (*'aegis'*) for her shield. But some say that there was only ever one Gorgon, who was the daughter of the sun, and before the war with the Titans Zeus slew her and made from her hide his own *aegis*-shield with which he was able to conjure up his thunderstorms.

Epitheus: That is a startling tale and one well told, Thaeo. But is there anything more to be told about Perseus?

Thaeo: Indeed, for Perseus sought to return to Argos and to Danae's father Acrisios, but when Acrisios learned of their coming he fled fearing the fulfillment of the oracle and went to the land of the Pelasgians. He came to Larissa where it happened that Perseus was competing in the pentathlon, at the very games being held by Teutamidas in honor of his guest Acrisios. Yet he had come to fear his grandson so greatly that he stayed far out of his way during every contest he participated in.

Yet it happened in the athletic contest, when Perseus threw the discus, that it flew so far it struck Acrisios upon his foot, thereby killing him at once. Perseus was very sorrowful when he learned of this, although he realized that the oracle had been thus fulfilled; the oracle which caused Acrisios through his life to distrust Perseus and his mother was ultimately fulfilled not through treachery but merely by an accident. So Perseus buried Acrisios outside of the city, but as a result of having been the cause of his death would not claim the kingdom of Argos for himself; so he traded this kingdom for that of Tiryns, then ruled by Megapenthes, the son of Acrisios's twin brother Proitos.[13]

So this brings the Perseus story to a close, yet I'm sure you can imagine how long we might be here if the story were to be told with every concocted detail intact, but for our purposes this seems more than adequate.

Epitheus: Surely it is.

CHAPTER 3

Thaeo: At this point let me retreat back to the episode that is of the greatest interest to us, by which I mean the beheading of Medusa by Perseus. For we learn that from this act was released both the winged horse Pegasus and the golden giant Chrysaor, which arises as a rather insignificant detail within the entire story. But let us consider that we can easily identify the constellation of the horse *Pegasus*, and that we also find nearby the other prominent figures as the constellations of *Andromeda*, *Cassiopeia*, and *Cepheus*.

Epitheus: Certainly.

Thaeo: So might we expect that there too should we should find the Gorgon herself?

Epitheus: It seems reasonable.

Thaeo: And though we do not find the name of Medusa among the constellations, there is a similar name which does appear and that is the name of Andromeda (*'andro-meda'*).

Epitheus: Truly.

Thaeo: While her name could mean 'one who thinks of men', let us consider that it might also carry the meaning of 'mortal Meda' so as to distinguish her from the 'immortal Meda' (*'theo-meda'*), for we know that Medusa is to have been the mortal among the Gorgons.

Epitheus: Surely.

Thaeo: And this name of 'immortal Meda' is known to us from the (ancient) Spartan town of Theometis, which would mean 'divine Metis'.

Epitheus: Yes.

Thaeo: In which case we could compare the name '*Medus*' (Medusa) with that of Metis, who as we know is the personification of wisdom, associated with the moon.

Epitheus: Truly.

Thaeo: Thus there might also be a link too between Medusa and the moon.[*] And this it seems would permit us to associate her with the role the moon plays in its medicinal influence, as in our words 'medical' or 'medicine', which then would each take their name from the moon ('*medis*').

Epitheus: Miraculous.

Thaeo: And we already know how powerfully the moon influences the harvesting of medicinal herbs.

Epitheus: Yes.

Thaeo: However, even if we might equate Metis with Medusa, and the name 'Medusa' with that of 'Andromeda', the characters of Andromeda and Medusa remain so very different and distinct from one another, for Perseus slays one and preserves the other; thus there is no reason to believe that these two would be identical.

Epitheus: No indeed.

Thaeo: Yet we might perceive it as relevant, at least, that the episodes involving Medusa and Andromeda are so closely linked within the myth; with both beginning with a beauteous woman (Cassiopeia and Medusa) raising the ire of a goddess by proclaiming that her own beauty surpasses that of the goddess.

Epitheus: Truly.

---

[*] The name of the goddess Meduna appears to combine of '*med*' ('mead') and '*luna*' ('moon'), although nothing else is known of her.

Thaeo: And that the slaying of the sea-dragon by Perseus in order to free Andromeda follows the story of the slaying of Medusa in order to free Pegasus; which is also not unlike the birth of Athena from the head of Zeus, as we considered before, whose mother as we know is Metis.[*]

Epitheus: Indeed.

Thaeo: And along with the similarity in the names of Medusa and Andromeda, we also have a similarity between the Gorgons with the Graiae, who were sometimes considered to be Gorgons themselves.[†] So it is possible to accept that the three episodes might once have been merely variations of the same story that were later assembled in the sequence: Perseus' encounter with the Graiae, his slaying of the Gorgon Medusa, and his freeing of Andromeda.

Epitheus: It is certainly possible.

Thaeo: And this would suggest that the constellation of *Andromeda* would then also be that of Medusa.

Epitheus: Seemingly.

Thaeo: Then let us consider the arrangement of the various constellations, reassigning them now based upon the story of the beheading of Medusa; for we can see that *Cepheus* ('head') lies higher (closer to the pole star) than does *Pegasus*. And considering their shapes and the position of the two in relation to one another, we could conjecture that they in fact constitute a head and body.

Epitheus: Indeed.

Thaeo: And as we had considered before the water-bearer *Aquarius*,[‡] the blonde Trojan youth brought to Olympus by Zeus to fill the cups

---

[*] See *The Eden Enigma: A Dialogue*
[†] The Graiae are sometimes called the sisters of the Gorgons (Apollodorus 2.4 § 2; see Hard 1998: 65), as daughters of Phorcus, and sometimes considered to be Gorgons themselves (Howey 1955: 157).
[‡] See *The Eden Enigma: A Dialogue*

of the gods with nectar, has the name of Ganymede, possessing the constituent *'mede'*, which we could also associate with the honeyed drink of the moon (mead).[*]

Epitheus: Certainly we could.

Thaeo: And just like Indra and the (drink of inspiration) *soma*, Zeus in the form of an eagle retrieved the mead-bearing boy from Mount Ida. And if we were to consider these two episodes as being once identical, we would have to believe that originally Ganymede did not become the server of the drinks but became the drink itself. And this recalls too the origin of the (Nordic) sacred mead produced from the killing of wise Kvasir.[†]

Epitheus: It does.

Thaeo: Then to consider the matter as we have progressed thus far, the constellations we have spoken of (*Andromeda, Pegasus*, and *Aquarius*) are associated with the word *'mede'*; though it manifests itself differently in the distinct forms of Andromeda, Medusa, and Ganymede. Yet should we regard this as mere coincidence?

Epitheus: It seems not, but I am also not entirely sure.

Thaeo: Then we shall continue, if we remain dedicated to seeking the answer. We should consider that the Mesopotamian constellation of the She-Goat (*Lyra*) represents a patroness of medicine and healing, and who also possesses the twin characteristics of giver of spirit (breath of life) and its antithesis of taking the spirit back, which makes her rather like the (Hindu) spirit god Shiva.[14]

Epitheus: Indeed.

Thaeo: This She-Goat is also deemed the custodian of the 'plant of life', and thus we find she might also be associated with the moon through her connection with health, remedial plants, and rebirth.[15]

---

[*] J. A. Edm. Veckenstedt ('Ganymedes', Libau, 1881) attempted to prove that the Phrygian Ganymede was the source of the mead.
[†] See *The Eden Enigma: A Dialogue*

Epitheus: That is a clear possibility.

Thaeo: And she too is known as the 'Great One' ('*Gula*'), and by her many features holds aspects which resemble both the Gorgon and also the goddess **QEDEM (EDEN)**.[16]

Epitheus: Truly.

Thaeo: And though not specifically associated with the 'Great Square' (of *Pegasus*), which is associated with Gula, she might likewise be identified with the goat-form of the Gorgon.

Epitheus: Certainly.

Thaeo: But only if we could equate the Gorgon with the 'Great Square' and the She-Goat with the Gorgon.

Epitheus: Equally true.

Thaeo: Then picking up where we left off before, might we then consider that the 'Great Square' can also be identified with the Gorgon Medusa?

Epitheus: It seems so, but could we be certain?

Thaeo: We would have to consider the matter further and with great care. Though we have noticed how both Andromeda and Ganymede are associated with constellations adjacent to *Pegasus* (*Andromeda* and *Aquarius*). And, as we considered, each of them bear very similar sounding names.

Epitheus: Yes, that is what we have so far.

Thaeo: Then there is one more thing we might be able to take into consideration; specifically that it is not only the horse Pegasus who springs forth from the Gorgon but also the giant Chrysaor ('golden blade'), who appears as a boy holding a golden sword. And we know that Chrysaor also becomes the father of another giant of renown named Geryon by the Oceanid Callirhoe ('mellifluous').

31

And you will know of Geryon already, perhaps, because he was further the subject of one of the twelve labors of Hercules, and thus it might be useful to provide a rendition of this, suited to the occasion, if you would like.

Epitheus: By all means.

Thaeo: Then I will start by telling you something of Hercules' pedigree, and we might best begin by going back again to the hero Perseus, for it was after his return to Mycenae that he is said to have had five sons named Alcaios, Sthenelos, Heleios, Mestor, and Electryon. (He also had a daughter named Gorgophone.) Alcaios had a son named Amphitryon who married his uncle Electryon's daughter Alcmene. And it was when Amphitryon was away in Thebes fighting against the Teleboans that Zeus visited the desirable Alcmene, taking on the visage of her own husband. Thus he was the recipient of her amorous embraces, and spent the night with her there in bed, lengthening the night by three times in order to fully satisfy himself.

So as a result of this when Amphitryon returned and found his wife took such paltry notice of him, and that when night came she was consumed with no great passion for him, he asked her why she gave him so little attention after so long of an absence. She then revealed to him the reason, and when he notified her that he had just now returned, it was thus clear to them that she had been visited by one of the gods.

It was after this that Zeus declared that the next child who was to be born would become king of all Mycenae, figuring that the next one born would be his own son. Yet Hera wanted to frustrate Zeus's plans in revenge for his dalliance with Alcmene, and was able to persuade Eileithyia (Greek goddess of birth) to hold up her progress and to speed up that of Nicippe the wife of Sthenelos, who bore her son Eurystheus in only seven months; thus he would according to the solemn declaration of Zeus rule all Mycenae. When Alcmene was finally due she gave birth to two boys: one who was named Alceides, the son of Zeus, and the other Iphicles, the son of Amphitryon.

Hera lost no time in attempting to destroy this child of Zeus by sending against him two great serpents, but even as an infant he merely took them up into his hands and throttled them both, one in each fist, until they were dead. Yet the wrath of Hera was unceasing and even in Alceides' maturity she beset him with such madness that he was driven to throw his own children into the fire, and along with them two of his brother's children. Thus when Alceides' mind was cleared of his rage he sought to exile himself so as to cause no further misery to himself or others, and thus went to an oracle seeking advice. It was the oracle who first addressed him not as Alceides but as Hercules, and that it was required he settle in Tiryns and serve Eurystheus, the king of Mycenae, for twelve years and to perform twelve labors for him, after which, upon completing ten of them successfully, he would thereby be granted immortality and take his place among the gods.

So this was the situation that caused Hercules to endeavor to complete the twelve labors, one of which was the theft of Geryon's cattle. Geryon himself is described as being three men joined into one at the waist, and he owned a particular breed of red cattle which were watched over by the cattle-herd Eurytion and his two-headed dog Orthos, offspring of the serpents Typhon and Echidna.[*] When Hercules came to Erytheia he camped under Mount Abas and there Orthos sensed his proximity and came after him. But Hercules just brushed him off with his club, with such a blow that it finished off the vicious two-headed cur forever.

Then the herdsman Eurytion went in search of Orthos and him too Hercules destroyed. The son of Zeus then led off Geryon's cattle, but Menoites was also nearby, acting as herdsman for the cattle of Hades, and had seen what had befallen the herd. After telling him of it, Geryon swiftly made his way to that spot where the theft had occurred and tracked him, finding Hercules near the Anthemous River and there contested with him. However, one propitious arrow loosed from Hercules' bow buried itself into Geryon's center where his three bodies met and so this marked his end. Eventually the cattle were brought to King Eurystheus who dedicated and offered them up to the goddess Hera. And so this concludes the story of Geryon and the tenth labor of Hercules.

---

[*] Typhon is described as having a hundred heads and is said to be the son of Tartarus (Hell) and Terra (Earth), living in the realm of Tartarus. Typhon is paired with the serpentess Echidna who was sister of the Gorgons and of the dragon Ladon, and like Typhon had an upper human-half and a lower serpent-half (Howey 1955: 163).

Epitheus: Well done.

Thaeo: As far as Geryon's description of being three-bodied,* here we might recognize that the formation of the constellation *Orion* taken with that of *Gemini* could be viewed as the three bodies joined at the waist. We can clearly see that there are three bodies which appear to be so joined, the waist being the three belt-stars of *Orion*.

Epitheus: Surely.

Thaeo: Also, we find Geryon shown with the image of a winged boar upon his shield, which we could take to be his father Chrysaor (sometimes a winged boar). We might thus consider Chrysaor to be the constellation of the Great Boar (*Ursa Major*),[17†] which is near the *Gemini* constellation; while the constellation of *Taurus* (the bull) could be emblematic of the giant's cattle herds.

Epitheus: Yes.

Thaeo: And it seems to me we might also have explained another situation: where Athena keeps the Gorgon's head as an emblem upon her own shield, which would also aid us in our identification of Medusa with the *Pegasus* constellation.

Epitheus: How do you mean?

Thaeo: We might figure from this that the original place Athena held in relation to the Gorgon would be the same as Geryon in relation to Chrysaor, by which I mean that rather than being born from the head of Zeus, Athena might have been born from the head of the Gorgon.

Epitheus: That would be incredible if it were true, Thaeo! But how could it be proven?

---

* He is sometimes represented as the combined form of a human, a goat, and a ram.
† Chrysaor is specifically described as being immortal, meaning that as a constellation it would never set into the ocean, which is true of all circumpolar constellations, with *Ursa Major* being especially noteworthy among them.

34

Thaeo: There might possibly be a way to associate the Gorgon with Athena, because we have already suggested that the constellations of *Pegasus*, *Aquarius*, and *Andromeda* taken together might represent the headless Gorgon.

Epitheus: Yes.

Thaeo: And that we have seen that the Gorgon might be represented by characteristics which are either goat-like or serpent-like.[*]

Epitheus: Certainly.

Thaeo: Then there is another connection which could be made, when we were speaking last time of King Cecrops, who appears represented in the form of a man above and a sea-dragon below.[†]

Epitheus: I well recall.

Thaeo: And we know that Cecrops was to have founded the city of Athenae on the river Triton just as we know the goddess Athena was to have been born from the skull of Zeus and at the same time from out of the river Triton.

Epitheus: That is so.

Thaeo: Further we concluded that Cecrops' name was equivalent to that of **EUROPE**, the storm god associated with Europa, and thus is also equivalent to *aegis*-bearing Zeus.[‡]

Epitheus: Certainly.

---

[*] Melusine or Melusina from French folk tales, like Cecrops, was half-human and half-serpent and by her name is probably the same as Medusa. (see Howey 1955: 330)

[†] See *The Eden Enigma: A Dialogue*

[‡] The Samoan Jupiter was both father of the gods and creator of all things, who appeared as a half-man half-eel, where his bottom half lies in the ocean. (Howey 1955: 278)

Thaeo: Then it is also noteworthy that Cecrops is also associated with the constellation of *Aquarius*.[18] This we recognize from his upper-half being a man (*Pegasus*) and his lower-half being a fish (*Aquarius*), which arises from the appearance of the two constellations taken together.

Epitheus: Yes.

Thaeo: Thus if we are able to associate the *Pegasus* constellation with both Medusa and Cecrops we could consider that the form of the stars taken together resembles a beheading, as in the case of the beheading of Medusa, or the striking of the head of Zeus in the birth of Athena. And we have already mentioned the similarity between Medusa and Metis (mother of Athena).

So if we visualize the figure of Athena springing forth from the severed head of Zeus, where we take *Pegasus* to be the torso and *Cepheus* to be the head, the constellation which appears to be springing forth from the neck is that of *Cassiopeia*.[*] And as a constellation set within the path of the Milky Way, does this not remind us of Athena being said to have emerged from the river Triton?

Epitheus: Indeed it does.

Thaeo: This then would identify Cecrops (*Aquarius*) also as the father of Athena (*Cassiopeia*), who was to have sprung forth from his severed head (*Cepheus*); though we must consider that it also occurred when the constellation is taken to be the form of Zeus.

Epitheus: Truly.

Thaeo: Then we might come to consider that there exists a far deeper connection between Athena and her *aegis*-shield, being not merely held as a prize but as symbolic of her birth; which we could consider to be from the Gorgon's head rather than from the head of Zeus or Cecrops.

---

[*] The constellation of *Cassiopeia* is sometimes represented holding a staff topped by a crescent moon, which is quite emblematic of the moon goddess Athena.

36

Epitheus: That is difficult to deny.

Thaeo: And we considered last time how Athena is also the same as Atthis, the daughter of Cranaus, whose name we recognized to be the same as the Titan Cronos, who is likewise known to have regurgitated his own children.[*]

Epitheus: Indeed.

Thaeo: Then we have good reason to conclude that the beheading of the Gorgon was an act of birth not unlike the birth of Athena out of the head of Zeus, and that these represent merely variations upon the same conception: the arising of the constellation *Cassiopeia* from the beheading of the creature formed out of the constellations making up a torso in *Pegasus*, a tail in *Aquarius*, and a head in *Cepheus*.

Epitheus: You appear to be on the right track, Thaeo.

---

[*] See *The Eden Enigma: A Dialogue*

CHAPTER 4

Thaeo: Then let us further consider Chrysaor ('golden blade'), for this 'golden sword' seems like another described as having a 'golden hilt', which is wielded by the Saxon hero Beowulf. And although again we could not hear the entire tale from beginning to end, we might consider the relevant parts for the purposes of our discussion. But before beginning I will recount something of the events which transpired prior to the actual confrontation wherein the sword is employed.

It begins with a mighty marauding Dane named Shield Sheafson, who gained great influence over lands beyond the seas. Shield had a son named Beow, who being generous in fine gifts, even during his father's reign as king, won him a great many followers. Then after Shield passed on Beow ruled in his place, becoming the father of Halfdane who ruled after him. Halfdane himself had three sons named Heorogar, Hrothgar, and Halga, and a daughter named Yrsa who became queen to Onela the Swede.

Hrothgar attracted many fine men and so as his influence grew he ordered a great mead hall to be built that would also serve as his new assembly room, and to stand as a wonder for all time. Materials of all sorts were sought in kingdoms from every quarter of middle-earth until soon it stood with its high-gabled roof topped with horns, and christened by the king the hall of Heorot ('hart').[19] The account goes on to tell of the troubles that subsequently befell them.

> They enjoyed themselves festively and filled their horn-flagons full, then it followed that one, a beast from the belly of Hell, arose bringing baleful transgression. The grave-demon's given name was Grendel, a denizen of damp gravel, a trampler of turbid territory, a monarch upon the muddy marshland.[20]
>
> Under the cover of nocturnal gray Grendel made his way to the splendid ascendant hall, so as to look upon the ring-Danes as they lay after finishing their feasting and drinking. There he met those noble men for the first time face-to-face, reposing after retiring from their revelry, not mindful of mortal misery, nor sensing a soul's sorrow.
>
> At once that ungodly creature, grim and greedy, grabbed angrily from among their group thirty in number, right from the

floor where they had fallen into slumber, and fled with them to his foul fetid fen, gloating with glee, cavorting home with his collection of corpses, a sickening gain for his grim sin of gluttony.

Then bright beams broke, heralding the return of the sun from its slumber, shining starkly upon the savage skill of cold-hearted Grendel. When their first-meal was finished they fell into a fit of weary weeping, making it the unmerry occupation of the morning. The formidable lord looked thunderstruck, the merciful man was met with melancholy, feeling faint fortitude over the force of unleashed fury; tracing the night-terror's twisted track transfixed in him a sullen sadness that offered no salvation.

It was not long thereafter, but one night following, that the foul fiend again came to feast, filling himself full with even more fear-fraught slaughter. Obsessed by brutality he bucked all blame for his bloodshed. At that time one might easily meet a man who had moved himself to a place where he should be more safe, finding a bed among the betrothed. Since any could view for himself how violent and vile was the valiant hall's visitor. Any Dane who had not met death that day was dealt a more dutiful eye and kept to digs more distant than had been deemed healthy hitherto.

By this means Grendel marshaled himself over them, an illegitimate heir, facing up alone against a multitude of humanity, until the best of all halls now lay hollow and inhospitable. For a dozen winters of dreadful duration the Shielding lord had to bear this bitter burden. So such stories became celebrated near and far, as talk of it spread. Sad songs were sung of this sorry strapped sovereign, of the ravenous raiding, of the roiling rage of Grendel in his relentless war with Hrothgar. Without peace possible, unrelenting under the pleas of Dane princes, no wise head determined the demon would pay any duty for the destruction he delivered with those death-dealing claws. Thanes young and old might fall prey when the malign monster was out marching, hiding himself in the hinterland, stalking for slaughter, in the pitch blackness upon the mist-enshrouded mire. But there was no telling which murky morass might prove to be the playground of those pernicious hell-hounds.[21]

Now a crew of warrior Geats led by Beowulf, son of Ecgtheow and nephew of Hygelac, king of the Geats, made their way by sea to the land of the Danes, and there they met and took up with Hrothgar within the hall of Heorot, and for a time the festivity returned to that forsaken place, as Beowulf pledged to conquer in his contest with this pernicious marsh-menace.

From under the misty banks of muck that unholy creature loomed. Grendel strode, carrying with him malice aimed at man, marauding with manifest malevolence, beneath overcast clouds, creeping until he came to the clearing where the hall of sheer walls shone off its gold gilding. It was not his virgin expedition to view Hrothgar's vaulted ceiling, though never in his days had he found more magnificent men, retainers of finer renown.

Malevolent and morose he moved in to mutilate all at that meetinghouse. The iron-fixed door flung freely from its fixtures at the moment he resolved to force it. With a maddened maw keen to chaw, he clawed a way through that indefensible door, and crept over the well-crafted floor, while casting a frightful light from eyes that flared rage like reddish flames upon that fine company of comrades.

The noble clan slept as a unit, witless and unaware, which delighted his gut to the fullest, foreseeing the carnage that lay afoot, a frenzied feeding that would fill him until first-light. He regaled at rending life from them, to banquet upon blood, to occupy his belly with bodies. Yet Fate that night showed herself to be his unfaithful ally, for neither was he destined to slake his savagery nor satisfy his thirst.

Hygelac's kinsman was keenly observing to see how he might order his attack. Not long was he caused to wait, for the severe creature struck with swift terror, bearing down upon the benches to one of his sleeping companions, biting through, breaching his flesh, gobbling gobs of grisly gore, leaving only a cadaveric carcass; having made a meal for himself, not missing a single morsel of carpal or clavicle.

Emboldened now, he browsed the benches further to the napping knave offered next for nourishment. With enclawed appendages raised to gorge the glib-girded Geat, Beowulf was thus balefully beset when with unequalled quickness he leaned lithely, binding Grendel's limb in a firm armlock. Fixing it with the full force of his fist, so that the earl of evil knew now he had not faced such a fearsome foe upon the face of the earth. Grendel was bitten by a fright he had never felt before, because he could not break himself free. Nothing more would he have liked than to find a way to flee, so eager was he to dash to his disgusting den, to the underworld of the ungodly. He hadn't come to grips with anything like this Geat's grasp. Then Beowulf recalled from before his evening's boasts and rose up from his bench to secure his severest hold. The scoundrel's sinews were straining, his finger-bones breaking, yet the combatant was unrelenting. The terror of Heorot was searching earnestly for an escape, expectant eyes hoping to espy an easy way back to the depths of his dwelling. Now the fraught flesh that fixed his fingers was fragmenting. This proved an adverse visit to the hall of Heorot; how the timbers shook and sang, the hall-dwelling Danes were gulping a god-awful drink. Great surprise reigned, as the engaged duelers dashed and dented, that the hall itself escaped demolition.[22]

Then a chilling cry broke to high heaven, which caused every Danish warrior to wince. The volume penetrated to the viands of these veteran victors, a grievous guttural strain, a venting of the vanquished. The howl from a careworn kid of Hel's kitchen, entwined in the embrace of a mere mortal who was by far the mightiest among men throughout the time in which he lived. The illustrious hero did not imagine that this thing should be allowed to go free, nor did he think its lasting life would be a blessing to any living soul. Beowulf's men wielded world-weary weapons, setting upon the beast, seeking to preserve the life of their illustrious lord, to save their Geat leader, as long as they might last. Brave warriors who heaved halberds to hack his hairy hide, who sought a way to strike through to his very soul, did not know their screaming steel might never prevail, for every battle-weapon in service avowed itself to be sans bite against that supernatural foe.

Yet the severing of spirit from body, on that day of his life, was to be for him a reign of pain, and that fellow would ferry the strange spirit away to find friendship among fiends upon far forsaken lands. He that had caused such great carnage, who had inflicted so much worldly injury, found a body that did not obey his will, but it served a new master, the hand of Hygelac's man. As long as they were locked together, neither would vouchsafe the other's victory. Then a rapid pain rose up within the terrible terrorizer, and straining flesh split wide open at the shoulder: muscles severed, bones shattered, and sinews split. It was Beowulf who had bested the brute. Now being free he fled, forced by the mortal anguish in his heart back to his old haunt, the sullen stinking swamp, making for his mirthless mire. He knew dearly that on that day the dealing of death had been delivered. The Danes meanwhile emerged out of that engagement with a heartfelt cheer, that the one who had come to them from afar with cunning and clarity had cleansed Hrothgar's hall once and for all.

Beowulf emerged well satisfied from his single night's work, to do a deed worthy of great renown. To the East-Danes the Geat leader had done what he had promised to do; he relieved them all of their anxieties, all their bitter sorrows, every cruel violation they had suffered and endured, not a paltry plague had passed them by. The sure sign of its expulsion was at hand, the arm and shoulder, Grendel's tremendous grasp, that Beowulf fixed ascendant among the vaulted arches.

When morning dawned a wealth of warriors were spawned, so it is said, to gather around that hall of wealth; chieftains who came from both close and distant lands to witness and wonder at the wound-worker's tracks. There was no remorse among any who came to point out his trail, where with frame shot and body spent in strides he went, and after a clash of cruelty had made his escape, leaving a trail of gore that led all the way to the demon's lake. The blood-surging waters were proof, there still boiling and swirling, with battle-red it bled from the wound dealt to it, for in the misery of impending death there he had hidden. Then there too, without comfort, in his bog home he met his end, his rabid soul lost to the world as ravenous Hel embraced him.[23]

They all went into a sound sleep, but one among them was ill-fated in his tranquil time, something that had become familiar to them during the duration that Grendel visited the gilded hall, as he cavorted in cruelty until his end finally came, a retribution of death in return for his incursions. But then it was made clear to all after this battle was over that another, yet alive, arose to avenge that abhorrent antagonist. This demonic matron was Grendel's own mother, grieving over the heart's wound she attributed to their wrongs.[24]

Carrying herself across the heath to Heorot, entering the hall where the Danes lay here and there in peaceful repose. A harsh reversal of fortune came when that fierce mother of Grendel set foot on their floor. The extent of the fury she unleashed was only less measured by how far a woman's strength might be matched with a man's, vigorously armed with a blade: one forged and treated by the hammer, a blood-slaked edge with hungry teeth that cleaves the firm boar-crest from atop the helmet.

The reaction within the hall was a hoard of hard-edged blades that were grabbed from the benches, as many wide shields were raised and hefted, with no thought given to the use of helmets or hard mail-coats when they were, in shock, suddenly awakened. The Queen of Hel now beset was eager to make her escape, being gripped by a fear to save her own self. Quickly she grabbed one of these nobles, lashed him within the flex of her fingers, before she made her way back to her marshy mansion. This man that she took was the most trusted of Hrothgar, one he counted as the closest of comrades among any who lived between the two oceans. This most admirable of men became the victim of her pitiful slaughter, caught when at rest in peaceful slumber. But Beowulf was not bivouacked among them there, for after having received his reward he had been granted a different lodging. A cry arose from that cavernous hall as they saw that their prize, Grendel's clawed hand, had been snatched from its place by that hell-hag. Thus emerged a fresh curse that beset their great haven; it was a hard bargain for both groups that they need pay with the spirits of their dearest companions. The noble king, that old gray war-chief, was stricken with grief, when he gathered that this great gentleman was gone, murdered and no more.

Beowulf was brought, summoned to the royal house, the best among the bunch, before the breaking of dawn, entering with a band of his noble troops, in to where the wise king was waiting.[25]

Then Hrothgar's hair-braided horse was dressed in a halter and tack. The high prince mounted onto his steed to lead the force of his troops. Everywhere through the wood the way taken by that wolfish woman, plain to perceive, could be seen running across

43

the ground; where she had scurried straight to the swamps, dragging the cadaver of their close companion, the noble lord who had once been Hrothgar's trusted officer. The noble king was climbing up steep rock-strewn scree, through narrow paths that could not be paced by two or more abreast, where a cliff face descended to the doom of a watery serpents' pool. He rode on ahead with a small party of his men, those who were good for scouting, and they soon surveyed the sad wood, where the mountain trees grew sideways over a damp gravelway of gray granite. Where the water beneath was but a boiling and blood-infested brew. It was a debilitating blow to all the Danes, and to their Shielding friends, a pain that penetrated their breasts and which tightened their throats, when at the foot of that crag, on that pale lapping shore, the head of Aeschere was beheld.

Where the water was a welter of crimson blood, all men looked with keen eyes, then promptly the horn was sounded, an unruffled requiem to remember the fallen. All the troops settled there on the rocky shore to wait. Within the whirling pool they watched a plethora of pernicious serpents, sea-dragons foraging in the mire, and above them on the cliff face a race of reptiles reposing restlessly amid the rocks. At the offspring of dawn these serpents and monsters rose to plague the sea-ways, becoming the menace of mariners. As soon as the blaring horn sounded they scurried off along every line of escape, riled and writhesome they raced. One of the Geat's rose with his bow and rapidly let sling an arrow that caught one in its blood-chamber, forever dealing death to its days of swimming those ship-weary seas. This one among them had been making off with less haste when it came to its end. Though fast it might have been within the waves, it was now faced with weapons, waging war with the barbs of boar-pikes, menaced and mangled then speared through the gut, and dragged up onto the craggy bank, that wondrous denizen of the deep. The surly victors gazed upon the strange visitor with curious looks.

Then Beowulf prepared himself, getting dressed in his battle-gear, not occupied at all with thoughts for his life. He would take as his companion, to explore the watery depths with him, a splendidly wrought mail of full fit and fine form, fashioned by men's felicitous fingers, which would shield his vital trunk from any bodily harm; that the fever-charged maul might not penetrate his blood-chamber, nor an evil embrace of wounding waylay him. While his burnished boar-crested helm was to keep its master's head from danger, that treasure the forge-worker fought for from out of the fire, with noble fittings and figures, likewise destined for the depths, that must surely stir up the sea; never had it yielded to the wielded bladed weapon.

One thing more was necessary; there was great need for it by the Geat at a time such as this, which the King's man presented. The name of this fine long-hilted sword was Hrunting, surpassed by none other among any ancient weapon. It had a fine edge of iron, its engravings a filigree of vines of poisonous fronds, battle tempered by enemies' blood, which had never missed its mark for its master when making merry with him who dared enter and maraud in foreign kingdoms. No damsel in the doing of distinguished deeds.[26]

After concluding his speech that storm-Geat king, disinclined to engage in any further discussion, was wont to be on his way and begin his audacious scheme. The wide-deep rapidly received the battle-ready warrior and for a long while he endured the descent before his perception peered upon the bottom of that foul bog. The savage and salacious she-demon, a devouring deep-dweller for a hundred summers and winters, sensed at once that a surface-dweller was surveying her submarine stronghold, somewhere from the waters above. So stretching forth her searching hand she struck out, seizing him with all her strength, and without delay dealt a death grip aimed at vacating his vital viscera. But his weighty war-coat protected him from her pernicious prodding pincers, which penetrated little the links of his veritably invulnerable vestment.

Once her feet felt the sandy fen's floor, then the bayou-wolf bore that regent of rings back to her boggy abode. But no matter how brave Beowulf might have been, he was unable to wield his weapon to wage underwater war; for the fighter's fragrance unleashed a furious force of sea-fiends who infested the waters in a feeding-frenzy focused upon his mortal frame, to rip and rend with their terrible-tusks his tooth-tortured tarp of mail. Then the Dane-servant soon saw that he had descended down into a hellish hall–which one, one cannot be sure–but where the water no

longer whirled about him. Nor with its secure ceiling was he not
freed from the floods affliction, where he perceived the flare of a
fire, a pallid beam blazing brightly.

And the good Geat saw the menace of that morass, the mighty
matron of murk, at once he swiftly swung out with his sword
towards that hag from Hel, not revoking the rage of his right arm,
as that war-singing ring-emblazoned razor came crashing down to
cleave her skull. Then the venerable visitor found that his battle-
torch refused to rend, to render redemption, but rather the blade
recoiled and foiled the brave man's day of reckoning. In how
many combats had this wonder weapon been wielded, to halve a
helmet and hack the war-jacket of the hard-pressed? In all its
brilliant career never before had this war-bullion had its battle-
mercies bested.

Regaining resolution, not forsaking his courageous quest for
fame, Hygelac's kin then cast aside the filigree-encrusted form–
that most admirably adorned–so it stuck into the soil, its iron still
sheer and sharp. Instead he was forced to put trust in his own
frame, the muscles of his mighty hands; that which all men must
do who desire to test their mettle in battle, to win undying
distinction, forgetting for the moment his mortal coil.

Now eager for engagement, the war-prince of the Geats took a
hard grip around the shoulder of Grendel's bearer. The combat-
hardened champion, now enraged, threw the awesome foe down
onto the floor, yet she graciously gave him payment with her
hands, in the form of tearing talons that trapped him within a
tenacious embrace. Then that foot-soldier faltered, strength left
this man of force and he tumbled. She firmly fixed her guest to
the floor, then pulled out her short-piece to pierce him, a
shimmering broad-blade that would bring her ripe revenge upon
him for the loss of her only boy. Striking for his shoulder it was
the tight mesh of mail that shielded his soul, to tease the tip and
bother the blade, enduring every attempt at entry. Surely that
would have spelled the end for this son of Ecgtheow, beyond a
bed of better ground, had it not been for his battle-shirt, had not
its well-meshed links borne the brunt.[27]

Managing to get back upon his feet Beowulf spied among a
stash of arms a glorious gilded grip, a giant's unbending blade of
bygone days, which would bring honor to any thane worthy of the

name. A wondrous weapon, but one that was more than any mere mortal might charge with into the melee; both good and gallant, wrought by giant hands, he gripped its ringed hilt. The brave man of the Shieldings was bold-faced and brazen, drawing back this ring-decorated thing he lashed out with a lust, no more looking after life. Bringing it down with such a blow that it buried itself deep within the creature's collar bone, breaking through her neck-links, the blade proceeded straight through the troubled tearing flesh, and her body heaved and hit upon the ground. Beowulf felt full vainglory at the feat of that bloody blade.

Then a light blazed, a beam shone within, just as from the sky shines with brilliance heaven's brightest candle. He then glanced about the hall and walked warily along the wall. With his rage-weapon raised, hilt held high for hewing, Hygelac's hero was fuming and focused, the blade had not yet become one without use to the battle-thane. He fervently wished to reimburse Grendel for all of the evil doings he had dealt the west-Danes, for on more than one venture had he harassed the happy men of Hrothgar, devouring them in their dreams; a dozen and three of the Danesmen and even more had he hefted and hauled away, as a terrible treasure. Battle-brave Beowulf had paid him back for his brutalities, for there he spied slouching the slaughter-sorry foe; Grendel's body lay settled and soulless. For the grapple at Heorot had given him grievous injury, now the corpse was cut and its guts gushed from the sword-Geat's swift stroke; then he heaved hard to sever trunk from head.

At that very second the sages of Hrothgar suddenly saw, while looking at the lake, a raging of waves that bubbled up like froth from a cauldron, rising with water the color of blood. These grizzle-bearded men gathered about brave Hrothgar and spoke as one: they did not expect the deed-hero would come back, returning in victory for a triumphant homecoming to his majesty. It was believed by many that the bog-beast had beaten Beowulf. Then when came the ninth-hour of the day,[*] the brave band of Shieldings abandoned their beach-head, and that treasure trooper made his way for home. The Geats were perturbed and peered

---

[*] Three o'clock in the afternoon

into the pool, those who still hoped but hardly expected to see their heroic lord and comrade again.[28]

Then Beowulf's sword-blade began to bleed away like melting ice, the corrosive battle blood was to blame, which caused the weapon to vanish. The great tempest-Geat gazed at the gold gathered there in great heaps, yet of treasure he took from that soggy grotto only Grendel's head and the remaining gold hilt of that sword; emblazoned with emeralds, its intricately inscribed blade had entirely dissolved; from scalding-hot blood, that peculiar poisonous soul of the one who had perished down below. Soon, however, the one who had persisted in peril through the perishing of his opponents was back in the foul murk, ascending through the watery abyss. Those wide waters were no longer tainted by turbulent terror, where foreign spirits gave up their ghosts, where they let lapse their lease upon this life.

The master of mariners then made his way back to land, stalwartly swimming to the shoreline, satisfied with his sea treasure, the heavy head he hefted. That stoic band of soldiers surrounded him, satisfied to see their great lord again, safe and sound. Then they immediately freed the stoic man from his helmet and mail-coat. The lake which lay under the lithesome clouds was tranquil, but traces of the terror remained lingering within the ripples.

They set off at once, going along the foot-paths, with great life they wended the pathways of this world, ones that their feet found familiar. The bold-hearted boys were like kings as they bore that burdensome brain-case from the beach-cliff. Four shared the task of transporting Grendel's tremendous head to the treasure hall, spiked upon a spear. All filled to the hilt with a full vigor until they had filed all the way to the fine fortress. The fearless battle-fevered Geat footmen, fourteen of them with their liege lord among them paraded proudly, and in no time were passing over the plain that led to the stately mead mansion.[29]

So here Grendel himself is immune to injury by any blade, just as (the Norse god of light) Balder could not be harmed by any weapon, save for the mistletoe.* Yet does this not also make the episode

---

* The mistletoe is sometimes known as the Mistletoe Sword.

similar to the contest of Hercules with the Nemean Lion, which you might recall was also one of his twelve labors?

Epitheus: I do.

Thaeo: Then as you well know Hercules was sent by King Eurystheus to bring the pelt of the Nemean lion back to him as a prize. But this lion was no ordinary creature for he too was invulnerable to all weapons, and like the dog Orthos was the offspring of the serpent Typhon. The beast was born and nurtured upon the moon, being cared for by the goddess Hera, until he grew so large that the moon shook him off and he fell down to earth like a fallen star, where he began to menace the people of Nemea.

On his way to battle the lion, Hercules stayed with Molorchos in Cleonai, who was then eager to offer a sacrifice to the gods; but Hercules asked that he delay his sacrifice for thirty days, at the end of which he would know if he had been successful in his task. That if he came back safely after his contest with the lion that he might then make his sacrifice to Zeus the Savior, but otherwise to make the offering to Hercules the fallen hero. Molorchos agreed to wait for thirty days, so Hercules prepared himself and travelled from there until he came to the town of Nemea.

From there he inquired where he might find the beast and all directed him up into the mountains, so upon making preparations to track down the beast there were none who wished him well who did not also consider that they were well-wishing him to his doom. Yet armed to the hilt he went up and tracked the lion to a cave that had two entrances. When the beast came out after him he quickly drew an arrow to shoot, but every one of his bronze-tipped arrows hit off its invulnerable coat, deflected as if off a bare rock. Thus putting his weapon aside he managed to strike primal fear into the beast by raising his fearsome club, bellowing, and charging against it.

So the lion took refuge within the cave, but Hercules would gain nothing by going in after it, if it should then make its escape out of the other hole. So he piled great boulders to close the other entrance before he went into the cave to confront the creature. Unable to use his weapons he was forced to engage it in a contest of strength. He fought the creature's claws and fangs with his wit and mettle, and applying wrestling tactics was soon able to bear down upon it so as to get his arm around the beast's neck. Pinching it then within his thick muscled arm he held himself firm against it until the animal had been strangled to death.[30]

The massive beast was heavy and though he carried it upon his back out of the cave, he knew he need only transport the beast's hide back to Eurystheus. Yet still even in death its skin resisted all manner of weapon, so Hercules used one of its own toe claws to slit up its belly, and drew off the hide; then rolling it up bore it upon his back all the way to Cleonai. Hercules had been gone for thirty days, and just as Molorchos was preparing to sacrifice the next day to Hercules the fallen hero, Molorchos witnessed his return and was joyful, instead making his offering to merciful Zeus. Yet when Hercules left Molorchos and returned to Mycenae with the lion's hide, Eurystheus had clearly not expected him to return and was so distressed at hearing the announcement of Hercules' sudden appearance at the gate, that he refused him entry into the city from that day forth.[31]

So here we find a beast that menaces the town of Nemea just as Grendel attacks the hall of Heorot. Hercules follows the beast back to his cave just as Beowulf follows the beast into his subterranean lair; and likewise, just as with Grendel, the Lion is invulnerable to all conventional weapons and thus must be engaged in a match of strength.

And similar also to Grendel, the Lion loses one of its claws, which Hercules uses to remove its own skin.[*] Although when Beowulf confronts Grendel he is said to tear off the monster's entire arm and shoulder or his clawed right hand, it also mentions how he first applied his strength to break the beast's fingers. And there is no reason to think that this does not recollect the use of the monster's own severed claw as the only effective weapon against him.

Epitheus: No indeed.

---

[*] The Hindu god Shiva is known to have skinned a tiger with the nail of his little finger, then used the skin as his prayer blanket.

CHAPTER 5

Thaeo: So in the story about Beowulf he first wrestles Grendel just as Hercules does the Nemean lion, then tears off the beasts arm while Hercules merely completes the process by strangulation. Yet afterwards, when Hercules skins the animal with its own claw, this suggests the same episode arising in both tales, where the contestant in tearing off the creature's claw is then able to use it to vanquish the beast.

Epitheus: Truly.

Thaeo: Then we must presume that initially Beowulf would have called upon all of his mortal strength so as to break off the beast's vulnerable digit and then use this claw as the only weapon that might kill the beast; and, as we said, that stress is placed upon him breaking the bones of his fingers, prior to where it says that his entire arm was ripped off.

Epitheus: As you say.

Thaeo: Then there is a similar recounting of events arising in the tale of Biarki, also known as Bodvar ('warlike'), who is the son of a mother and father who both hold the name of bears; for it tells of a king in Norway named Hring, who ruled in the Uppdales (highlands), who had a son named Bjorn ('bear'). And after his queen died he sent some of his men south to seek a new wife, but embarking on this enterprise they were kept back by a strong headwind and were driven north to Finnmark (Lapland). When they reached the shore they disembarked and found there a house. Within that house there were two beautiful women: Ingebjorg and her daughter Hvit, the child of the Lapp King who was then off at war. So they asked Hvit if she would be willing to become the wife of King Hring. The decision was left to her mother who decided to send her off with the men without her father's approval, saying in effect, "Nothing ventured, nothing gained." The girl was from neither a rich nor a royal family but nevertheless, upon seeing her, the king accepted her at once as his wife.

Not far from where the king lived there was a wealthy farmer whose wife gave birth to a daughter named Bera ('she-bear'). When they were still children Bera and Bjorn played with one another and thus became very close. As they grew up they would often meet because each was so very fond of the other.

As Bjorn grew into manhood he took on greater responsibilities as heir to the throne, while the wicked Queen Hvit was not well liked by her people and once, when the king was setting out to go to war, the queen asked him if Bjorn might remain with her so as to rule the kingdom in his absence. Though Hvit was attracted to Bjorn the feelings were not mutual. But she was fed up with being tied to the old king and encouraged Bjorn to sleep with her while the king was gone. He was outraged by the idea and slapped the queen across the face, telling her to go. She reproved him for his obstinacy and hit him across the face with her witch's gloves, casting a spell upon him whereby he metamorphosed into a huge gray bear. Thus he became a fearsome and savage beast, and although many searched for Bjorn afterwards he could never be found.

When the bear once came onto the king's lands to attack his cattle, and killing a great number of them, Bera was near and approached him more closely. When she was near him he immediately gave up his savagery and she, thinking it was Bjorn, followed the bear back to its cave. There Bjorn again appeared to her in the form of a man, and explained that whereas he was forced to become a bear by day he remained a man during the night. So from then on Bera sought him out and stayed with him during the night. This continued until he experienced premonitions of his own death at the hands of the king's men. And he warned Bera that the queen was a mighty troll and would encourage her to eat some of his bear meat, advising her that she must not eat even the smallest bit.

Indeed in the morning Bjorn turned into a bear, and when he left Bera followed and saw the king's men surround him. He harmed some of them and killed every one of the dogs in their troop, but after tearing apart the man nearest the king he lay down in exhaustion and the party of men killed him. Bera was brought with the rest of the hunting party to the king's palace where they made a feast upon the bear's meat. Bera avoided the feast by staying in the queen's chamber, but when the queen came in with some of the bear meat on a tray she encouraged her to eat some of it. Putting pressure on the girl to overcome her abstinence, she finally cut off a very small piece for her and, as a matter of politeness to the queen, she ate it, but refused to take any more. The queen became unpleasant, telling her that perhaps this small amount would be enough, and frightened her with a great outburst of cruel cackling.

Bera then went home to her father where she soon discovered that she was now pregnant, although it turned out to be quite a difficult one for her. After her term she gave birth to three boys who were no ordinary men: the first appeared human to the midriff but had the legs and feet of an elk, so he was named Elk-Frodi ('elk-wise'); the next son had the ankles and feet of a dog and was thus named Thorir Hound's Foot; while the third showed no deformity at all and he was named Biarki ('little bear') the warlike ('*bodvar*').[*]

The brothers grew until each one had attained his destiny: Elk-Frodi became a highwayman, Thorir became the king of a foreign land, while when Biarki was eighteen he learned from his mother of the evil of Queen Hvit. And he went to his grandfather who made offers to him if only he would spare his wife's life, but Biarki would not tolerate her continued ill-contrivances within the kingdom. So Bera and Hring accompanied him to the queen's chamber, watching as he threw a leather satchel over her head, tied it around her neck, and then dragged her through the streets until she was dead, driven down into deepest Hel. Biarki (Bodvar) then was intent to make a journey to Denmark and so traveled until he was not too far from the town of Hleidargard (Leire).

A heavy downpour fell one day that soaked Bodvar through, while his horse, having been driven very hard, was walking wearily beneath him. And travel was slowed by the condition of the ground which had become a thick mud. The rainstorm continued relentlessly even as the night grew dark, but Bodvar was unrelenting until his horse stumbled upon something quite large. After he dismounted he took a look around and found that they had come upon a house. Finding the door he knocked upon it and the man who lived within the house emerged. Bodvar asked if he might get shelter there for the night and the farmer replied that he would not deny his request as it was the middle of

---

[*] In '*Biarkarimur*' he is described as having a single bear's claw on his toe.

the night and he was clearly a weary traveler. So Bodvar remained there through the night and was treated with hospitality by the farmer and his wife. Upon the following day he asked many questions about King Hrolf's campaigns and those of his troops. And asked them how many miles it remained to Hleidargard.

"From here it is but a short distance," replied the farmer. "Have you determined to travel there today?"

"Surely," replied Bodvar, "this is what I am most determined to do."

The farmer stated, "Then no doubt you would fit right in, because you are clearly a large and strong man and there they believe themselves to be the greatest of warriors."

But the woman of the house was overcome with weeping, which marked her behavior any time mention was made of King Hrolf and his horde at Hleidargard.

So Bodvar asked her, "Why do you cry, carefree old woman?"

The old woman replied, "It is because my husband and I have a son named Hott, and one day he went to the royal palace for some fun and games but there the king's men merely mocked and ridiculed him. He was not able to stand up for himself, so they grabbed him and tossed him into a great bone pile. And it became their custom during meals that when they had finished taking the meat off the bone they would throw it as hard as they could in his direction. And at times when the bone struck him he ended up severely welted and bruised. I do not even know whether he be alive or dead, but would beg you as compensation for your fair treatment here, that when you are there you will not throw the largest of bones at him but only the smaller ones, unless, of course, he be dead already."

Bodvar replied, "I will certainly honor your simple request, and I do not believe it suits a warrior to batter people with bones or to make war upon children and men of little might."

The old woman said, "You will do well for yourself, because you possess a strong arm and certainly, if you do not withhold your blows, any adversary you face would find no deliverance."

So leaving them behind Bodvar continued on to Hleidargard and once he had come to the king's palace he boldly stabled his horse in a stall amongst the king's most prized mounts. Then he came into the king's hall where there were but a few men sitting. And he found a seat at the end of the bench nearby the entryway, and had only been there for a short time before he heard noises emerging from near the corner of the room. Looking towards the sound Bodvar saw there a great pile of banquet bones, from which a quite begrimed hand emerged.

Bodvar strode to the corner and inquired, "Who makes this pile of bones his home?"

A man answered timidly from within, "Good sir, my name is Hott."

Bodvar asked of him, "What are you doing over here? What are you up to?"

Hott replied, "Good sir, I am building a protective wall for myself."

"I think both you and your protective wall are pathetic," Bodvar said before he grabbed the man's arm and pulled him out from within the pile of bones.

Hott cried out like a madman, "You're acting clearly to bring about my quick death, because I had made provision for my own defense, but now my protective wall lies in pieces on the floor, the one I had formed high so as to shield myself from all of your projectiles. Because of this wall none of the dire blows intended for me did reach me, even though the wall was, as of yet, unfinished."

Bodvar said to him, "No longer will you work on your protective wall."

Hott answered, "Good sir, do you intend to bring my life to an end now?"

But Bodvar only told him to keep his mouth shut and carried him off, taking him out of the hall to a nearby lake, although few paid any attention to what Bodvar was now up to. There he had Hott wash thoroughly and then returned with him to his place on the bench, to the seat he had occupied before, and set Hott there beside himself. Yet Hott was so frightened that every one of his bones was shaking, even though it appeared to him that this man was acting as his benefactor.

Later in the evening a large body of men entered the hall, who were the warriors of King Hrolf. They saw Hott seated with the men at the benches and believed that any man who had done this must truly be courageous of heart. When Hott looked at his former foes he could only wince when remembering the pain they had caused. Fearing for his life he began to amble back towards his bone heap, but Bodvar grabbed him and would not let go. Hott thought that if he could only get back to his bone pile he would not be so vulnerable to their abuses.

The king's warriors were quick to resume their former habit, at first throwing the smaller bones across the room to where Bodvar and Hott were sitting. But while Hott, expecting at any time to feel the pain of one of their thrown bones, was so fearful that he could neither eat nor drink. Bodvar paid them no attention at all, however, as though nothing untoward was brewing.

Hott noticed and warned Bodvar, "Good sir, that is no paltry joint bone aimed to injure us."

But Bodvar told Hott to keep quiet and when it flew towards them he caught the joint bone in his flexed hand, which came with the entire leg bone attached, and threw it back with great force. It struck the very man who had thrown it, so hard that he was immediately killed, which caused the rest of the king's men to gasp in horror.

Afterwards King Hrolf and his retainers who resided within the fortress heard of the formidable man who had come into the king's hall and who had killed one of his warriors. The others that were there now lobbied to have the man put to death. Yet the king asked if his follower had been killed without cause. They replied to him that it was nearly so. And after they explained themselves the truth eventually emerged, causing King Hrolf to declare that under no circumstances must this visitor be put to death, saying: "You have developed a bad habit amongst yourselves of throwing your meat bones at blameless men. This not only brings disgrace to me but by doing so you also dishonor yourselves. Often I have reprimanded you concerning this habit, but you have refused to change your ways. This man whom you attacked I gauge is not your inferior, so summon him here that I might learn who he is and why he is here."

Bodvar was brought before the king and greeted him with great felicity. The king asked him his name.

Bodvar replied, "Your men refer to me as 'Hott's protector', but my real name is Bodvar."

Then the king asked, "How much are you prepared to pay in compensation for the death of my man?"

And Bodvar answered, "What he received is what he deserved."

The king asked him, "Would you like then to become my man in his place?"

And Bodvar replied, "I could not refuse such an offer, but as things are I will not do so unless Hott is taken too, for the two of us will not stand apart. And that we must both sit at a position closer to you than the man who was killed, otherwise we will both leave."

So the king said, "I do not recognize much worthiness in Hott, but I will not deny him food at my table."

Bodvar then chose a seat on the benches as he wished, rather than that of the other man who was killed. To do this he lifted three men up from their seats and moved them further down, then he and Hott took their places. They were much farther into the hall than they had been before when near the door. And the other men considered Bodvar was not easy to confront though a great deal of resentment formed against him.

As Yuletide approached a manifest foreboding overcame the men there, and Bodvar inquired of Hott why they had become so anxious.

Hott replied, "They are fearful because for the past two winters a great baleful beast has terrorized the hall. A monster that has wings upon its back and oftentimes is seen flying. And for the two years it has come here it has caused a good deal of damage. Weapons are useless against the creature and of the king's warriors who have sought to slay it, even the best among them, have never come home."

Bodvar said, "Then this hall is not so well defended as I'd thought, if one lone animal could cause so much destruction to the king's lands and livestock."

Hott said, "This creature is no mere animal, but rather it is the most fearsome of trolls."

When Yule eve arrived the king said to his troops, "This night my wish is that you men keep still, and make not a sound. None of you should attempt to confront this creature in combat, because

57

I do not wish to lose any of you to this formidable foe. And I will leave the livestock to its own fate." And they all solemnly swore to do as the king asked.

But Bodvar had sneaked away during the night and Hott went along with him, though not until being forced to do so, stating that in going out he was being taken to his death. Bodvar had told him that it would rather be for the better. When they went from the hall Hott was so frightened that Bodvar was required to carry him, until they spied the baleful beast. And as soon as Hott set his eyes upon it he began to scream in his loudest voice, bawling that the creature was going to eat him.

Bodvar said to him, "Keep quiet, you dog," and tossed him down upon the heather and there he remained, neither frightened but little, nor brave enough to make the trek back home. But Bodvar went forward to attack the beast, but his sword became sluggish, remaining stuck within its sheath. Yet by grabbing his scabbard hard and with a prodigious pull he caused it to be freed, but so that in its egress from the sheath it shrieked severely. Then he hefted his handle and struck beneath the creature's shoulder, delivering it with such swiftness that it speedily sought the beast's blood-chamber, causing the demon to fall dead upon the moor.

When the contest was complete Bodvar then made his way to where Hott still sat, lifted him up, and carried him to where the beast was lying.

Hott was shaking terribly and Bodvar said to him, "You must drink the beast's blood." But at first Hott was not willing to do so, though he was too terrified to do anything else. Bodvar then made him take two large gulps of the blood and in addition had him eat a bit of the demon's heart. Then after that Bodvar raised Hott to his feet and there they prodded and parried blades with one another for quite some time.

Then Bodvar said to him, "Now that you have grown to be so strong I imagine from now on you won't be so fearful of King Hrolf's men."

To which Hott replied, "From this day forward I will have no fear of them, nor of you."

Bodvar said to him, "Then, my friend, things have turned out the better for you. So now let us return to the beast and prop him up in such a way that the king's men will believe that it must still be alive." And this they did before returning home. But they did not speak a word of these events to anyone else, and so no one learned of what had occurred.

Then in the morning the king inquired of any news about the creature and whether it had visited them again during the night. And he was given word that all of his livestock remained unharmed within their pens. So the king gave orders to his troops to seek out evidence as to whether the creature had been there, and these armed men departed but very soon returned. They told him that the beast was coming upon them in a ravenous rampage against the fortress at that very moment. So the king ordered his warriors to fight courageously, that each according to his might and mettle do what he could to defeat the beast. And at the king's command the men made themselves ready.

When the king set his eyes upon the creature he eventually said, "It does not appear to be moving, but which of you is willing to take this opportunity to attack it right now?"

Bodvar replied, "That would no doubt quell the curiosity of the most courageous amongst us. Hott, my lad, you can dispel the slurs against you that men have made, saying that you show neither will nor courage. Since no one else is quick to do so, why not go and kill the creature yourself and gain fame for it."

The king said to Hott, "I cannot say from where you've found this newfound nerve, Hott, however there has clearly been a great change in you and in such a short span of time."

Hott said to the king, "In order to carry out this deed would you lend me the sword Golden Hilt, the one you now hold, then either I will kill the beast or meet my death this day."

King Hrolf replied, "This sword is only to be wielded by a man who shows both strength in his body and nobility in his spirit."

Hott replied, "Then you must assume, Majesty, that I am made of such stuff."

The King responded, "But how would one know? Unless far more is different about you than mere appearances would suggest, but truly not many would believe that you are no different than you were before. So take the sword and it will serve you well if my perception of you proves true."

59

So then Hott took the sword and set out to confront the beast. And as soon as it was within his reach he struck it at once, so that the monster's body fell vanquished to the ground.

Then Bodvar said to the king, "Majesty, see now what he has accomplished."

The king answered, "He is certainly quite different, that I cannot deny, but I am sure that Hott by himself was not the one who killed the creature, but rather I believe you are the one who is responsible for it."

And Bodvar replied, "You may be right."

Then the king declared, "I was aware that when you appeared amongst us that hardly one could presume to be your equal, but I would consider your greatest feat to be making a brave champion out of this man Hott. Previously he had always been deemed a man who would be forever beset by ill-fortune. But I do not wish him to be called Hott from this day forward, but instead that he be called Hialti ('hilt'), so that he will now be known by the name of the sword Golden Hilt."

This concludes the story of Bodvar and his brothers.[32]

Epitheus: Splendid, Thaeo.

CHAPTER 6

Thaeo: Notice that here both Hvit and the dragon are described as being powerful trolls, just as we find with the demon Grendel and his mother.

Epitheus: Yes, it seemed very similar to the slaying of Grendel's mother with the sword 'golden hilt'.

Thaeo: Yet, as you surely noticed, there are other details that are not present within both, such as the drinking of the beast's blood and the setting up of the body. But they do agree, however, that the creature is killed during the first encounter whereas it is only a symbolic killing which follows, as with Beowulf when he defeats Grendel then later goes to his lair and severs off his head.

Epitheus: True enough.

Thaeo: Though I am inclined to think that we might do better at this point if we were to determine what might have inspired the original story.

Epitheus: But what do you mean?

Thaeo: I mean to say that we could identify the role of each character if we understood better what each character represents. For instance, we might consider the name of the beast Grendel is not very far from that of 'Earandel', which is a name for the Morning Star.[*] Thus we could conclude that the character of Grendel might also be associated with this star.

Epitheus: Certainly.

Thaeo: And we could likewise associate him with a character (in Norse myth) by the name of Aurvandil, from whom we attain the star name 'Aurvandil's Toe'. It is the (Nordic) god Thor who relates the episode of how he created this star, subsequent to his confrontation

---

[*] This is the planet *Venus* as seen from Earth.

with the giant Hrungnir; which I would be inclined to believe is nothing less than another take on the slaying of Grendel. Thus it might be well worth relating, if you would like to hear of it.

Epitheus: By all means.

Thaeo: Then I will tell the entirety of it,

> It began when Odin rode his swift steed Sleipnir into Giantland and there came to the house of a burly giant called Hrungnir ('combatant'). Hrungnir asked what sort of person he was, wearing his gilded helmet and able, as he was, to traverse both land and sea. Odin replied that it was because of his unrivaled horse, then swearing by his own head that there was no better horse to be found in all of Giantland. Hrungnir agreed that it was a fine stallion indeed, but he countered that his own horse Gullfaxi ('gold-mane') was a far superior mount than his. And when Odin set his eye upon this exceptional horse he bolted off at once and a livid Hrungnir leapt upon his own steed and galloped off in pursuit, intending to make him pay for his arrogant boasting.
>
> Odin galloped away at such a great speed that he was able to keep just ahead of him, and when they rushed over the next high hill Hrungnir was charging in such a great giant-rage that, before he knew what had happened, he had followed Odin straight through the gates of Asgard. When he reached the doors of Valhall the Aesir were friendly enough towards him, however, and to avert his rage Odin invited him inside for a drink to slake his thirst.
>
> Hrungnir entered the hall and demanded to be served at once. So they brought out for him several enormous goblets brimming with beer, which were normally used by Thor when he was drinking. He drained each one of them and afterwards became drunk enough that there was then no end to his boasting. Freyia was the only one among the Aesir who was still willing to refill his empty goblets, and he stridently declared that he would drink all of the Aesir's ale before he was through. Then Hrungnir told them that he was going to pick up the entire edifice of Valhall and carry it back with him to Giantland upon his shoulders. Then he

was going to kill all of the gods and bury Asgard beneath the ground, taking as his prize the goddesses Freyia and Thor's wife Sif, before he headed home.

When the Aesir had had enough of listening to his nonsense they called upon the name of Thor, and at once he came striding into the hall with his hammer raised aloft. Thor took in the situation and with high ire wanted to know who had been responsible for inviting one of the treacherous race of giants to drink among them; who had given him sanctuary as their guest within the hall of the slain; and why the goddess Freyia would, like an ordinary serving wench, be serving him drink as upon one of their feasting-days. Giving Thor an unfriendly stare, Hrungnir replied that Odin himself had invited him in for a drink and that while he remained he stayed under his protection. Thor blasted back that after he was through with him Hrungnir would be plenty sorry he ever accepted Odin's invitation.

"I did a very foolish thing," Hrungnir said, "leaving my shield and whetstone at home. For if I had my weapons with me we could surely resolve this in a duel right here and now, but as things stand you could be called a rotten blackguard if you were to kill me when I was unarmed. It would be a far greater test of your mettle if you would dare agree to fight me in single combat upon the plain of the stone-town wall."

Thor would not wish anything to hinder his going into single combat, for no one had ever challenged him to enter into a duel before, so he readily accepted. Hrungnir then went on his way and rode quickly until he had reached his home in Giantland. Hrungnir's visit to Asgard was much spoken of among the giants and about the meeting that was to take place between himself and the mighty Thor. But the giants believed that they had a great stake in the outcome, as to which one emerged the victor, for they would find themselves at the mercy of Thor's hammer if Hrungnir were killed in the contest, for he was the strongest one among them all.

The troubled giants then made a man out of clay at stone-town wall, who was nine-leagues high and three broad at the armpits. Yet there was not a heart large enough to be found among the giants in which to animate his form. So they took a mare and removed its heart, inserting it within the clay creation. But this proved to be not so stalwart when staring in the face of Thor. Hrungnir himself had a heart that was famous, which was composed of solid rock and sharp with three spikes. His head was also made of stone and so was his shield, which was both broad and deep. When he stood there at stone-town wall in expectation of Thor's arrival he held his shield in front of him, while resting the whetstone weapon, a club that looked very formidable, upon his shoulder. To his side stood the giant of clay named Mokkurkalfi ('weak-legged') whose own heart was quivering and, it is said, that when he first set his eyes upon thunderous Thor that he immediately wetted himself.

When Thor had gone to meet Hrungnir for the duel he took along with him his squire Thialfi. Thialfi ran ahead of Thor to where Hrungnir was and said to him, "You're not standing so as to properly defend yourself, for you're holding your shield in front of you. Thor saw you standing like that and decided to approach you from beneath, so you must realize that he's going to attack you from the ground."

So at this Hrungnir placed his shield on the ground and stood upon it, and now held his whetstone weapon in both hands. Then he heard a loud thundering and saw a great deal of lightning before Thor appeared in view exhibiting a terrible rage. He was approaching at great speed, brandishing his hammer Miollnir. Thor threw it when he was still at a good distance away from Hrungnir. The giant raised back and threw his whetstone in reply, and the two weapons met in mid-flight and crashed together, leaving the whetstone cleaved in two. One of these pieces fell down to the earth and from it all whetstone rocks have come. The other fragment flew into Thor's forehead, causing him to topple to the ground. But his hammer found its mark nonetheless, hitting Hrungnir's head square in the middle, which broke his skull into fragments. But his body fell forward so that when he landed his leg pinned down Thor on his neck.

Thialfi had engaged Mokkurkalfi in combat, but his defeat was nothing noteworthy. After this Thialfi approached Thor so as to attempt to raise Hrungnir's vast limb from over him, but was unable to make any headway. Afterwards the other Aesir made haste to get there, hearing that Thor had been downed, each one in turn making an attempt to raise the great leg but not one of them could budge it a single inch.

Then Thor's son Magni ('mighty'), son of the giantess Iarnsaxa, arrived and, though he was only three-years old at the time, threw off Hrungnir's leg as if it were nothing, saying to his father, "Isn't it too bad, Dad, that I came here so late. For I rather suspect I might have easily sent this giant down into Hel myself with but one blow from my fist."

Thor stood and greeted his son with fondness, saying that he would certainly mature some day into a very mighty man. Then Thor said to his son, "I think that you should have Hrungnir's horse Gullfaxi as a gift."

But Odin thought it improper for Thor to give such a miraculous horse to the son of a giantess rather than to his own father. Yet, according to Thor's decision, to Magni it went. Thor then returned to his home of *Thrudheim* ('Mighty House'), but with the whetstone still lodged deeply in his forehead. But a spell-worker was summoned named Groa, who was the wife of the valiant Aurvandil. She knew the proper spells and chanted them over Thor until the whetstone began to loosen. Thor could feel this and thought to himself that the whetstone fragment would soon be gone, much to his relief. Wishing to reward Groa for her work, and to give her something to be happy about, he told her news of her long-lost husband, saying that when he had made his way south out of Giantland he carried Aurvandil upon his back in a basket across the Elivagar River.[*] Yet on the way one of his toes was sticking out of the basket and had frozen solid, so Thor broke off the frost-bitten toe and threw it up into the sky so as to make the star known as 'Aurvandil's Toe'.

Thor pointed out this star to her as proof of what he had told her, and said that it would not be too long before Aurvandil would be home. Groa became so excited at this news that she could hardly remember her spells and so could no longer loosen the whetstone any further, so there it remained lodged within

---

[*] Elivagar ('stormy sea') is the river which divides Middle-Earth from Giantland, though here Giantland's position in the north clearly equates it with the Underworld. The river is likely to have been the one that surrounded the entire world. (Simek 1993: 73, 'Elivagar') In Greek myth it is the river Styx and in Indian myth the river Rasa.

Thor's head. And because of this we are not permitted to toss whetstones about, for this causes the one in Thor's forehead to shift, which causes him great pain.[33]

And that is the extent of the tale, and as you can see the battle of Thor against Hrungnir is placed in proximity with that of Aurvandil's toe, though the two are not coincident within the story.[*] But we might only conclude that the star he created would be the Morning Star, which by its white color and oblong shape would surely bring to mind a toe that had been frost-bitten.

Epitheus: Certainly.

Thaeo: Though I also notice a possible connection between Thor's squire Thialfi and Biarki's companion Hialti, who at least share similar names if not similar roles; for Thialfi here takes down the clay giant Mokkurkalfi in the same manner that Hialti defeats the propped up monster after drinking its blood.

Epitheus: Truly, he does.

Thaeo: Then also consider Hercules and Hylas, for they too show a similarity with Thor and Thialfi.[†] And Hercules was to have possessed a godly strength that he might have gained from his battle with the Nemean Lion, which as we know was his first labor.

Epitheus: Indeed.

Thaeo: We also find that Hercules and Thor (Thorkillus) can be related through the (hypothetical) name of **THER**, though also perhaps through their characteristics, for we find that both are known as the slayer of monsters, and that the club of Hercules could be easily compared to Thor's hammer. And we know that Hercules was

---

[*] This could arise from their having at one point been developed out of a single episode, where at the conclusion of Thor's duel there was made reference to the appearance of the star as a consequence.

[†] Hylas is the youthful companion of Hercules, but does not appear in his twelve labors. Linguistically, (T)hercul-es is related to Thorkill-us (Thor), and (T)hyl-as related to Thial-fi and (T)hial-ti.

carried from his funeral pyre upon a cloud of crashing thunder, being, as he was, the son of Zeus.[34]

Epitheus: Just so.

Thaeo: Likewise, we saw before the emphasis placed upon the heroic character taking on the form of a bear, where Biarki is the son of two parents named 'bear'. And it is actually stated that the beast Biarki fought with was not a dragon but rather a great bear. Likewise, in the same manner after defeating it, Biarki has Hialti drink some of its blood so as to gain the bear's strength.[35] Thus we have here a contest between a savage bear and a bear-hero who himself possesses tremendous strength.

Epitheus: Truly.

Thaeo: And although Grendel's mother is never named, we do know that the wife of Orvendil is named Gerutha,[36] which is the same as Bertha (the Germanic sun/earth goddess). This is also comparable to the name of the wife of Orendel (Erentel) whose name is Breide.[*]

Epitheus: Fascinating.

Thaeo: Then being equivalent to the (Germanic) sun goddess, we might consider that Grendel's mother would be a goddess of death who resided beneath the fens at night, which fits the name of the dwelling place of Odin's wife Frigg (the Nordic Bertha) which is called *Fensalir* ('fen hall').[†]

---

[*] Grimm summarizes the exploits of Orendel: "He suffers shipwreck on a voyage, takes shelter with a master fisherman, *Eisen*, earns the seamless coat of his master, and afterwards wins frau *Breide*, the fairest of women: king *Eigel* of Trier was his father's name." (Grimm 2004: 374)

[†] Later traditions put Asgard, the realm of the gods, in the sky; while in earlier times, when the gods were regarded as the sun and the moon, they were believed to inhabit both the heaven and the underworld. The sun is sometimes imagined to have gone into the water and below the world causing the swamps to glow. The moon was to have served the same purpose, thus the origin of the name 'Fenrir', as well as of jack-o'-lantern and will-o'-wisp (*ignis fatuus*).

Epitheus: One could hardly doubt it.

Thaeo: Thus there must have been a reason why bogs came to be associated with the sun. And we might think this could have arisen from the light which sometimes appears above marshes at night (*ignis fatuus*), and could be viewed as a reflection from the sun's subterranean dwelling wherein she resided at night, which certainly fits with Fensalir.* This is certainly what is meant when the poet says, "Night brings with it the most singular event, for there the water glows."[37]

Epitheus: Most singular.

Thaeo: Then the marsh was the abode of the sun at night, but was likewise held to be particularly sacred because it also acted as a gateway to the underworld.†

Epitheus: Yes.

Thaeo: Thus this might take us back to the meaning of Grendel's name, which could simply derive from 'green dell' or 'green devil'.

Epitheus: That would be appropriate.

Thaeo: Then from this we can associate the sun goddess (Bertha) with the Morning Star (Orendel), who is viewed as being either her husband or her son.

Epitheus: So it seems.

---

* Another name for the city of Bath was *Aquae-Solis* which essentially means 'watery sun', no doubt because the sun was believed to dwell beneath the hot springs at night. Sulis (Sol) was the goddess of hot springs for the same reason.
† The underworld is often conceived in Germanic folklore as being a vast green meadow. The realm of the Canaanite god Death was said to lie within a swamp.

Thaeo: And if we have already included the sun and Morning Star, then might we expect the personage of the moon must also be present?

Epitheus: One must assume it would.

Thaeo: And we know already that the Nemean lion was to have fallen down from the moon, while the goddess Nemea is given as the daughter of Zeus and the moon goddess Selene. But Nemea is also associated with the moon through her names Pandeia ('all bright') and Erse, (Greek) goddess of the dew ('*herse*').[*]

Epitheus: Certainly.

Thaeo: And might Erse's name also be related to '*ursa*', meaning bear?

Epitheus: Surely it might.

Thaeo: With Erse being the same goddess as Nemea, and Nemea being the daughter of Selene, the mother of the Nemean lion, whose nurse we know was Hera, the queen of heaven.

Epitheus: Yes indeed.

Thaeo: Then the beast we have also identified as a denizen of the moon, cared for by the moon goddess (Hera or Selene) before falling down to the land of Nemea.

Epitheus: Clearly so.

---

[*] There are two other goddesses who might be associated with Herse: one is Erce the mother of earth, Perseis the wife of Helios, Perses the father of Hekate, and Perseis (Hekate), as well as Persephone ('*Perse-phone*') herself. Erce might also be linked to Frau Herke from Saxon folklore (Simek 1993: 75, 'Erce').

69

Thaeo: So if we believe that the mire beast was also to have come from the moon, we would expect it to have taken the appearance of a bear.[*]

Epitheus: Certainly.

Thaeo: And since we are observing the heavenly bodies subsequent to the bear's confrontation with his adversary, whereby we view the Morning Star to have been his claw, appearing in close proximity to the sun, then we would also expect to see the bear as it was after the contest had transpired. By which I mean that it would be after he had been beheaded.

Epitheus: Yes, truly.

Thaeo: And is this then, in fact, what we observe?

Epitheus: It is, indeed, just as you say.

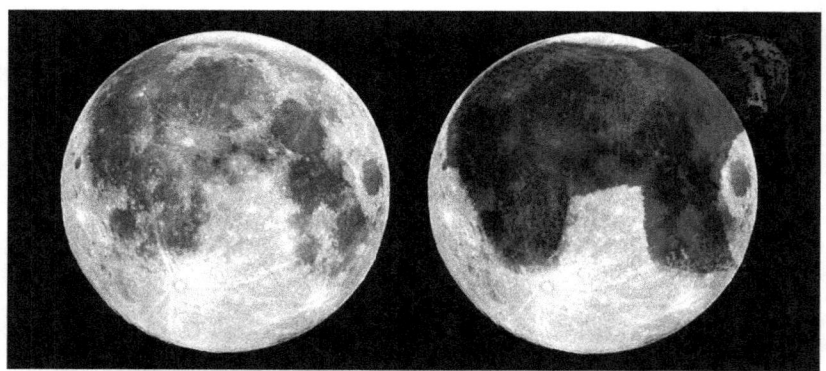

Headless bear visible upon the Moon, the beheaded beast.

Thaeo: Then having identified this bear upon the moon we have likewise justly confirmed that the story was designed to explain why a headless bear could be seen upon the moon?

---

[*] Bogs were believed to be the dwelling place of bears.

70

Epitheus: It seems undeniable.

Thaeo: And then when we look upon the moon reversed from this we see upon it the figure of the moon goddess, his mother or caregiver, whom we are already familiar with as the 'queen of heaven'.[*]

Epitheus: Indeed.

Thaeo: Then there is something else we might add in reference to the giant Hrungnir. For he is said to have been standing upon his shield at the moment he was struck down by Thor's hurtling hammer. And as we know both the sun and moon disks are often likened to shields and thus the appearance of a headless bear upon the face of the moon equates with the giant Hrungnir standing upon his shield (the moon disk).

Epitheus: Amazing.

Thaeo: And we might conclude that not only are the episodes of the two contests merely similar, but that Hrungnir is the very same figure as Grendel, and then so too we might surmise that Beowulf is then equivalent to Thor, as the god of thunder.

Epitheus: It would seem to be precisely as you say, Thaeo.

---

[*] See *The Eden Enigma: A Dialogue*

CHAPTER 7

Thaeo: Though we have satisfied ourselves by identifying the voracious foe, appearing as a figure upon the moon, it is suggested too that its own claw, which was used to vanquish him, was thrown up into the sky to become the Morning Star. This we can conclude both from the name for the Morning Star 'Earandel' and the description of its origins as being 'Aurvandil's Toe'.

And this creature's mother was the goddess of the sun, who was thought to reside beneath the swamps at night. And although we haven't any trace of the goddess in the story of the Nemean lion, we might compare her to its mother (Selene or Echidna) or to the vengeful Hera, who was the beast's caregiver and who also appears as the divine adversary of Hercules. Likewise, a goddess fails to appear in the story of Thor's duel with Hrungnir, although we do find the wife of Aurvandil named Groa ('grow').

Epitheus: Well put.

Thaeo: And as we have identified a bear upon face of the moon, it makes me think back to Queen Hvit, who is the one responsible for killing the father of Biarki (Beowulf), for her name means 'white' (*'hvit'*) and this could associate her with the whiteness of the moon.[*] And as we might regard the bear to be a threat that fell down from the moon, might we also consider his mother could be the featureless moon disk itself?

Epitheus: We might well consider it.

Thaeo: Though Queen Hvit may reflect yet another tradition, where the moon and sun were two sisters, one however who outshone the other. Thus the original moon was white and featureless like her sister (the sun) but also far less radiant. It is possible then that Hvit is the original inspiration for Grendel's mother, who with his aid trapped the sun to keep it from outshining her own pale beauty. And perhaps this is the original concept behind the story of Snow White, which I could tell if you would like to hear it.

---

[*] Heimdall, the Norse god of the moon, was known as the 'white god'.

Epitheus: Please.

Thaeo: Then I will tell as much of it as I can.

Once upon a time, when snowflakes were falling like feathers from the sky at mid-winter, there was a queen sitting by her ebony-framed window. As she sat there sewing by herself she glanced out the window at the gathering snow, which caused her to accidentally jab her finger with the needle causing three drops of blood to fall. Yet the color red upon the white of the newly fallen snow was so striking to her, that she mused to herself, "Oh, if only I had a child who was as white as snow and as red as blood, with hair as black as ebony." Then not long after this it came to pass that she gave birth to a little daughter who was as white as snow and as red as blood, with hair as black as ebony, so they named her Little Snow White. Yet as soon as the girl had been born the queen died and her husband the king took a new wife.

Little Snow White's step mother, the new queen, was a striking but vain woman, and because of this she was filled with a great deal of pride and jealousy, and could not tolerate any other woman being considered a greater beauty than she. The queen possessed a magic mirror and each morning she would stand before it and look upon herself saying, "O mirror, mirror, upon my wall, who in the land is fairest of all?"

To which the mirror always answered, "You, my queen, are the fairest by far."

So as long as she heard this she remained pleased and her arrogance was satisfied, since she was aware that the mirror could only speak the truth.

But as Snow White matured she became year-by-year a greater and greater beauty to behold, so that when she was seven-years old she had a loveliness that far outshone the light of the sun, and surpassed the beauty of her step-mother the Queen. So on that day when the Queen asked her mirror again, "O mirror, mirror, upon my wall, who in the land is fairest of all?"

The mirror answered her, "You, my queen, are fair 'tis true, but Snow White is a thousand times fairer than you."

At this the Queen felt flustered, like a ruler deposed, and became green with envy at Little Snow White. So from that time forward whenever she looked upon Snow White's beauty her heart heaved within her frame, so great was the growing spite she held for that little child. Her cruel envy and wicked pride became a sickness within her, so that it twisted itself like a vine around her heart, until she could no longer find any peace, neither day nor night.

So she summoned to herself a huntsman and said to him, "You will lead Snow White deep into the woods, for I cannot bear to look upon her ever again. And to provide me proof that the deed is done, you must bring her liver and lungs back to me."

The huntsman obeyed the Queen and took fair Snow White out deep into the woods. Unsheathing his hunting knife he was about to use it to strike at her innocent heart. But then her eyes filled with welling tears and she begged upon her knees, "Oh my dear friend, please let me live and I promise that I will run off into the wild woods and never return."

Because the girl was so sweet and gentle the huntsman could not bring himself to do her any harm, and so he said to her, "Then run off, dear child." But then he thought to himself that the wild animals would be her death in any case, but for him it was like a heavy burden had been lifted from his chest, since now he did not have to kill her by his own hand. After this an immature wild boar came leaping by and so he went after it and killed it. He cut out its liver and lungs and took them back to the Queen, to provide her with proof that Snow White was dead. She made the cook boil them in brine and serve them to her for dinner, and the vile villainess ate them, thinking that she was consuming the liver and lungs of Little Snow White.

Now the anguished girl was all by herself in the immense dark forest, so full of fear that all she could do was gaze at the raging leaves upon the trees, for she had no idea where she could be. So there was nothing else for her to do but keep running. And she cut up her feet on jagged stones, tore her dress upon sharp thorns, and wild beasts sprung at her from all directions, but without being able to inflict any injury upon her. She ran until her little feet could carry her no further, then just as the last light of evening was beginning to fade she spied in a small clearing a little house and lumbered inside to rest herself there.

Everything within, like the little house itself, was quite small, but it was so tidy and clean that no one would think it not so. In the middle of the floor sat a little table with a tiny white tablecloth and seven tiny plates; each of the plates had a little spoon, knife and fork; and there were seven little cups too. Upon the plates was food and bread, and within the cups was something to drink. Along the wall there were seven little beds lined in a row, each covered with the whitest of white sheets.

Snow White was so hungry and thirsty that she could not help but eat from each one of the plates a small amount of the vegetables and bread, and to drink from each one of the cups a small amount of wine. But after eating she was so tired that she walked to the beds to allow her weary limbs to rest. She went to the first but this one wasn't quite right, it was far too long, the next was far too short, the one after that was too hard, the next one was too soft, the one after that was too narrow, the next one too wide, until she finally reached the seventh bed and this one was just right for her. So she stayed there tucked inside and fell into a deep sleep.

Then at night, when it had become fully dark, the owners of the little house returned. They were seven diminutive men who mined ore from the mountains. They came in and lit their seven tiny candles, and when the light from them cast itself about the room they recognized that things had been disturbed from the way they had been left.

The first said, "Who's been sitting in my chair?"

The second said, "Who's been eating off my plate?"

The third said, "Who's been eating some of my bread?"

The fourth said, "Who's been nibbling my vegetables?"

The fifth said, "Who's been jabbing with my fork?"

The sixth said, "Who's been slicing with my knife?"

The seventh said, "Who's been drinking from my cup?"

Then the first went over to his bed and there saw a small depression in it, and he said, "Who's been resting in my bed?"

And the others came running up to him and they all shouted, "Someone has been resting in my bed, too."

All but the seventh, who looking into his bed found Little Snow White lying there fast asleep. The other dwarfs ran up to him and gasped together. Then they returned with their seven little candles and cast their light upon Snow White's little figure. "Oh my! Oh merciful heavens!" they exclaimed, "This girl is such a beauty!"

They were so delighted by her looks that they did not even attempt to wake her, but allowed her to stay dozing there within the bed. So the seventh dwarf had to share a bed with his companions, spending one hour in each of theirs until the night was finished.

When Snow White awoke the next morning she saw the seven dwarfs around her and was dreadfully frightened, but they asked in a very friendly way, "What is your name?"

"Snow White," she replied meekly.

"And how did you come to find our house?" the dwarfs inquired further.

So she told them that her step-mother had tried to kill her by sending her out into the woods, but the huntsman sent to do the deed had spared her life, and when she had run for an entire day she found herself at their little house.

The dwarfs said to her, "If you will take care of our home for us, and cook our food, and make our beds, and wash our clothes, and sew and knit for us, and keep everything neat and tidy, then you may remain here with us as long as you wish, and you shall find nothing wanting."

Snow White replied, "Yes, I will do it with all my heart."

So Snow White took care of their little house for them and every morning they went off to the mountains where they went searching for ores and gold, and when they returned home in the evening she had their little meals ready for them. But during the day she was all alone in the empty house, and so the dear dwarfs had warned her before setting off, "Beware of your mother, for she will eventually come to know that you are living here with us. So never let anyone in when we are gone, under any circumstances."

The Queen, who believed that she had eaten Snow White's liver and lungs, at once believed that she was again the fairest of all. When she walked before her mirror and asked, "O mirror,

76

mirror, upon my wall, who in the land is the fairest of all?" the mirror answered her, "You, my queen, are fair 'tis true, but Snow White, who lives beyond the seven mountains with the seven dwarfs, is still a thousand times fairer than you."

When the Queen heard what the mirror had said, she fidgeted and shook with rage screaming, "Snow White shall die, even if it costs me my own life!" And she went off into her hidden room, where she allowed admittance to no one but herself, and there she concocted from her wares a poison apple. By appearances it was very appetizing, with a deep red side and a pale white side, so anyone who looked upon it would no doubt wish to eat it. But anyone who took even the merest bite of the red side would suffer by immediately falling down dead, for the apple had been so devilishly crafted that only the red half of it was poisoned. Then applying makeup to her face she disguised herself to look like a poor peasant woman, and travelled over the seven mountains to the home of the seven dwarfs. When she arrived she rapped upon the little door.

Snow White peeped out of the window and said to her, "I am not permitted to let anyone enter, for the dwarfs have forbidden me from doing so."

"That's fine with me," answered the Queen, "because I'll soon find someone else who will want one of my apples and I'll be rid of them. But here, you may have one of them to try."

"No, I am not allowed to take anything," said Snow White.

"But what are you afraid of, that the apple is poisoned?" asked the old peasant. "Then watch, I will cut the apple in half and you may eat the red half and I will eat the white."

Snow White desired so much the perfect-looking apple and when she saw the peasant woman eating half of it and appearing to be unharmed, she wanted the other half desperately and reached her dainty hand out of the window and took it. Yet she had barely taken a bite of the poisoned half when she slipped down lifeless to the floor.

The Queen looked at her now with a malicious eye and cackled greatly, shouting, "You who are white as snow, red as blood, and black as ebony, the dwarfs cannot do anything to save you now!"

Then having gotten back to her room the Queen asked her mirror again, "O mirror, mirror, upon my wall, who in the land is the fairest of all?"

And the mirror answered her, "You, my queen, are the fairest by far." And now her envious heart was content as greatly, at least, as a green heart can be.

Now by this time the dwarfs had come home that evening and found Snow White lying on the floor, she was not breathing and appeared to be dead. They lifted her and looked for anything that might be poisoning her. They unlaced her dress, they brushed her hair, they washed her body in water and wine, but nothing worked to revive her. The dear child was surely dead and so she remained to all outward appearances. So they laid her out upon a bier and all seven of them sat down next to her, mourning her passing with tears for fully three days. They had planned to bury her, but she still looked as rosy as one who was yet alive and she still possessed her lovely red cheeks.

They said to themselves, "How can we bury her within the dark earth," and so they made a coffin of transparent glass, so that her body could be viewed from every side. They put her inside and upon it wrote her name in golden letters, "Princess Snow White". Then they set the casket upon a mountain and one of them always remained with her and watched over her body there. The forest animals too came and mourned the passing of Snow White: first came an owl, then came a raven, and finally came a dove.

Snow White's body remained lying in the coffin for a very long time but she remained incorruptible, looking as if she were merely sleeping. And she was still as white as snow, and as red as blood, and with hair as black as ebony.

Then it so happened that a prince had entered the woods, and came upon the house of the seven dwarfs, seeking shelter with them for the night. When he was near the mountain he had spied the glass coffin with a beautiful girl inside and read what was written upon it in gold letters.

And he spoke to the dwarfs, saying, "Please give this coffin to me and I will give you in return for it whatever you might wish to have."

The dwarfs answered, "We will never sell it, not for all the gold in the world."

So he said to them, "But I would not be able to go on living if I could no longer look upon this little Princess Snow White. Give it to me and I avow that I will honor her and cherish her as my most adored one."

Thus he spoke and the merciful dwarfs felt great pity for him and let him have the coffin without accepting any payment for it. The prince made arrangements for his servants to carry it away upon their shoulders. But as they were moving along one of them stumbled upon some branches and this caused the piece of poisoned apple lodged in Snow White's throat to loosen. Soon after this she stirred, opened her eyes, and lifting the lid of the coffin she sat up, resurrected.

"Great heavens, where could I be?" she cried out.

The prince answered her with great joy, "You are here with me." And he told her everything that had happened, and then said "I love you more than any cherished thing in the entire world. Please, return with me to my father's palace and there I will make you my wife." Snow White loved him so and thus she eagerly went with him. They planned a great wedding that was both grand and splendid. All of the dwarfs were invited to attend the feast, as was Snow White's evil step-mother, though she did not know it was for her step-daughter, whom she thought to be dead. And after the Queen had dressed in her elegant gown and made herself up to go to the feast, she stepped before her mirror and asked, "O mirror, mirror, upon my wall, who in the land is the fairest of all?"

The mirror answered her yet again, "You, my queen, are fair 'tis true, but the young queen is a thousand times fairer than you."

The wicked woman cursed aloud and she became greatly troubled, so much so that she did not know what to do next. At first she thought she would not go to the wedding at all, but she became restless and had to go herself to look upon this young beauty. When she arrived she gazed upon her and recognized Little Snow White and was stunned into stillness.

At the wedding dance they prepared a special prize for the Queen. They had beforehand placed a pair of iron shoes within the fire's blazing coals and these, when they were nice and hot, were brought out with tongs and placed in front of the evil Queen. She was forced to put them on and in the red-hot shoes forced to dance until she fell down dead.[38]

So we see that the Evil Queen does not wish Snow White to outshine her in beauty so she seeks to do away with her. And do we have enough here to recognize that Snow White does represent the sun?[*] For is it not said that year after year she grew in splendor until at the age of seven she became as bright as the sun?

Epitheus: Truly.

Thaeo: And we also see that after Snow White's quiescence the seven dwarfs and animals come to mourn her, before she rises again from her sleep resurrected, which is quite similar to the passing of the (Nordic) god of light Balder into the underworld.[†]

Epitheus: Indeed.

Thaeo: And that when Grendel's mother is beheaded a bright light appears that is said to shine like the sun,[39] which might also provide an explanation comparable with the beheading of the Gorgon; though here we presume the sun goddess is taking her place again in the sky, being liberated from the wound in her neck.

Epitheus: So it would appear.

Thaeo: And this we might also relate back to what we know of the giant Hrungnir, for it is said that he was also the abductor of Thor's daughter Thrud ('ruddy'), who might likewise represent the sun.

Epitheus: That would seem entirely possible.

Thaeo: Then from this we might understand better the strange matter of the given sequence, wherein Grendel is mortally wounded yet

---

[*] This could even explain the Morning Star as being the fragment of apple which lodged in her throat.
[†] See *The Eden Enigma: A Dialogue*

when Beowulf goes down to his lair in the underworld he instead fights with and defeats Grendel's mother.

Epitheus: Certainly.

Thaeo: So then it could be that the sun goddess was not intended to be Grendel's mother but rather her captive. And the sun goddess is freed after the head of Grendel's mother is severed from her body, the implication being that the demoness had swallowed the sun.

Epitheus: Truly, it seems to be so.

Thaeo: Thus we might surmise the reason Grendel arrives at midwinter is that this is also the time when the sun itself is swallowed into darkness, and thus in beheading the Yule beast the sun is released and born again into the world.*

Epitheus: Indeed.

Thaeo: And here Grendel represents the slain beast of mid-winter, which again makes his contest with Beowulf similar to that between the brothers Balder and Hod.

Epitheus: Yes, it does.

Thaeo: Then we might also consider that the beast, being the 'green devil' (Grendel), might also make him emblematic of the spirit of growth. And we could identify his killing at mid-winter to herald the return of the sun and ultimately of the return of spring. For does not each of these stories emphasize that the beast made his appearance at this same time of year, since the dragon which Bodvar confronted arrived at Yule, the Green Knight at King Arthur's court came at

---

* The story of the slaying of Grendel by Beowulf is clearly similar to the ubiquitous 'Bear Son' tale, where the hero is often himself the son of a bear. He appears as a hero with the strength of a bear (a strength which Beowulf clearly possesses), and thus is able to combat the demonic creature and kill it in its lair, while subsequently releasing three princesses. The release of the three princesses may be indicative of the freeing of the sun represented as the sun-disk, the dusk and dawn.

Christmas,[*] and even the story of Snow White begins with a reference to it being mid-winter.

Epitheus: Truly.

Thaeo: While the contest that is associated with Grendel's mother, where her neck is severed and a great light arises as bright as the sun, reminds us more of the story of Snow White, where the sun is kept quiescent until freed by the prince.

Epitheus: Clearly so.

Thaeo: So we would have to recognize one variation where there is a demonic son and his mother: the son being the moon and the mother being the sun, and another where there are two sisters: the wicked moon and the beautiful sun.

Epitheus: Yes.

Thaeo: And these would suggest different approaches to what is essentially the same story, based around the disappearance of the sun at the time of the winter *solstice*.

Epitheus: That would appear to be entirely the case.

Thaeo: Then should now we attempt to make some sense of them?

Epitheus: By all means.

Thaeo: Then first we identified Grendel's mother as the sun goddess Bertha, who herself is said to have wielded an iron knife, and thus was known as 'Iron Bertha'. And we find Grendel's mother also wielding an iron knife in her combat against Beowulf, which thereby

---

[*] 'Sir Gawain and the Green Knight' bears many similarities to the story of Grendel. This familiar Yule creature could also be the origin of Krampus ('claw') the Christmas beast of Germania.

makes her the likeness of the giantess Iarnsaxa ('iron knife'), which is probably merely an epithet for Bertha.[*]

Epitheus: Truly.

Thaeo: But in other cases it was a creature akin to Grendel himself, and thus viewed to be a male rather than a female demon.

Epitheus: Yes.

Thaeo: While the situation we considered before suggests that there was a mother (moon) who gave birth to a daughter (sun) more beautiful than herself, and this is like what is represented within the story of Snow White.

Epitheus: I would have to agree.

Thaeo: And this again suggests to me the idea that (the Greek goddess of wisdom) Athena was the daughter of the Gorgon Medusa, being swallowed by her out of envy and then freed again when Medusa was beheaded.

Epitheus: That would certainly make them similar.

Thaeo: Although, as we are familiar with it, the figure who gave birth to Athena was rather great Zeus, even though she was also the daughter of Metis. Thus in one case we have Zeus swallowing Metis and giving birth to Athena, when he is struck upon the head with an axe, whereas we are also suggesting another circumstance with Medusa giving birth to Athena when she was beheaded.

Epitheus: That is the extent of it.

Thaeo: But we also previously associated both Athena and Medusa with the moon rather than with the sun.

---

[*] Iarnsaxa is Thor's wife, also named Sif, a goddess known for her long golden tresses

Epitheus: True.

Thaeo: So we might not equate this easily with either of the other two variations.

Epitheus: No.

Thaeo: Though it is interesting that Athena is the one who lends Perseus the mirror which he uses to attack the Gorgon, which reminds us of the mirror possessed by the Evil Queen; and also that there is a contest of sorts between the Queen and Snow White as to whose beauty is superior, just as we found occurred between Athena and Medusa.

So in some ways Athena is more like the Evil Queen, since she is the one who possesses the mirror and in a vain fit condemns the beautiful Medusa to live within a deep cave on the western edge of Ocean, just as Snow White is condemned to flee into the depths of the forest.

Epitheus: That makes sense.

Thaeo: So in this case we would be right in suggesting that the Evil Queen would be associated with the moon, as we already suggested would be compatible with Queen Hvit, and which would also make her like the moon goddess Athena.

Epitheus: That is hard to deny.

Thaeo: Likewise, we also know that Athena is very closely associated with the Gorgon, since as we saw she places its head upon her shield and breastplate. And the name of Athena's mother 'Metis' too being equivalent to 'Medusa' would suggest that they filled precisely the same role, for the goddess Metis was, like the Gorgon's head, taken to be a symbol of 'divine wisdom'.

Epitheus: Very good.

Thaeo: But if the Gorgon swallowed her daughter out of a belief that she would outshine her, this also harkens to the warning given to

Zeus that his own son would usurp his position. Thus it appears that two different stories may have been combined, wherein the story of Medusa might have been equated with that of the Gorgon.

Epitheus: But what do you mean?

Thaeo: What I mean to say is that in order to reconcile the two we would have to assume that the Gorgon had been the one who swallowed the sun, where the sun was a daughter of the moon goddess (Athena). The moon goddess would then have been born from the Gorgon before she herself gave birth to the sun; but then when she saw that her daughter far outshone her, she became envious of her beauty and condemned her to be swallowed by the Gorgon, her own mother. Then when the Gorgon was beheaded the sun sprang from her neck, just as we suggested was so with the beheading of Grendel's mother.

Epitheus: It does make sense, but can we assume the Gorgon Medusa, like Grendel's mother, represents the sun?

Thaeo: It may be difficult to reconcile Medusa's name with the sun, for if it arises from '*mede-ursa*' it would mean 'mead bear'. Thus if she took the form of a bear to swallow her daughter the sun, she would herself have been a moon goddess.

Epitheus: Yes.

Thaeo: And with Perseus slaying the sea-dragon to free Andromeda ('*meda*'), she too would, like Medusa, be linked through her name to the moon rather than to the sun.

Epitheus: That is undeniable.

Thaeo: Yet Perseus ('*erse*') might himself have taken the form of a bear ('*ursa*'), who by beheading the Gorgon somewhat resembles Beowulf, who by beheading the goddess releases the sun again to shine. Thus the story of Perseus provides us with similarities to both the story of Beowulf and that of Snow White, but without any mention of freeing the bright sun (Snow White) nor the pale moon

(Athena), but rather there emerge Medusa's sons Pegasus and Chrysaor.

Epitheus: That is correct.

Thaeo: But let us see if we can simplify the discussion somewhat, if we assume that the story of Medusa rather relates to the image of the woman seated upon the moon. And taking note of her appearance she is both sitting rigidly and holding something within her hand.

And so as to explain this image of a woman upon the moon, people may have devised the explanation that it was the work of an envious rival. And we might also view this to have been the original fate of the Evil Queen, who was thus punished for the evil deeds which arose from her exceptional vanity. Thus she is also like the beautiful Medusa who was cursed by Athena to take on the appearance of a Gorgon. So that when this woman in the moon picked up her mirror to glance upon her own great beauty she saw instead her own horrid reflection as a Gorgon and was immediately turned to stone. This would, at least, tie up the different elements of the story and explain why this exquisite lady appears petrified when sitting upon the moon.[*] Though there is no beheading involved here, but the lovely lady is only given the frightful appearance of a Gorgon.[†]

Epitheus: That seems clear enough upon reflection.

Thaeo: And this story might actually be quite distinct from the tale of the beheading of the Gorgon, which may have involved the birth of the goddess Athena. Medusa (rather than the Gorgon) is instead far more like the first woman created by Hephaistos, who was also the woman seated upon the moon and, like Medusa, rivaled the beauty of the goddesses.[‡]

---

[*] Praetorius says, "superstitious people assert that the black flecks in the moon are a man who gathered wood on the Sabbath, and is therefore turned to stone." (Fischart quoted in Harley 1970: 23)
[†] This might explain why Medusa is depicted with beautiful features yet with hair in the form of serpents, for it is the influence of the serpents which was believed to turn people to stone.
[‡] A reference to the first woman Pandora

So then the tale of Andromeda might have been this very same story. But in order for it to be consistent, Andromeda would have to have been cursed in some different manner, and thus is offered in sacrifice to the sea-dragon Cetus; until Perseus comes to her rescue and lifts the curse by slaying the monster.

Epitheus: Stupendous.

Thaeo: Then let us go on by considering a further the story concerning Perseus when he goes to Larissa to take part in the games that Teutamidas had staged to honor his guest Acrisios. For then we know that Perseus accidently hit Acrisios in his foot with a discus thereby killing him.

Epitheus: Yes.

Thaeo: But then as Perseus is responsible for the death of Acrisios from a blow to his foot, we also know that Paris is the one who kills the hero Achilles with an arrow shot into his heel.

Epitheus: That is so.

Thaeo: Then might we equate Perseus here with Paris and Acrisios with Achilles?

Epitheus: That would appear to be valid.

Thaeo: And we know that Achilles' heel was the only part of him which was mortal.

Epitheus: Yes.

Thaeo: And does this not remind us too of the beast which was invulnerable but for only one of its claws?

Epitheus: Clearly it does.

Thaeo: So shall we then attempt to make sense of these various instances, which all appear to be so highly correlated?

Epitheus: By all means.

Thaeo: Then if we were to make an identification of Acrisios with Achilles, and the slaying of Acrisios by Perseus with that of Grendel by Beowulf, we would have to equate the vulnerable heel of Achilles with the vulnerable claw of the moon bear.

Epitheus: Inevitably.

Thaeo: And when the divine Thetis attempts to make her child (Achilles) invulnerable, she holds him by the heel when dipping him into the turbid waters of the river Styx.[*]

Epitheus: True enough.

Thaeo: And by the same token we would have to consider that Grendel's mother likewise attempted to make her own son invulnerable by some similar procedure; for like Achilles, his mother must have held him by a single claw to give him immortality in a way that caused this one claw to remain mortal.

Epitheus: That seems hardly dismissible.

Thaeo: Then when the hero arrives, he attacks her son by using all of his mortal strength to tear off the beast's only vulnerable digit, and then uses this claw as the weapon to slay him, slitting him up with it and then wearing afterwards the invulnerable bear skin himself.

Epitheus: Indeed.

Thaeo: Then with this bear skin to protect himself, resembling the impenetrable mail suit worn by Beowulf, he invades the lair of the night hag, engages her in combat, and beheads her so as to set the sun free. And so the body of the headless bear is to be seen upon the moon, and the bear's claw is to be seen near the sun as the Morning Star.

---

[*] Thetis the ocean nymph is sometimes equated with Metis.

88

Epitheus: That seems right-headed.

Thaeo: This hero we imagine to also have possessed the strength of a bear, and likewise by accomplishing this proves his mettle, and thus became the supreme god above others, the thunderstorm who rules the sky, as are the mighty gods Zeus and Thor.

Epitheus: Well done.

Thaeo: And though we have seen several instances where the various details have been confused or recombined, in identifying the ultimate source we find the story was meant only to characterize and explain the presence of the heavenly bodies.

Epitheus: Surely.

Thaeo: Thus does this not imply that the Grendel story, as are the others we have considered, is truly a creation story?

Epitheus: I cannot say otherwise, Thaeo.

Thaeo: And this story of a contest between two bears at the very beginning of time could then be related to the dual constellations of the Great Bear (*Ursa Major*) and Little Bear (*Ursa Minor*), for we know that Biarki's name means 'little bear' and that his adversary was a huge invulnerable bear, whom we can surely equate with Grendel.

Epitheus: Surely.

Thaeo: Thus the images of these two were emblazoned upon the heavens by the gods so as to recall the characters involved in the early creation of the universe, whereas the heavenly objects (moon, sun, and Morning Star) are still to be seen as cosmic remnants of these elemental events.

Epitheus: Well put.

Thaeo: So then the sun goddess was viewed as a fierce figure residing in the underworld, but who perhaps also possessed an alternate and benevolent side. So if we were considering the creature to be a sun deity, we would have to presume that it represented the old sun and that through its beheading she would thus release a new sun, the sun of the New Year at the winter solstice.

Epitheus: Stupendous.

Thaeo: Then we have a similar situation with the beheading of the Gorgon by Perseus. But we have seemingly identified two stories that were later combined: one being the punishment of the beautiful Medusa by Athena, being made to resemble a Gorgon so that she ended up sitting upon the moon, gazing into a mirror upon her own reflection, which turned her to stone.[*] The other is the beheading of the Gorgon by Perseus, an act which, as we suggested, may originally have given birth to Athena. And by this we might presume that some confusion of the two stories led to their eventual combination: where the beauteous woman punished by Athena was combined with the mortal Gorgon beheaded by Perseus.[†]

Epitheus: That seems very possible.

Thaeo: And the beheading of the Gorgon is also similar to the birth of Athena from Metis, whose name appears to be identical with 'Medusa' (the Gorgon). So Athena here appears to be the daughter of the Gorgon, where both mother and daughter are associated with the moon.

Epitheus: Very true.

---

[*] This could make her any one of a number of goddesses associated with the moon, Pandora among them. Often recognized to be a bride, the wreath worn on the head of the 'woman on the moon' could just as easily have been viewed as a crown of serpents. The mirror was also a familiar object of the goddess Venus.

[†] This is substantiated by the Gorgons being described as three sisters. Medusa being given the appearance of a Gorgon would not then have been one of these sisters; though it is difficult to determine whether the name 'Medusa' originally applied to the beautiful woman or to the Gorgon.

Thaeo: But might we also say the same of the queen Cassiopeia?

Epitheus: What do you mean?

Thaeo: We have spoken here of three similar figures: Medusa who boasts that her beauty surpasses that of the goddess Athena; Cassiopeia who likewise boasts that her beauty surpasses that of the queen of heaven (Hera); and Princess Snow White who is regarded by the magic mirror as being many-times more beautiful than the Evil Queen.

Epitheus: Yes.

Thaeo: Thus we might likewise recognize that both Hera and Athena are goddesses of the moon. And just as Medusa was given the appearance of a Gorgon by an irate Athena, we might figure too that Cassiopeia shared a similar fate at the hands of a vengeful Hera. Thus we would have to imagine that she is the one who had been swallowed by the Gorgon, and that it was not Andromeda who was saved by Perseus but Cassiopeia herself, who by beheading this mortal Gorgon ('*Meda*') thus freed the beautiful girl from within her.

Epitheus: Amazing.

Thaeo: And this not only resembles the birth of Athena from Metis but, as we said earlier, if the constellation of *Cassiopeia* represents Athena springing from the Gorgon's head; in this case, it also truly represents the queen herself. And since we might derive Cassiopeia's name from the Phoenician '*Quassiu-peaer*', meaning 'rosy-cheeked',[40] we also find her to be very like the princess Snow White.

Epitheus: That is difficult to refute, Thaeo.

CHAPTER 8

Thaeo: I too might mention that among the Scythians there were a collection of warriors who imbibed the *soma* and raged like wild berserkers ('bear-shirts') known as the *haumavarga* ('*haoma* wolves').[41] This word is also not far from the fearsome adversary of Gilgamesh, the beast Humbaba. And we might even attempt to create a hypothetical name that falls between the two, which would be **HUMABARBA**.

And we already know that both of the sacred drinks *soma* and *haoma* are associated with the moon and were ultimately believed to have been brought down from there by the eagle, as was the sacred mead (Mead of Poetry). Likewise, in Mesopotamia the wolf was called *barbaru* (in Akkadian), and there too a wolf was their moon god named *Asim-babbar* ('luminous one').[42]

Epitheus: Tremendous.

Thaeo: And the reason I bring this up is because it is not only relevant to what we have been speaking of but it also reminds me of an interesting story that Soleos told us some time ago. Soleos said,

"The giantess Angrboda by (the Norse fire giant) Loki had three children, one being the wolf Fenrir, one being Iormungand the serpent, and the third being a girl named Hel. These three were living in Giantland, being brought up there by their mother, until oracles received by the gods predicted that when they grew to full size they would menace the world. This they believed, knowing the bad nature of their mother, but even more so because they well knew the character of their father. Thus it was that Odin ordered that the three be seized at once and brought to him that he might determine what should be done with them.

When they were brought to him he immediately cast the serpent into the ocean which surrounds the land and thus he became known as the Midgard Serpent. This serpent grew in the middle of the ocean until it was long enough to bite its own tail. Odin then cast Hel into deep *Niflheim* (Otherworld), but at the same time she was given the responsibility to manage room and board for all those who came there from any of the nine worlds, having died of sickness or old age.

Odin judged that the wolf might stay there among the Aesir, yet still only the brave (sky) god Tyr was courageous enough to approach it closely enough to feed it.[*] But after the Aesir gods became aware that it was growing so greatly day by day, and knowing that it was fated to cause them injury in the future, decided to bind him with a strong iron fetter called Leyding. Yet this proved to be no trouble for the beast, who quickly broke himself free. So the Aesir devised another iron fetter which they called Dromi. Though this was two-times stronger than the last, the wolf had too become even more formidable in the meantime, so he was able to break apart the fetter into far-flying fragments. This is why to "free from Leyding" or to "escape from Dromi" were used as expressions for achieving something which took a great deal of effort.

Yet the gods, though praising the triumph of the wolf in his presence, were increasingly fearful that nothing they might devise would be enough to permanently bind him. So Odin decided to send Frey's envoy, Skirnir by name, into the world of the dark-elves to seek from the dwarfs a fetter formed with the black arts. This they made for them out of six ingredients: the sound from a cat's footfalls, the beard of a woman, the roots of a mountain, the sinews of a bear, the breath of a fish, and the spittle of a bird. The fetter they produced was called Gleipnir and in appearance it did not look strong or formidable at all, but rather more like a silken ribbon.

When Skirnir brought it to the Aesir they thanked him greatly, took the silky strap and presented it to the wolf, telling him that it was of far greater strength than it appeared. The Aesir then passed it among themselves and each tried to tear it apart by pulling on it with both hands, but none could cause it to tear in the least. They claimed that they thought the wolf with his tremendous strength might do so. But the wolf suspected some sort of trickery might be involved, so they told him that if he proved too weak to break the slender band that he would hardly

---

[*] This is similar to the story of Hercules bringing up the hound of Hades. (see Pausanias iii, 25.5)

be such a threat to the gods that they would not immediately free him. The beast still did not think that they would come to his aid soon enough, so agreed to do so only if one of them made a pledge by placing his hand within the wolf's mouth. The Aesir, however, were each reluctant to offer his hand as a security, knowing full well that he would lose it as soon as their deception became known. Yet Tyr fearlessly stepped forward and without qualm placed his right hand within the wolf's mouth. So now the gods were allowed to place the band around the wolf's legs, but this time as the beast struggled the slim band became stronger and tighter, and the more that he struggled the stronger and tighter it became. Every one of the Aesir was gleeful, seeing that the wolf was finally trapped, all but Tyr who felt the wolf's cruel bite that took away his hand.[*]

The Aesir then transported the wolf to a lake called *Amsvartnir* ('black one'), taking it out to an island that was called *Lyngvi* ('heather covered'). Then they threaded the cord Gelgia ('fetter'), which hung from Gleipnir, through a large slab of stone called Gioll ('loud') which they then pounded deep into the ground with the large rock called Thviti ('pounder'), which they then forced down on top of it to act as an anchor. The wolf was enraged and stretched wide his mouth, trying to snap them up. So they pushed into his mouth a sword to prop open his jaws. Now he howls with fearsome cries, while the dribble which runs out from his mouth became the source of the river Van."[43]

The name of this wolf is Fenrir ('fen dweller') meaning that he is a wolf who lived in the fens, just as we saw with the beast Grendel.[†]

Epitheus: Indeed.

Thaeo: And Soleos also said, "Fenrir is similar to the dog Garm who is Tyr's adversary at *Ragnarok* (Norse Armageddon), where each

---

[*] Psalm 137 contains a curse for failing to honor a pledge, with the phrase, "may my right hand shrivel". This is metaphorically intended in retribution against one's own capriciousness or lack of honor, while in Norse society the loss of a hand was a common punishment for perjury.

[†] Likewise a wolf appears out of a swamp in *The Metamorphoses* of Ovid (chapter xi).

kills the other after a devastating contest. Garm too is bound before a place called 'deep cave' and like Fenrir is freed at Ragnarok.[44] And this Garm is also like Moongarm, who appears upon the moon's face, who is seemingly to be equivalent to Fenrir, since to be seen along with the wolf is the image of a hand within its throat."[*]

Wolf upon the Moon: Fenrir or Moongarm.

Epitheus: That is very satisfying.

Thaeo: Yet this brings to mind something else that was also a matter of discussion with Soleos at that time, and it likewise has something to do with our discussion. It related to the beheading of a wise giant named Mimir who guards a well which lies near the root of the ash tree Yggdrasill, the one which extends into the domain of the frost giants, which would mean to the north.[45] This was a well of mead and known as a source of wisdom and inspiration.

Soleos told us, "Odin sought the knowledge that was to be acquired by taking a drink from the well called Mimir's well.[†] The

---

[*] It is possible to suppose that *Amsvartnir* ('black one') meant the night sky and that the island *Lyngvi* was the moon. This is difficult to prove but is justified since the sun and moon motivate many other Norse mythological traditions. In folk belief the moon was thought to shine more brightly over bogs.

[†] In Snorri's *Edda* it seems the term for heaven, 'storm-Mimir', means rain, and 'winter-Mimir' means ice, and the term for a sword 'flesh-Mimir'

giant Mimir, or Mim, was considered to be of great wisdom because he drank from the well every morning with his drinking horn. But Mimir did offer Odin a single draught from the well, but only if he gave one of his eyes in return, which he did willingly. This episode serves to explain the sun and moon, where Odin's remaining eye is the sun and so his sacrificed eye became the moon.[*] And this is similar to the Egyptian sun gods Ra and Horus, whose eyes were also viewed to be the sun and moon, called either the 'Eyes of Ra' or the 'Eyes of Horus'.[†] Odin claims later that he beheaded this giant Sokkmimir ('deep Mimir') when he boasts,

> I went by the name of Svidur and Svidrir when I was at Sokkmimir's hall, where I tricked that ancient giant and became the lone slayer of Midvidnir's famous son.[46‡]

And we might learn more of this circumstance in another case where Odin goes to visit a wise giant with whom he engages in a contest of knowledge. And in this cerebral duel each wagers his head upon the outcome.

> Odin travelled to test the knowledge of the widely wise giant
> He went until he came to the great hall owned by Im's father
> Odin entered and said to the giant, 'Greetings, Vafthrudnir!
> At long last I have entered your hall to see you face to face.

---

means blood. So the name Mimir is used as a substitute for 'water'. Mimir's name also arises in the German river Mimling and the Swedish river Mimeså near Mimessjö. (MacCulloch 1964: 169)

[*] As to why it is believed he sacrificed his eye into a well, this can be known by the way that sunlight cast into a well begins as a crescent and then grows until the sun is overhead and then diminishes again. Such light resembles the changing phases of the moon, thus suggesting that his other eye must have been left in a well. The giant himself is to be seen upon the face of the moon, as the 'man in the moon'. An Etruscan mythological motif shows a wolf within a well, which also appears to relate to Moongarm (see Bonfante 2006: 53).

[†] One of the Eyes of Horus was injured by Set and this was the moon. Within the Greek Magical Papyri the sun Helios is referred to as the 'Eye of Zeus' (PGM II. 88-89; see Betz 1992: 15).

[‡] Sokkmimir's father's name 'Midvidnir' could mean 'mead robber' ('*miodvitnir*'). (Simek 1993: 215)

The first thing I must know, are you merely wise or truly wise?'
'Who is the man within my hall to whom I address myself,
For he will not leave alive if he does not prove to be the wiser.'
'Gagnrad is my name, and after much walking I'm so thirsty
I have come a long way and need the hospitality of your hall.'
'Gagnrad, why do you speak to me from a place in the dirt?
Rather seat yourself here in the hall, and there we will spar
To see who knows more, the ancient wise one or his guest.'[47]

So although this giant's name is Vafthrudnir ('great riddler'), it is likely to be merely an epithet for Mimir. And although the story here does not conclude with the beheading of the giant, we can see that it is surely anticipated at the end."

And I said, "Surely, that is clearly meant."

And then Soleos gave us the passages which tell us what transpired after the fall of Mimir,

"Mental runes you must know if you wish to become more wise than any man. Hropt (Odin) was the one who made and engraved them, and gave them their meaning. This came from the drink that dripped from the skull of Heiddraupnir ('bright cropper') and from the drinking horn of Hoddrofnir ('hoard-tearer').[*]

Odin stood on the ridge gripping Brimir's sword within his hand, wearing his helmet on his head. Mim's head then spoke the first wise words, relating to him the sacred runes. Then every rune that had been engraved was stripped off and sent far away, flowing in every direction along with the sacred mead. They found their way to the Aesir, and the elves, some to the wise Vanir, others to the abode of men."[48]

Thus the mead that came from the moon and the wise head of Mimir were the keys to attaining the sacred runes. This beheading is also like one related to the sacred soma, for its secret was told only to Dadhyanc. And Indra threatened Dadhyanc that if he told the secret to anyone else he would cut off his head. The Asvins ('horsemen'),[†]

---

[*] The skull Heiddraupnir is visible on the surface of the moon, and the moon's phases can be likened to a drinking horn for the same reason the phases might resemble light cast into a well.

[†] The twin sons of the sun

97

who wished Dadhyanc to tell them the secret, came up with a means to frustrate Indra's plans, by replacing Dadhyanc's own head with a horse's head before he disclosed the secret to them. So after Dadhyanc told them the secret, Indra cut off the horse's head and then the Asvins restored his former head to him. The horse's head is said to have fallen into a spring where, like Mimir's severed head, it continued to prophesy.

So like the mead, the soma dwells within a celestial well, and both the horse's head and Mimir's head are also found to be visible upon the moon. Though we do not know how Odin came to possess Brimir's sword, he clearly used it to behead the giant Mimir. And it is possible then that this is meant to be Mimir's sword, as the name 'Mimir' is often used by giant forgers of swords.[*] It might be possible then to reinforce this identification by recognizing that Brimir came to live in a beer hall in the Otherworld, when it says,

> To the north upon the dark-moon plain there was a golden hall which belonged to Sindri's descendants, while upon uncold ('*okolnir*') plain stood another hall; this is the beer hall of the giant Brimir.[49]

And we also know that Mimir drinks mead from out of his well, and this puts Brimir into something of a comparable situation."

And I replied, "Truly it does."

Then Soleos said, "This beheading also makes Mimir similar to the primordial giant Ymir, the one who is killed by Odin and his brothers and from whose body the world was created. And Ymir is also equateable with Brimir, the very one whose sword Odin possesses, and which he might have come to possess after killing its owner. Thus they all appear to be different names for the same primordial giant who still lives on in the netherworld."

And I said, "It would seem to be as you say, Soleos."

And he said, "The Persians (in the *Avesta*) tell us of a similar being named Yima, the son of Vivanghvant; while the Hindus (in the

---

[*] The master smith who made incredible swords with special powers was Mimir in *Thidriks-saga*, Miming in Saxo, and Mime the old in the German hero-saga *Biterolf* (MacCulloch 1964: 169). Snorri includes the sword name Mimung among his list of swords (Sturluson '*Skaldskaparmal*' 75; see Faulkes 1987: 159).

Vedas) speak of (the Hindu giant) Yama, the son of Vivasvant, known as the first to go upon the way to the Otherworld. The giant Ymir is likewise the first mortal to be slain and, going to the underworld, there became its king.[*] But of Yama it says.

> Beneath the tree with beautiful leaves where Yama drinks with the gods, there our father, the head of our family, turns with longing to the ancient ones.[50]

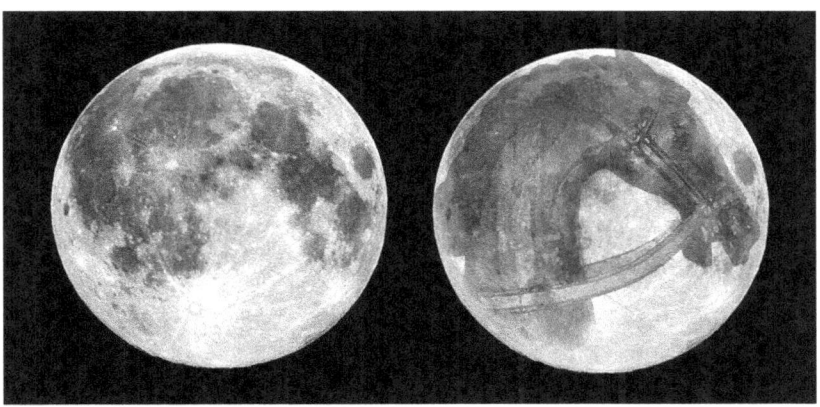

Dadhyanc's horse head upon the Moon.

And Yima we are told is the king of a remote realm, a marvelous land where there is neither cold nor suffering, and this realm appears to be the same 'uncold place' associated with the giant Brimir. And this beautiful-leaved tree would appear to be the very same as the (Nordic) World Tree Yggdrasill; while among the Greeks there was thought to lie beyond the North Wind a land covered by a grove of trees called *Hyperborea*."[51]

And I said, "Assuredly."

---

[*] The primal giant was the king of the Otherworld and thus shares a certain correspondence with the deity of fire, the Norse Loki and the Hindu Agni. "It is certain that in the Veda Yama is often treated as a god. He is the friend of Agni and sometimes is identified with him" (Keith 1964: 313). It is not clear whether at some point the Otherworld and the Underworld were distinct but most often they are equated.

99

Then he said, "And while the well of Mimir lies beneath the World Tree, Yggdrasill, there is also mention of another tree called Mimameid (Mimi's tree), which appears to be the very same."[52]*

And I said, "So it would seem."

And he said, "And because the Otherworld was located to the north and downward, this would place the tree's axis close to the North Pole, where the apex of the tree would be the Pole Star."[†]

And I said, "That makes perfect sense, Soleos."

And he said, "So if you wish I could recount the Nordic creation story, wherein the character of Ymir first appears."

And I said, "Please."

So he said, "It says, in the beginning,

Ice and frost from Niflheim blew over the region called Ginnungagap ('generative abyss'),[53] and at its southern extent it was melted into a vapor by the hot sparks which flew from out of the fiery world of Muspell. The increasing heat caused the drops to simmer and from this interplay was born a man called Ymir ('hermaphrodite'). Ymir slept and sweated and from beneath his left arm were formed a man and a woman, and one of his legs with the other brought forth a son who became the ancestor of all frost giants.

When frost turned into droplets there formed from this a cow called Audhumla, and from her teats flowed four rivers of milk that fed Ymir. She stood licking the salty blocks of ice and as she did so, even upon the first day, by evening had uncovered a head of hair; by the second day the man's entire head could be seen; while on the third day the entire man was released from this ice, and he was called Buri.

Buri was big and beautiful in appearance, in addition to being very strong. He had a son named Bor, who with his wife Bestla,

---

* Here the giant is called Fiolsvid ('knows-much'), which is an epithet for Mimir. Mimi's tree is probably the same as Hoddmimir's wood, in which hide the last two humans Lif and Lifthrasir to save themselves during Ragnarok, the mythical end of the world.

† Even in Greek mythology the axis of the sky, held up by Atlas, was sometimes said to lie in Hyperborea. There Hercules went to seek the golden apples and took them after slaying the tree's guardian snake. (Apollodorus 2.5 § 11; see Hard 1998: 83)

the daughter of Bolthorn, had three sons: Odin, Vili, and Ve. It was Bor's sons who together killed the giant Ymir. And when they felled Ymir such a quantity of blood poured forth from the death wound that it drowned the entire race of frost giants, but for one named Bergelmir who escaped with all of his household. He climbed onto his ark with his wife and was thus saved, and they became the ancestors of all frost giants.

Here we find that Ymir had a descendant who becomes the father of all frost giants.[*] And although it is not said that Ymir gave rise to humankind, according to Caesar the Gauls' progenitor giant was equated with Dis Pater ('rich father'). And according to Tacitus the German tribes descended from a line that began with a being named Tuisto, the son of Earth, whose own son Mannus was the father of the three Germanic tribes. And this is similar to Thor the son of Iord ('earth'), whose own son was named Magni; and like the Hindu self-born one Prthu, from whose son Manu, brother of Yama, all humans were descended.

So let us compare these two who emerge from the earth, Tuisto and Thor, and also Prthu ('*thu*'); and there is a similarity among their sons' names Manu, Mannus, and Magni. While we also have the three progenitors of man, being 'Dis Pater', Manu, and Mannus. And we could reduce this into a simple sequence of the Earth giving birth to Thunder, who then had a son named 'Man' who then became the father of humankind.

Though we also have the emergence of a primordial giant, and we have already seen the equivalence in their names: Ymir, Yama, and Yima which all mean 'twin', which too is the meaning carried in the name of Tuisto ('*twi*'). Likewise, we might consider too that Mimir's name also contains this meaning of 'double' (mimic); so all of these essentially contain a root-form meaning of 'hermaphrodite'. And among them we find that Thor, Ymir, and Tuisto are all said to be born from the earth, while Prthu is known as being 'self-born'.

And in Persia, Yima was said to be the first who pressed the sacred drink *haoma*,[54] while the name Billing (an alternate of 'Gilling') is the giant whose son (Suttung) acquires the Mead of

---

[*] The three generations of giants were Aurgelmir (Ymir), Thrudgelmir, and Bergelmir

Poetry, and his name likewise means 'hermaphrodite'. Thus we have uncovered yet another link between the primeval giant and the sacred drink, as there is between Mimir and the mead and, generally speaking, between Yima and the moon as the haoma."

And I asked him, "What precisely do you mean by this, Soleos?"

And he said, "We have found that the primeval giant is closely associated with the intoxicating drink we presume is to be found upon the moon, whether it be Brimir and his beer hall, Billing and the Mead of Poetry, Mimir and his well of mead, Yama and the soma, or indeed Yima and the haoma. And we find that each of these also becomes a source of prophetic wisdom."

And I said, "Indeed, that is so." And that appears to be all that could be said concerning this, but there is also a similar and well-known episode out of Greek lore, concerning the Titan Cronos, which might be relevant here if you would like to hear of that as well.

Epitheus: I most certainly would.

CHAPTER 9

Thaeo: To begin with I will tell of Cronos' birth and then of the confrontation he had with his father Ouranos,

> The first one to come forth from (the earth goddess) Gaia's womb spread out to cover her entirely in breadth and length; he was the star-speckled sky Ouranos, forming a firm floor for the great immortals. Next she bore the lofty heights and forest depths that are the cherished places of the blessed Nymphs, who occupy the land in the hills and those of the shady, far-spreading forests. Without mating by the ways of beauteous love she brought forth Pontos, the swirling, lonely sea. After this she settled down with Ouranos and this mixed union produced the river of Ocean, the vast swirling-sea Oceanus; also Koios, Krios, Hyperion, Iapetos, Theia and Rhea, Themis and Mnemosyne, gold-enwreathed Phoebe, and lovable Tethys the cherished. After these came the youngest child named Cronos, blessed with a cagey and conniving mind, the most awful of offspring; for he formed fearsome thoughts towards his illustrious father.[55]

These children of Ouranos were known as the Titans. And the matter between Ouranos and his son Cronos came to a head when Ouranos had sent some of Gaia's children (the Hecatonchires, the Gigantes, and the Cyclopes) down into deep Tartaros; and with this elevating her ire, she offered Cronos a means of defeating him.

> Forming herself a shear sickle of fearsome form, she poured forth her plan to her sons and so speaking egged them on, with a malicious intent enwrapping her heart, "You my sons, who are begotten by a careless father, if you were to do what I ask then it would be a fitting punishment against your vile father, for is he not the self-same one who created crime?"
>
> This she spoke, but they were not nurturing courageous hearts, and none dared open his lips to utter a word. It was only from the malicious heart of Cronos that she received a reply, "Dear mother, I will do what you ask, for there is no love lost between me and my father, for he *is* the self-same one who created crime."

This he said to her, and wide-bounded Gaia was pleased to the cockles of her heart and set off together with him, showing him a hiding spot from which to launch his attack. She placed within his hand the fearsome-edged sickle, then let him in on the plan she had devised. So vast Ouranos came, bearing night's spangled shroud; how he yearned for sweet embraces, as he spread out fully over Gaia to accept her love. Yet from its hiding spot surged a baleful left arm, sweeping up with a grip which perplex him. With one jab from the right, in clenched fingers with a fearsome-edged weapon wielded with accurate aim, Cronos severed off the outstretched penis of his father and his testicles too, throwing them aside with discourteous abandon. But not for nothing were they discarded from his bloodied hand, for the drops seeded the breast of Gaia, and as surely as the seasons appear so did she bear the fearful Furies (the Erinyes named Alecto, Tisiphone, and Megaira); and the race of gigantic Giants, girded with light-gleaming armor, with formidable sharp shafts in their grips; and also the celebrated ash-tree Nymphs.[56*]

Then because he had performed this courageous act, Cronos was made the new sovereign in his father's place and his reign became known as the Golden Age—as during that age there was no need for rules of law since morality was second nature to all, and it was a time when men lived among the gods. Yet finding the Hecatonchires, the Gigantes, and the Cyclopes to be just as troublesome to him, Cronos simply banished them back into Tartaros, where they were permanently bound and guarded by the dragon Campe.

Then Cronos married one of his sisters, Rhea, and she became pregnant with his children. But his parents Gaia and Ouranos betokened a prophecy that one of his own sons would usurp his kingdom. So to prevent this, at the moment his children were being born, Cronos swallowed them down just as soon as they came: Hestia first, then Demeter, Hera, and Pluto. Poseidon came next, but he escaped this fate when his mother hid him amongst a flock of sheep, where he was fed by Arne, and she gave Cronos a goat to consume in his place. As all her other children had been swallowed up by their father, Rhea was in a fearful frenzy and

---

* The goddess Aphrodite is also said to have been born from this.

fled while still carrying Zeus within her, who seeing the fate of his siblings had remained inside.

So she fled to the mountains of Ida and there bore Zeus, and it is said that from this event sprung the seven rivers of Arcadia.[*] She then said it was time for Gaia to give birth, and holding aloft her staff she brought it down and cleaved Mount Lycaon, thus releasing a momentous flood with which she bathed the infant. And then he was given into the hands of the nymph Neda and her sisters Theisoa and Hagno, who nursed him before Neda secreted him away to a Cretan cave, and in whose honor Rhea named the bourn she had given birth to, the Neda.[57]

In Crete Zeus was cared for by the three nymphs Adrasteia, Adamanthea, and Ida; and there they fed him on the milk of the goat-nymph Amaltheia and her goat named Aega.[†] But Cronos still heard the sounds the child made and came seeking him. So Rhea took the swaddling clothes of Zeus and wrapped up within them a stone, called the *omphalos* ('naval') stone,[‡] presenting this as his youngest child, and so he swallowed it down thinking it to be his newborn son.

Thus Zeus continued to live there amongst the nymphs on Ida, and when fully grown he sought the aid of one of the daughters of Oceanus named Metis. She passed on to Zeus a drug that when fed to Cronos caused him to expel his children one by one, starting with the stone and the goat, and then came all the others: Pluto, Hera, Demeter, and Hestia. Zeus also released the Hecatonchires, the Gigantes, and the Cyclopes and they in return equipped the gods with weapons with which to attack the Titans: thunderbolts for Zeus, a trident for Poseidon, and a helmet of invisibility for Pluto.

Zeus then led the gods into a war against the Titans called the *Titanomachy* and this fighting is said to have continued for ten years.[58] However, the gods with the aid of their allies proved victorious, and after the gods had defeated the Titans many were sent down into Tartaros; except for Atlas, Epimetheus,

---

[*] These are given by Callimachus as the Ladon, Erymanthus, Iaon, Melas, Carnion, Crathis, and Metope. ('Hymn to Zeus'; see Mair 2006: 39)

[†] Otherwise Zeus is said to have been born within a cave on Mount Ida in Crete.

[‡] Or the Abadir stone

Menoetius, Oceanus, Prometheus, and last of all Cronos. For Cronos, his wife instead prepared a banquet. But after getting himself drunk upon the honeyed mead that had been prepared for the feast, Cronos was captured and taken to the cave of Nyx ('night') where he was bound in chains. There he still lies asleep, drunk on honey, dreaming and prophesying to the goddess Nyx. Upon receiving them, Nyx chants out these visions, while beyond the cave mouth Adrasteia (Nemesis) dances the universe into motion to the cadence of her chanting, banging her cymbals and beating upon her drum (*tympanon*).[59]

Epitheus: Well done.

Thaeo: So what we might do, I think, is to take this along with the birth of Athena, where Zeus is warned that there will follow the birth of a powerful son by Metis, and so as to avert this usurpation he swallows her down, only to give birth to the goddess Athena from his own head. These in reality appear merely to be variations of the same story, for each involves a similar act of birth: whether it be the Furies and Nymphs (from Ouranos), the Olympian gods (from Cronos), or Athena (from Zeus).

Epitheus: Assuredly.

Thaeo: Thus we can see that there is little distinction among the three acts, the castration of Ouranos, the disgorging of Cronos, and the wound to the head of Zeus; the last two of them resembling a beheading though not explicitly so. In this sense then, they are giving birth in the same manner as with the beheading of the Gorgon and that of Grendel's mother.

Epitheus: Superb, Thaeo, and most astonishing; but I find this interesting too because of what you said before concerning Cronos lying asleep, drunk and prophesying; and too of Mimir drinking by his well; as well as the others you mentioned, for these remind me of something I had perhaps not fully appreciated before, and it concerns what occupied Noah after the Great Flood, and this I am able to recall from memory well, for it says of him,

Noah was the first man to till the ground, and he planted a vineyard from which he made wine and drank enough of it so that he became quite drunk from it and so lay down naked within his tent. His youngest son Ham saw his father's nakedness and called to his two brothers who were outside of the tent. Noah's other two sons, Shem and Japheth, entered and took a blanket which they set upon their shoulders and, walking backwards with it, were thus able to cover their father without looking upon his nakedness, for they averted their gaze. So the conclusion of this is that because Ham, the father of the Canaanite people, had perceived his father's nakedness that Noah proclaimed that Canaan would henceforth be the slave to his two brothers.[60]

It is not otherwise clear what purpose this story serves, but it appears to me now to be related to the one you have just told; for it specifically says that Noah got drunk, as Cronos gets drunk at the feast which makes him prophesy, just as here Noah is prophesying the future of his sons' descendants.

Thaeo: Very good, and as you said it might too be similar to the two giants Ymir and Mimir, the first of whom was beheaded and the other who when slain was the source of the momentous flood which wiped out the frost giants. So then it might be interesting to proceed by reading the entire account of Noah's flood.

Epitheus: I should be able to tell it from memory, Thaeo, for there is perhaps no story that I am more familiar with, due to the appeal it had for me when I was a boy; for when we were younger my brother and I even used to act it out while he spoke the narration. But I would like to preface the event with an account of the ancient race of the Nephilim. This begins at a very early time after the creation, when it says,

In the age when humans were reproducing upon the surface of the earth, they had given birth to daughters, and their daughters aroused the sons of God and so they came and took the ones they desired at their pleasure.

And Yahweh said, "My breath will not remain in man forever, for he is a being of flesh and blood, so I will make his years no more than a hundred and twenty."

The Nephilim lived upon the earth in those days, when the sons of God had intercourse with the daughters of man, and to them children were born. These mighty men were the heroes of bygone days.

Yahweh, however, saw that iniquity ruled upon the face of the earth, that the thoughts within their hearts were always intentions towards evil and malice. And Yahweh regretted the day that he had made man upon the earth, and this caused a bitter pain to gird his heart. So Yahweh said, "I will wipe them out, all the humans I created upon the earth, everything I regret having made; man and animal, creeping critters, birds in the sky; all of them I shall wipe from the face of the earth."

But Noah among the humans was righteous in Yahweh's eyes. These are the records of Noah. Noah was a moral man and without guilt among the men of his generation; he walked in the ways of God. And as we saw before he had three sons named Shem, Ham, and Japheth.

The earth in God's eyes had become corrupt, a world swelling with hatred and violence. He looked over the earth and, as it was, it was backward everywhere he could see, for the beings of flesh and blood upon the earth had become vile in their behavior. God said to Noah, "I have decided to bring an end to all beings of flesh and blood, for the world is swelling with hatred and violence because of them. Know then that I intend to destroy them along with the entire earth. So make for yourself an ark out of gopher wood, and make divisions within the ark, and cover it with pitch both inside and out. This is the design by which you will construct it: the ark's length is to be 300 cubits, its width is to be 50 cubits, and its height is to be 30 cubits. Make a window for the ark that is one cubit from the top, and make a door for the ark upon its side; construct it with three decks.

Know that I am going to bring about a deluge to cover the earth, to destroy all beings of flesh and blood, all which have the breath of life beneath the sky, so that everything that lives upon the earth will perish. But I will make a pact with you, so that you will go into the ark, you and your wife, and your sons with you, and your son's wives with them. And you will bring with you two of every living thing, bring one male and one female of every species upon earth into the ark with you, to save them from extinction. The different species of birds, the different species of animals, the different species of creeping critters upon the ground, two of each kind will you bring with you, to save them from extinction. Also you must bring with you every thing that is used for food, keep a stockpile of it, and it will come to serve as food for you and for them." So Noah did everything according to God's direction.

Then Yahweh said to Noah, "Go on board the ark, you and everyone in your household, for I have witnessed the right conduct you have performed before me within this generation. Take seven pairs of every clean animal with you into the ark, a male and his mate; and bring with you a pair of every unclean animal, one male and his mate. Also bring with you seven pairs of each of the birds who inhabit the sky, both male and female, so as to keep their species alive on the surface of the earth. Because in seven days time I will make a heavy rain fall upon the earth, lasting forty days and forty nights, and I will extinguish all who are left upon the surface of the earth."[*]

And Noah did everything according to God's direction. Noah was six-hundred years old when the waters of the flood came to the world. Noah together with his sons and his wife and his sons' wives boarded the ark prior to the coming of the flood. Of pure animals and animals that are not pure, and of birds, and of every critter that creeps upon the ground; they came in twos, male and female, and went into the ark with Noah, just as God had commanded him to do. And in seven days the waters did come upon the earth in the form of a flood. It happened in the six-hundredth year of Noah's life, within the second month, upon the seventeenth day of the month, that all the springs of the great abyss burst forth and the gates of heaven were opened wide. And cascading rain battered the land for forty days and forty nights. On that very same day Noah boarded the ark with his sons; Shem,

---

[*] According to Hesiod the *Pleiades* were hidden from view for 40 days and 40 nights (Hesiod, '*Works and Days*' 385; see Lattimore 1991: 65), and they are known as the 'watery stars' because they heralded the rainy season (winter).

Ham, and Japheth; and Noah's wife; and the three wives of his sons. And every species of wild beast and every species of domestic animal, and every species of creeping critter that crawls upon the earth, and every species of bird and every flying thing went with Noah into the ark in twos, all beings which possessed the breath of life. They were brought aboard, male and female of every species went into the ark as God had commanded him, and Yahweh sealed him up inside.

The flood waters persisted upon the earth for forty days, and they greatly increased and bore up the ark, and it was lifted from the ground. The water rose and became deep over the land, while the ark was afloat upon the waves. The waters rose so much upon the earth that they covered every high mountain under heaven; and even rose over the mountains, submerging them beneath fifteen cubits of water. And every being that inhabited the earth: the birds, the domestic animals, the wild beasts, every flocking creature that swarms upon the earth, and every human being died; all that had the breath of life in their nostrils, everything upon the earth perished. He destroyed all that existed upon the surface of the earth, both man and beast, creeping critter, and birds of the sky, all of them were extinguished from the world. Only Noah survived, he and those who were with him aboard the ark. And the waters rose upon the earth for a hundred and fifty days.

God remembered Noah and all of the wild beasts and all of the domestic animals that were with him within the ark, and God blew a wind over the earth so that the waters receded. The springs of the abyss and the gates of heaven were shut and the rains from heaven were contained, and the waters drained away from the earth, continuously receding. And at the end of one-hundred and fifty days the waters withdrew, and the ark came to rest upon the mountains of Ararat in the seventh month, on the seventeenth day of the month. And the waters continued to withdraw until the tenth month; the tops of the mountains could be seen in the tenth month, on the first day of the month.

At the end of forty days Noah opened the window of the ark, the one he himself had made, and he released a raven, and it flew hither and thither until the waters had dried from over the land. He then released a dove, in order to determine if the waters had left the surface of the earth, but the dove could not find a place to perch and she returned back to the ark, for the waters were still upon the surface of the entire world. So he put forth his hand and took her and brought her into the ark with him. After another seven days he released the dove again from the ark, and in the evening she came back again to him; and there, in her beak, was a newly plucked olive leaf; thus Noah knew that the waters had decreased upon the earth. So he waited another seven days and released the dove again, but she no longer returned to him.

In the six-hundred-and-first year, within the first month, on the first day of the month, the waters had dried from the earth; and Noah lifted the roof of the ark and looked out, and he saw that the surface of the ground was dry. Within the second month, on the twenty-seventh day of the month, the earth was completely dry. God spoke to Noah, saying, "Disembark from the ark, you and your wife, and your sons and your sons' wives with them. Bring out every living thing that is there with you; all beings, birds and animals, and every creeping critter that scurries upon land; that they might reproduce abundantly upon the earth, and be fruitful and multiply over the entire world."

Thus Noah emerged, and his sons and his wife and his son's wives with him. And every living thing, every creeping critter, every bird, and everything that inhabits the earth, was brought forth in groups from out of the ark.

Then Noah constructed an altar to Yahweh, and he took one of every pure animal and every pure bird and offered it in sacrifice, as a burnt offering upon the altar. And Yahweh smelled the pleasant smoke rising and said to himself, "I will never again blame the ground on account of the humans, for the inclinations of their hearts are evil even from when they are young, and I will never again extinguish every living thing as I have done. As long as the earth exists there will be planting and harvest, cold and heat, summer and winter, day and night."

God then blessed Noah and his sons, and said to them, "Be fertile and reproduce and populate the earth. Every beast on earth will be alarmed by you and frightened by you, along with every bird in the sky and everything that crawls upon the ground and every fish of the sea. They are given into your hands. Every animate thing will be your food as I have given you, and every growing plant, though you must not eat the flesh with its life, by

111

which I mean the blood. Those who do, know that I will seek after your blood as a reckoning; I will seek it from every animal as well as from man. I will seek a human life from each man for the sake of his kinsman. For whoever will shed the blood of a man, by yet another man will his own blood be shed, for when God made man he created him in his own image. But you, be fertile and reproduce, give birth in great numbers and increase your population upon the earth."

Then God said to Noah, and his sons who were with him, "Know that I am going to establish my pact with you and your descendants, and with every living thing that is there with you: the birds, the domestic animals, and every wild beast upon the earth that is with you, to each and every one that came out of the ark, I will establish my pact with you, that all living beings will never again be decimated by flood waters, never again shall I send a flood to wipe out the entire earth."

And then God said, "This is the symbol of the pact which is made between me and you and every living being that is there with you, and to all future generations. I have set my bow up in the clouds, and there it will symbolize the pact between me and the earth. So that when I send clouds over the earth and my bow is seen among the clouds, I will remember the pact that I made with you and every living thing, all animal life; and the waters shall never become a flood sent to extinguish all living beings. When this bow appears in the clouds, I will see it and remember the eternal pact between God and every living thing, of all animal life, that inhabits the earth." God said to Noah, "This is the symbol of the pact that I have made between myself and all beings that inhabit the earth."

The sons of Noah who disembarked from the ark were Shem, Ham, and Japheth. And Ham was the progenitor of Canaan. These three were the sons of Noah and from them the entire world was populated.[61]

So that is the extent of it, and here we would pick up right at the point I had mentioned before, where Noah plants his vineyard.

Thaeo: Very good, and in the spirit of things it is only right that I contribute what I can, in this case relating the flood of Deucalion ('sweet-wine sailor'). Deucalion was the son of Prometheus and Pronoia who lived in Phthia, and the flood is said to have occurred during the reign of Cranaus, when Zeus wished to eliminate the Race of Bronze. For after the Golden Age of Cronos, whose inhabitants became the good spirits who live above the ground, came the Silver Age. And the men of this age were corrupt and refused to worship the gods, and they became the benevolent spirits who live beneath the earth. After this the men of the age which followed, the Bronze Age, were very warlike; so Zeus determined to wipe them out and send them all down into Hades.

This arose specifically because of the hubris and lack of piety on behalf of the Pelasgians, for King Lycaon of Arcadia had been tested by Zeus, who came to them in the form of a simple itinerant laborer. When he was invited to their feast he witnessed their slaughtering of a local boy, whose entrails were then added to the meal prepared for Zeus, which had been suggested by the eldest son Mainalos as a means to test him to see whether or not he were a god. Zeus viewed this act with revulsion and in response tipped the table so that the place then became known as Trapezous.

Then great Zeus sent thunderbolts against Lycaon and his sons, all but the youngest Nyctimos who was saved by Gaia, who stilled the anger of Zeus in time to save the boy. Yet he still in vengeance turned Lycaon into a wolf and it was when his son Nyctimos succeeded to the throne that Zeus unleashed the fury of the flood, but it was truly brought on by the corrupt behavior of Lycaon and his other sons.

However, before Zeus unleashed the flood Prometheus alerted his son to build for himself a chest, which he did; and took his wife, who was also his sister, along with him. And, like Noah, Deucalion was a man distinguished by his exceptional righteousness. Then Zeus sent great rains down from heaven which flooded most of Greece, and as a result destroyed the entirety of humanity except for those who took refuge in the high mountains. Then it is said that the mountains of Thessaly parted, which flooded all the lands beyond the Isthmus and the Peloponnese. But Deucalion survived the flood within his chest for nine days and nine nights, until he was washed up upon Mount Parnassos, where he remained inside until the rains ceased. Zeus then caused the wind to blow so as to make the waters subside, and there Deucalion offered a sacrifice to Zeus the Savior.

Epitheus: Splendid.

Thaeo: Then we too must not forget the story of the flood of Atrahasis, if you would like to hear of that too.

Epitheus: I certainly would.

Thaeo: Atrahasis, whose name means 'greatly wise' ('*atra-hasis*'), is merely another name for Utnapishtim who, as you might recall, appeared in the story of Gilgamesh. But I will tell of things only from the time after the gods sent plagues down to mankind, which was done so as to reduce his numbers upon the earth; after which they settled upon a different plan to drown him forever in a great flood. The (water) god Enki had sworn an oath with the rest of them not to tell any living soul of its coming, yet he recognized the faithful dedication of his devotee Atrahasis and sent him a warning during his sleep in the form of a dream. Yet Atrahasis didn't comprehend the meaning of this baleful and incredible portent, thus he spoke to his god through the reed wall of his temple.

> Atrahasis raised his voice to be heard, speaking to his master,
> "Lord, please make known to me the meaning of my dream
> Tell me plainly that I might understand its implications."
> Enki raised his voice to be heard, speaking to his servant,
> "You say, 'It should be made known to me while dreaming'
> So pay heed to the substance that I will pass along to you.
> Wall, hear every utterance! Reed hut, attend to every word!
>
> "Take apart your house and with the timbers construct a boat
> Put aside your property for the sake of saving living things
> The boat you construct must be sized with proper proportion
> The length of it and the width of it should be equivalent
> Put a roof upon it, like that which covers the deep Apsu,
> Cover it all so that even the sun might not peek inside!
> Construct within it both upper decks and lower decks
> The ropes must be made durable enough to endure strain,
> The bitumen must be made strong, to lend it sturdiness
> For I will make the rains fall upon you where you stand,
> Descending like a wealth of fowl, like a treasure of fish."

114

Atrahasis opened up the sand timer to fill it with sand,
Enki told him the amount of sand that would be required
Enough to last the duration of the flood, for seven nights
Atrahasis heard every word that Enki had spoken to him

He brought together the elders, who assembled at his door
Atrahasis raised his voice to them that he might be heard,
"My lord Enki is not popular right now with your lord Ellil
The two gods are in the midst of a feud with one another
Thus they have caused me to be driven from my house
But because I have always treated Enki with devotion,
He spoke concerning this trial which I am to undergo
No longer will I be able to remain within your city walls
Never again might I set my feet upon Ellil's dear land
But down into the Apsu must I travel, to be with Enki
This is what he spoke to me and this is what I must do.[62]
If I do this then he will make it rain abundantly for you,
He will send down a wealth of fowl and a treasure of fish
He will shower a downpour in prosperity, a cornucopia
In the morning it will spread over you like thick syrup
In the evening you will drown in an abundance of heaps."[63]

Thus when the first sign of dawn appeared the next day
The elders assembled together the entire people there
The carpenter with his axe, the reed worker with his stone
The young children came with the stocks of bitumen
The poor folks fetched everything else that was required[64]
On the fifth day he was able to lay out the frame's form
It spanned over the area of an acre, with walls ten poles high
Then he designed its form, drew out the plan for her decks
To feed the workmen every week he slaughtered an ox
To feed them every day he slaughtered a fine fat sheep
Giving them ale and beer as if there were no tomorrow
Pouring out oil and wine to the workers as if it were water
Every day was like the feast at the New Year's Day festival
When the sun appeared on the final day he gave them balm
By the time the sun had set that day the boat was complete[65]

Everything that inhabited the meadows he had brought in,
Everything that inhabited the wild spaces he brought in:
Pure ones and impure ones, and tall ones and short ones
Fat ones and skinny ones, and large ones and small ones
He chose from among these and put them aboard the boat
Birds that are in the skies, the moaning cattle of Shakkan
The savage beasts that roam throughout the wild expanses
He chose from among these and put them aboard the boat
And he took with him every manner of skilled craftsman

He then brought all of his people together within his barn
Inviting them to join him before disembarking, to feast
They were seated when he sneaked his family on board
While they were all eating and while they were drinking
He did not keep still, but kept going out and coming back in,
He was crushed, his heart was breaking, he was vomiting
Then the cast of the sky altered and the clouds rumbled
When he heard that sound he closed up the door with pitch
During that entire span, as he was sealing around the door,
He could hear the storm god booming within the clouds
The winds whipped around the ship, even as he climbed up,
When he cut through the mooring rope and freed his boat[66]

The next day there came lowering gray clouds over the sky,
An ominous gloom arose and approached like a tempest,
And an unnatural darkness prevailed over the landscape
This brought the Anzu-bird forth, flapping and screeching
Overhead the sky resounded; all of the people gazed aloft
Anzu was scratching at heaven with his fearsome claws
Lightning blazed the sky and earthquakes struck the land
He broke through the firmament and formed a gaping hole
From this hole in the firmament the torrent's fury poured
The Flood-weapon was unleashed upon the people like a war
They lost sight of one another within the cascading rain
The storm surge roared like a charging, bellowing bull
The wind sounded like a howling ass in the wilderness
Thick dark enveloped the entire earth, the sun was not seen
The people became like a white-sheep offering to the gods
Every one of them was consumed by the turbulent purge[67]

116

Even the gods were alarmed by the full force of the flood
They retreated to the safety of the highest heaven of Anu
Where they cowered like dogs from the crash of the deluge
The flood surge wreaked havoc, was raging out of control,
Anu lost his mind; the gods, his sons, shook around him[68]

The lips of the great mother goddess, Nintu, were salty
All the gods, the Anunna, were left hungry and thirsty
But the divine midwife, wise Mami , gazed out and cried,
"Bring sunlight back to them so that they might see!
How could I, within the very assembly of the gods,
How could I ever have consented to their destruction?
Ellil had a callous enough nature to command this evil
He should have withdrawn that command, like Tiruru
They lash out with anguished curses directed at me
Now they have become like white lambs of sacrifice,
Beyond my control, for how could I live with this loss?
My busy din upon earth has been reduced to silence
What must I do, must I hide myself beyond the sky?
To live evermore in a cloister, cut off from my kith,
With what reason then did Anu accept this decision?
It came about from the command to his obedient sons
He didn't deliberate the matter, he just ordered a flood
And brought the people to a sad and sorry destruction
He conspired to bring about their pitiless decimation
Now their shining faces will never again see the light."
The gods cowered like dogs from the crash of the deluge
The flood surge wreaked havoc, was raging out of control,
Anu lost his mind; the gods, his sons, shook around him
Nintu was screaming and wailing like woman in travail
"Would a genuine father have unleashed the wild waters
To meet their end clogging up the river like dragonflies?
Their bodies wash upon the banks like overturned boats
They bobble like a raft abandoned in the wilderness
I have seen them there, I have wept over their corpses!
Will there be an end to the tears that I shed for them?"
Nintu wailed and expressed her feelings of grief fully
The gods joined her in weeping for the vanished country
She was overcome with heartache, but could find no beer

117

The same spot where she wept, so the great gods did too
Managing in their speech only the sound of bleating sheep
Parched with thirst, from their lips came only emptiness
For the duration of seven entire days and seven nights
Whirling water, the storm wind, and the flood prevailed[69]

When the next day arrived the tempest, flood, and fury,
Which had been thrashing like a mother straining in birth,
All suddenly expired, and the swirling sea became still,
The storm wind lessened, the raging torrent refrained
Atrahasis peeped out a gap to see what things were like,
All quiet, nowhere distinguishable a man from the mud
There was just the endless flood water, like a flat roof
He opened the window and light beamed onto his face
He knelt down and sat, then cried with tears cascading
He looked for the hills and for the banks of the ocean
Then he saw areas of land breaking the surface of water

The boat settled itself upon the mountain of Nimush
It took hold of the craft and would not let it wander
For the first and second day, for the third and fourth day
For the fifth and sixth day, the boat did not move an inch
Then upon the seventh day Atrahasis released a dove–
It flew out and came back, finding no place to perch,
Then he reached his hand forth and released a swallow–
The swallow flew here and there, then came back home
For there was no promising place it might alight upon
Then he reached his hand forth and released a raven–[*]
The raven flew, and seeing that the waters were receding
It settled to eat, preen, fluff itself, and did not return

He sent out everything in all directions, and sacrificed
Setting down the ritual offering on the mountain peak
Setting out the jars in seven columns and in seven rows
And into them he poured the oils of reed, pine, and myrtle[70]
The gods smelled the rising smoke, a pleasing fragrance

---

[*] Perhaps the idea of birds being sent out after a flood merely recalled their use by mariners seeking land.

They gathered over the offering like a swarm of flies
After they consumed the offering, Nintu rose and spoke,
"What could have come over Anu to make this decision?
And does Ellil have no shame coming to savor the smoke?
Without consideration the two of them sent down a flood
And brought the people to a sad and sorry destruction
They agreed to cause their dire and pitiless obliteration
Now their shining faces will never again look on the sun."
She approached the great flies which Anu had fashioned
"From now on man's burden will be a burden which I share
From now his fate will no longer be separated from my own
He must now save me from any harm, by offering sacrifice
And so let me rise every day in the morning for his sake
Recognize, O gods, that I will never forget this calamity!
May these big flies become *lapis lazuli* upon my necklace
I will eternally recall and never forget what happened here." [71]

Ellil then came to recognize the boat and realized that the god Enki had spoken to Atrahasis into the wall of the reed hut so as to warn him of the approaching flood. Enki admitted that he had acted in defiance of Ellil. They brought Nintu, who shaped the destinies of men, to bring about various means of infant mortality and population control to humankind.

So with the completion of this flood story we have three, and these also appear to agree quite closely in details with one another. But I would like to review the story of Noah's flood a little further, for there seemed to me to be several instances where there were noticeable disjoints and discrepancies.

Epitheus: Yes, I had noticed too.

119

CHAPTER 10

Thaeo: I will begin with examples that are the least refutable, even if they are not at first the most conspicuous, and after this I will then give further attention to each of the finer points.

Epitheus: That would be very welcome.

Thaeo: As I perceive it, the manner of the discrepancies lie most clearly within the time periods given for the duration of the flood, in which are provided a total number of days: one which states that after 7 days there will be a flood that lasts for 40 days and 40 nights, and the other which says that the flood waters rose for 150 days and continued upon the earth until the tenth month. Then, in addition, we have mention of the specific number of years, months, and days which record a chronological progression, as when it says,

> In the six-hundredth year of Noah's life, in the second month, on the seventeenth day of the month the fountains of the abyss burst and the gates of heaven were opened.[72]

> In the seventh month, on the seventeenth day of the month, the ark settled down upon the mountains of Ararat.[73]

> The waters continued to recede until the tenth month; in the tenth month, on the first day of the month, the peaks of mountains were seen.[74]

> In the six-hundred-and-first year, in the first month, the first day of the month, the waters had dried from the surface of the earth.[75]

And,

> In the second month, on the twenty-seventh day of the month, the earth had completely dried.[76]

Epitheus: That is so.

Thaeo: Then let us set these out before us in simple terms. The flood begins in month 2, day 17, of the year 600; the ark comes to rest in month 7, day 17, of the year 600; mountains are seen in month 10, day 1, of the year 600; the waters are gone in month 1, day 1, of the year 601; and the earth is fully dry in month 2, day 27, of the year 601.[*]

Thus if we compare this to the mention that the water rose for fully 150 days they might be reconciled with the period from the time the flood begins to the time when the ark came to rest, which is five months (from month 2, day 17 to month 7, day 16), if we take each month to be equivalent to 30 days.

Epitheus: Yes, that corresponds nicely.

Thaeo: Yet even though this is the time during which the waters were at their height, the water continues to recede until the tenth month. This must mean either the 10th month of the year or the 10th month of the flood.

Epitheus: Yes.

Thaeo: However, if the 10th month of the year is meant it would not equate, since here it says that on the first day of the 10th month that only the mountains were to be seen, it is not until the 1st month of the next year that the waters are entirely gone from the earth. So we must conclude that they meant it continued for 150 days and finally ended in the 10th month after the flood began.

Epitheus: So it must.

---

[*] When we consider that the full moon appeared on the 15th of the month, then the 17th was the first day of the visibly waning moon. Thus we can regard that the 1st was the new moon, and if the month was 28 days long, the 27th would be the final day of the waning moon before the new moon came on the 28th. Thus there is a clear lunar meaning behind the days associated with the flood. The 'Book of Jubilees' says that after Adam had been tending the Garden of Eden for 7 years that it was also upon the 17th day of the second month that the serpent spoke to Eve. (see Barnstone 1984: 12)

Thaeo: Though if you notice this now makes it out of context with our prior statement.

Epitheus: What do you mean?

Thaeo: Let us take the latter case, where it says that the flood lasted for 150 days and the waters continued to recede until the 10th month; for if we assume that each month is 30 days long, which we must do in order to reconcile the two, then the period of the 10th month (during which it ends) must fall between day 271 and day 300 of the flood.

Epitheus: Certainly.

Thaeo: Thus the flood could not have lasted any longer than 300 days.

Epitheus: Agreed.

Thaeo: But let us take the other case, assuming again that each month is 30 days long; the period given for the first five months would be the same 150 days, as we calculated before. Then to the first day of the next year, when the flood waters finished receding (with an extra 5 intercalated days at the end of the year to make it 365 days per year), would add another 170 days, which adds up to 320 days.

Epitheus: Yes.

Thaeo: As you can see this is clearly beyond our upper limit of 300 days.[*]

Epitheus: That is irrefutable.

---

[*] This arises merely because in the one case the waters recede until the 10th month of the flood, whereas in the other this does not occur until the 11th month.

Thaeo: Then if we continue to the 27th day of the 2nd month we would have to add an additional 56 days, which brings us to a total duration of 376 days.

Epitheus: That would be correct.

Thaeo: But also consider that the duration of the flood (taking a month as 30 days) comes to one year (365 days) with an additional 11 days.

Epitheus: Yes.

Thaeo: And I surmise the reason for these eleven extra days must lie in the fault of one of our stated assumptions.

Epitheus: Which assumption would that be?

Thaeo: That in order to equate the one with the other, we made the assumption that both must be using months which are 30 days long.

Epitheus: I see.

Thaeo: We might assume then, accepting a different duration for each month, that the 11 days would makes sense, since the meaning certainly arises from the length of the lunar year of 354 days,[*] which is 11 days shorter than the length of a solar year (365 days). Thus this calendar presumes that each month is not 30 days in duration, but that they are either 29 or 30 days (averaging at 29.5 days, thus $12 \times 29.5 = 354$ days).

Epitheus: That must be the solution.

Thaeo: Yet this means that when we recalculate the duration of the flood with this month length (average 29.5 days) it no longer would last for a period of 150 days but only 148 days.

---

[*] It is well known that the lunar year was in use among the Hebrews (see 'Book of Jubilees' 6:32-38).

Epitheus: Yes, it would.

Thaeo: Thus they might not be reconciled precisely with one another.

Epitheus: No, clearly not.

Thaeo: Though we still might assume that they were only stating things approximately.

Epitheus: That is true.

Thaeo: But we end up with one dating scheme which calculates the waters to have been upon the earth for no more than 10 months, while in the other case the waters were upon the earth for 320 days, thus requiring 10 months that were 32 days each in order to equate them. And even if we could accept a longer month, we could not do so without producing a discrepancy (of 10 days) between the period of 150 days that is stated and the period of 5 months (5 x 32 = 160 days).

Epitheus: That is certain.

Thaeo: Then let me also bring up one further minor discrepancy that makes things even more difficult for us. That there yet remain two other durations given for the flood: one case speaks of it lasting for '40 days and 40 nights', while another speaks to it having continued for '40 days'. This might be a trivial distinction, but nonetheless I would like to proceed through a further consideration of the details. And for this we might begin by investigating the division that arises from the authorship of each of the two major accounts (Priestly and Jahwist).[*] Let us start with the first (Priestly), and here we should be able to divide them up by paying attention to the durations for the flood as we have found them to be.

Epitheus: Very well.

Thaeo: First, if we look, we have precisely the same expression of the earth being corrupt (6:11 and 6:12), and of the earth being one filled with violence (6:11 and 6:13). Then also speaking of how they will all be destroyed (6:13 and 6:17). Since in the first instance the third comment follows immediately after the other two, then in the second instance the content occupying the gap (from 6:13 until it completes in 6:17) must arise from the first instance rather than the second.[*]

Epitheus: Yes.

Thaeo: The next difference is that the second instance speaks of each animal entering "two of every kind" where the first instance uses the slightly different phrase "two followed by two", thus these stanzas (7:8 and 7:9) must come from the first, which later repeats (7:15). Then there is the stanza (7:24 and 8:3) that gives the duration of the flood as 150 days, while it also mentions that the waters receded in the 10th month (8:5).

Then we find another set of repetitions (9:1 and 9:7), and likewise mention of the covenant is again given with repetitions (9:14-15 and 9:17 compared to 9:9-13 and 9:16). Since the second instance is more generally embellished, then anywhere we find expressions which are considerably less we will assign to the first instance.

Thus we have completed our analysis of the first account (Priestly), and as the bulk of it derives from the second instance I will begin by divulging that one first.

Noah was a moral man and without blame among those of his generation; and Noah had three sons named Shem, Ham, and Japheth. God looked over the earth and clearly it had become corrupt, for all beings upon the earth had perverted their dealings with one another.

God said to Noah, "I have decided to put an end to all beings of flesh, for because of them upon the earth there is nothing but violence. Know that I will cause a flood to flow upon the earth, to bring an end to all beings of flesh under the heavens in which

---

[*] Essentially, if these first three comments are parallel between the first and second instance they must also be similarly sequential.

resides the breath of life. Everything that lives upon the earth shall perish. But with you I shall make a covenant; and you, your sons, your wife, and your sons' wives with you, will go into the ark. The birds of their kinds, the animals of their kinds, every thing that creeps upon the ground of its kind, two of each species shall enter along with you, so that they will survive. Also, take along with you every kind of stuff for eating, and stockpile it, and it will serve as your food and their food." And Noah did these things; he performed them all just as God had commanded him.

Upon the six-hundredth year of Noah's life, in the second month, on the seventeenth day of the month; upon that day the springs of the abyss burst open, and the gates of heaven were released. On the very day this happened Noah and his sons; Shem, Ham, and Japheth; and Noah's wife; and the three wives of his sons; boarded the ark with him: they and every animal of its kind, and all domestic animals of their kind, and everything that creeps upon the ground of its kind, and every bird of its kind, every flying fowl of every kind. And they that came in, male and female of every being of flesh, entered just as God had commanded him; and every being of flesh that lived upon the earth perished: all birds, all domestic animals, all wild beasts, all flocking creatures that flock over the earth, and every human being.

But God remembered Noah and all the wild beasts and all the domestic animals that were with him aboard the ark, and God caused a wind to blow over the world and the waters diminished. The springs of the abyss and the gates of heaven were closed, and upon the seventh month, on the seventeenth day of the month, the ark settled upon the mountains of Ararat. On the tenth month, on the first day of the month, the peaks of mountains could be seen. In the first month, on the first day of the month, of the six-hundred-and-first year, the waters had gone from the surface of the earth. And upon the second month, on the twenty-seventh day of the month, the land itself was dry.

Then God spoke to Noah, saying, "Disembark from the ark, you and your wife, your sons and your sons' wives with you. And bring along every living thing that is with you, of all beings of flesh: birds and animals and everything that creeps upon the

126

ground, that they might reproduce over the earth, be prolific and repopulate the world.

Thus Noah disembarked, with his sons and his wife, and his sons' wives with him. And every wild beast, and everything that creeps, and every bird, and everything that walks upon the ground came out of the ark in groups.

And God said to Noah and to his sons who were with him, "And you too, be prolific and reproduce, increase yourselves upon the earth and repopulate it. Recognize that I am establishing my covenant with you and your descendants who come after you; and with every living thing there with you: birds, domestic animals, and every wild beast of the world that is with you, as many as came out of the ark. I will make my covenant with you that I will never again destroy all beings of flesh with a great flood, nor shall a flood ever come again to destroy the world."

And God said, "As a sign of this covenant that I have made with you and every living thing that is there with you, and all future generations, I have set my bow into the clouds, and it will remain as a sign of the covenant made between me and the earth. When the bow appears in the clouds I will see it and remember the eternal covenant God has made with every living thing of all beings of flesh that live upon the earth."

Then to identify the next, we only need concern ourselves with the phrases which remain, leaving us with,

Noah walked in the ways of God, but the world was corrupt in God's sight, and the land was abundant in violence. [God said to Noah,] "Know that I will destroy them all from the earth. Make for yourself an ark of gopher wood, and construct rooms within the ark, and use pitch to seal it both inside and out. This is how you should build it: the ark's length should be three-hundred cubits, its breadth should be fifty cubits, and its height should be thirty cubits. And construct a roof for the ark, and make it a cubit high; and put a door in the side of the ark, and build it with three decks, one above the other. And of everything that lives, of every being of flesh, you shall bring from among them two of every kind into the ark, so that they will survive as you do; being a male and female of each."

127

Of animals that are clean and animals that are not clean, and of birds and of everything that creeps upon the ground, two followed by two, male and female went with Noah into the ark, just as God had commanded him to do. They went into the ark along with Noah, two followed by two of every being of flesh in which resided the breath of life; and everything that was on the dry land whose nostrils had the breath of life perished. And the waters were upon the earth for a hundred and fifty days. After a hundred and fifty days the waters started to recede, and continued to recede until the tenth month.

Then God blessed Noah and his sons, and said to them, "Be prolific and reproduce, and populate the earth. And when I make clouds form over the earth and the bow is to be seen among the clouds, I will recall my covenant with you and every living thing of all beings of flesh, that the waters shall never again come as a flood to destroy all living beings. This is the symbol of the covenant made between me and all beings of flesh that live upon the earth."

Now let us do the same with the other (Jahwist): (starting with 6:5) we have a continuous narrative until it mentions Noah escaping the waters of the flood (7:7), even though it continues again where the flood commences after seven days (7:10), after which there is mention of rain falling for 40 days and 40 nights (7:12). The second picks up again where it adds that Yahweh sealed him inside (7:16), continuing by stating that the flood lasted for 40 days (7:17). Then we can see the repetitions in this verse (7:17) and the next (7:18), which both convey that the waters rose and caused the ark to float. After this there comes another repetition (7:19 and 7:20) which conveys that the waters rose high and covered the mountains. The second concludes (8:6-7) by mentioning that at the end of 40 days Noah opened the window and sent forth a raven; while the first continues through the sacrifice (ending at 8:22).

Thus this completes the analysis of the second account, and the longer of the two can be easily separated out, in which the flood has a duration of 40 days and 40 nights.

Yahweh had seen that the evil of humanity prevailed upon the earth and that every conception that arose from the consideration of his heart was always wicked. And Yahweh regretted having made humans on earth and a pain beset his heart. So then Yahweh said, "I will destroy man, whom I created, from the surface of the earth, human and animal, and creatures that crawl and birds of the sky, for I regret that I made them."

But Noah was favored in Yahweh's eyes. Yahweh spoke to Noah, saying, "Board the ark, you and everyone of your household, for I have witnessed that you are morally upright in front of me among the people of this generation. Take along with you seven pairs of every animal that is clean, male and female, and a pair of all the animals that are not clean, male and female; and seven pairs of birds of the sky you will also take, male and female; so that they might survive on the surface of the earth. For in seven days I am going to send down rain upon the land for forty days and forty nights, and every living thing that I created I will destroy from the surface of the earth." And Noah performed everything as Yahweh had commanded him to do.

And after seven days the flood waters filled the world, and rain fell over the land for forty days and forty nights. The waters rose and spread greatly upon the earth, while the ark floated upon the surface of the waters. The waters rose so high over the level of earth that every high mountain under the whole of heaven was submerged. He destroyed every living thing that had lived on the surface of the ground, human and animal, and creatures that crawl, and birds of the sky, all were made extinct upon the earth. Only Noah remained, and those who were with him inside the ark.

Then the rains that fell out of the sky were held back and the waters continuously drained from the earth. Then he let go from there a dove so as to determine if the waters had reduced upon the surface of the world, but the dove found no perch and she came back to him in the ark, since the waters still covered the entire surface of the earth. So after seven more days he again let the dove go from the ark, but the dove returned in the evening. But there in her mouth was a newly cut leaf from an olive tree, so Noah knew that the waters had begun to subside from the world. After waiting another seven days he let go the dove again, and this time she did not return to him. And Noah lifted the cover of the ark and looked out, seeing that the surface of the ground was dry.

Then Noah made an altar to Yahweh, and taking every clean animal and every clean bird he made a burnt offering upon the altar. And when Yahweh smelled the sweet fragrance he thought to himself, "Never again will I blame the ground because of humankind, for the conceptions in man's thoughts are evil from the advent of his childhood, nor will I ever again destroy every living thing as I have done. As long as the earth remains there will be seedtime and harvest, cold and heat, summer and winter, day and night."

Now what remains are the passages which pertain to the flood that lasts for 40 days, which gives us the simplest story yet of the flood,

Noah went into the ark so as to escape the waters of the flood, and Yahweh sealed him inside. The flood persisted for forty days over the world; the waters rose and bore up the ark, which floated high over the earth. The waters rose over the tops of mountains, covering them to a depth of fifteen cubits. After forty days had passed, Noah opened the window of the ark that he had made and sent out a raven, and it flew back and forth until the waters had dried from the surface of the earth.

Epitheus: This is a very good piece of work you have done, Thaeo.

Thaeo: But we might also have cause to wonder at the dating scheme itself. For here we find, in the instance where we are provided with clear dates, that the flood is said to have begun in the 600th year of Noah's life. But all the other occurrences of this timescale contain no reference to Noah's age. So from this we might draw a different conclusion: that they must rather be marking time from the first day of the creation. Thus the flood ends on the first day of the 601st year after the date of creation, which means that the waters had entirely receded from the earth precisely 600 years after the first day of the creation.

Epitheus: That seems likely, now that you mention it.

CHAPTER 11

Thaeo: If we now consider each of these stories of Noah, we have lost the disjointed nature which had formerly been present.

Epitheus: Indeed.

Thaeo: The last of the descriptions of Noah's flood which we derived is also the simplest, and is perhaps the earliest, and which is also much closer to that of the frost-giant Bergelmir, who we encountered earlier. Him being the only one among the frost giants who survived, and this is also like the giant Nephilim, if we consider that from among them only Noah was to have survived.

Epitheus: Assuredly so.

Thaeo: And we could reconcile these by considering the common belief that the ancient heroes were of much larger stature than modern people.

Epitheus: Certainly.

Thaeo: And Bergelmir is also said to have been set within his box, as it says,

> Innumerable winters before the world came into being, Bergelmir was born; that is my first memory, when the wise giant was first placed within his box.[77]

This could mean he had ridden out the flood when he was but an infant.[*] And so we might too reconcile the story of Noah and Bergelmir if we were to assume that Noah was born on the very first day of the flood.

Epitheus: But might we consider such a thing?

---

[*] The Norse word for 'box' could equally mean 'crib' or 'coffin', though it speaks here of his birth.

Thaeo: There is something which makes me think so, if we recognize that the name of the one who escapes the flood is named 'Noah' or 'Noe' and this is similar to the word '*nova*' which means 'birth' or 'new'.

Epitheus: That is so.

Thaeo: And we find this not unlike Moses whose name also means 'birth' ('*mose*'). Moses being himself an infant floating upon the Nile in an ark made of bulrushes and formed like a cradle, before pharaoh's daughter Tharmuth had him drawn from its unremitting currents.[78*]

And we find here a prophecy brought to pharaoh from one of their holy scribes that a child would be born among the Israelites who would bring down the Egyptian kingdom and raise the Israelites into greatness, which is what caused all male children of the Israelites to be thrown into the Nile.[79] And this prediction is rather like what we had already found in the instance of Cronos, in relation to the prophecy concerning his son (Zeus), which caused him to swallow his own children.

Epitheus: True.

Thaeo: And we found before a similarity between Noah and Cronos, and now something which connects Noah with Moses, and Moses with Cronos.

Epitheus: Indeed.

Thaeo: Though also Noah and Atrahasis appear to be similar enough, perhaps to make us think they are, in fact, identical.

Epitheus: How might we say so?

Thaeo: Although it seems at first glance that their names are noticeably dissimilar, there is yet another name for Atrahasis we are

---

* The unnamed daughter of pharaoh in Exodus also goes by the name of Merris in 'Fragment 3' of Aptapanus, preserved in Eusebius, '*Praeparatio Evangelica*' 9.27.3. (see Charlesworth 2009, Vol. 2: 898)

familiar with, which is Utnapishtim.   And we can recognize that hidden within this phrase (*'ut-nap-ish-tim'* or *'uta-na-ish-tim'*) is the name of *'Nah'*.

Epitheus: Truly.

Thaeo: Though in considering the sound of his name alone, there is another personage who seems to me to be an even closer match to Atrahasis; for if we replace the 't' with a 'b' then the name becomes 'Abrahasis', which as you can hear is not too far from that of Abraham.

Epitheus: Astounding, but are you saying that they are the very same fellow?

Thaeo: We could certainly do our best at searching for similarities between the two.

Epitheus: In what way?

Thaeo: For instance, we are told that Noah made a burnt offering subsequent to the flood, while Abraham is also said to have constructed an altar to God and to have performed sacrifices there.[80*]

---

[*] After Abraham receives the fire and oven from Yahweh (Genesis 15), he makes a burnt offering and receives his covenant in the same month of the year that Yahweh had made his covenant with Noah ('Book of Jubilees' 14:20; see Charlesworth 2009, Vol. 2: 85). Abraham is said by Eupolemus (fragment retained in *'Praeparatio Evangelica* 9.17.3; see Charlesworth 2009, Vol. 2: 880) to be of the 10th generation of the city of Camarina, just as Noah is of the 10th generation given in Genesis. Likewise, the same speaks of Abraham learning and teaching the science of astrology in Phoenicia and Egypt (9.17.3-8, 9.18.2), and astrology was considered to be the science of the Watchers, or angels of God (those who came to the daughters of men in Genesis 6:4), and which was recovered after the flood (Jubilees 4:22 and 8:3). Those who escaped the Great Flood were giants (*'Praeparatio Evangelica'* 9.17.2), while Abraham's ancestry was among the giants, descended from Belos who had escaped the flood (9.18.2). Noah also appears to have been from among the race of giants but who found favor in God's sight (Genesis 6:1-9).

Epitheus: Yes.

Thaeo: And we can also compare Abraham directly to Atrahasis, for we find it said of Atrahasis that he stowed away a great amount of gold and silver aboard the ark along with cattle and other beasts.[81] While when Abraham goes to settle his lands he already is in the possession of a great deal of wealth in gold, silver, and cattle, we are told.[82]

Epitheus: Indeed.

Thaeo: Though if there is anything which might suggest that Abraham rode out a flood we should find it through an investigation of the various episodes of his life.

Epitheus: That would be agreeable to me.

Thaeo: Then examining the matter incisively we find that Yahweh tells Abraham, called 'Abram' here, to leave the unnamed country of his father and proceed to another land in order to become a great nation. So he goes through the land of Shechem to the oak of Moreh and Yahweh tells him that this land will be given to his descendants to occupy, and there Abram builds an altar to Yahweh. Then he proceeds to a mountain that is to the east of Bethel, camping with Bethel to his west and Ai to his east, and here too he builds an altar to Yahweh and is said to call upon his name.

He then goes down into Negeb, but with famine there proceeds down into Egypt. And it is mentioned at this point that he has a wife named Sarai, though he tells Pharaoh that she is his sister. But we will skip this episode because the detour places him back precisely where he started from, between Bethel and Ai. Here is where it says that Abram was very rich with cattle, silver, and gold; and here too his brother Lot enters the picture.* They both have many cattle and thus in order to avoid discord between their herdsmen they separate, one going west and the other going east. Then it says that Lot chose for himself the Jordan valley to the east and mentions the he favored the well-watered land that sprouted gardens in the direction of Zoar.

---

* Lot is said to be Abraham's brother in Genesis 14:14 and 14:16.

134

It then concludes by anticipating the story of Sodom and Gomorrah, saying that he placed his tent near Sodom, and adding that "the men who inhabited Sodom were extremely vile and great transgressors against Yahweh."[83]

Then we are struck by Yahweh suddenly speaking to Abram, saying, "Look up and out from where you stand to the north, to the south, to the east, and to the west; know that all the lands that you look upon I am giving to you and to your descendants forever. I will make your descendants like the dust of the earth, so that only if one could count all of the dust grains upon earth might the number of your descendants be counted. Stand and walk along and across the land, for it is yours."[84] Further it says that Abram moved his tent and sojourned near the oaks of Mamre, which are located in Hebron, and here he builds another altar to Yahweh.

Now, what follows is the episode we spoke of previously, an unrelated one where Abram is visited by Yahweh, who tells him to offer up the sacrifices, and gives him the flame and fire oven in return.[*] Then again Sarai is brought into the narrative, along with her Egyptian maid Hagar, and we presume this continues from where previously we heard about Sarai (chapter 12); and through Hagar, Abram has a son named Ishmael.

Yet the continuation of our narrative, after Lot had settled in Sodom, picks up again here; although Abram is said to have seen Yahweh while still tented near the oaks of Mamre,[†] we might presume this is done merely for the sake of consistency. Since the narrative continues from, "the men who inhabited Sodom were exceedingly vile and great transgressors against Yahweh". And here it says that Abram was seated at the door of his tent in the middle of the day and met there three holy men. One of the three is identified as Yahweh, to whom Abram makes his appeal to spare the people of Sodom. Two of the holy men go down to Sodom where Lot protects them from the depraved mob when they gather outside his door, as it says,

> Lot was seated out near the gate of Sodom and when he saw the lords coming he rose and went to them, bowing himself down to

---

[*] See *The Eden Enigma: A Dialogue*
[†] Genesis 18:1

135

the ground, and saying, "My lords, turn aside from your way, I implore you, and rather spend the night at the home of your servant. Take the time to wash your feet, and then in the morning you might rise up early and proceed on your way."

They replied to him, "No, we will instead take our place this night somewhere in the street."

But he implored with even more vigor, persuading them to turn aside and so they came into his house. He made for them a banquet and had unleavened loaves baked, and there they ate. But before they lay down to sleep, the men of the city, of Sodom, the youths and the aged, every person down to the last man, came and surrounded the house.

They called in to Lot, saying, "Where are the men who are tarrying with you tonight? Bring them out here so that we might sodomize them."

Lot went out his door to speak with the men, shutting it behind him, and saying, "I implore you, brothers, do not do this act of shame. Know that I have two virgin daughters here with me. I will bring them out here to you that you might do with them freely as you like, only do not do anything to harm these men, for they are now under the protection of my roof."

They replied, "Stand aside!" and to one another said, "This man is here to dwell amongst us and here he acts as our judge!" Then they said to him, "We'll be even more harsh with you than we will be with them." And they moved towards Lot and came forward to break down the door. But the lords reached forth from within the house and pulled Lot inside; then they barred the door, and cast blindness upon the men who were outside the door of the house, both great and small, so that they occupied themselves groping around to find the door.

Then the lords spoke to Lot, saying, "Are there any relations of yours who live here, any sons, sons-in-law, daughters, or anyone else you have who lives in this city? If so take them out of this place, for we are soon going to destroy it, because a great cry has risen up against these people before Yahweh, and Yahweh has sent us here to destroy it."

So Lot made his way out and went to his sons-in-law, who were going to marry his daughters, saying, "Rise and move yourselves away from here, for Yahweh will soon destroy this

136

city." Yet to his sons-in-law he seemed to be merely joking with them.

Yet when morning arose the angels prodded Lot, saying, "Rise, take your wife and your two daughters with you, so you might not be devoured when this city is punished."

But he delayed, so the men seized hold of him and his wife and his two daughters by the hand, for Yahweh was showing his mercy towards them, and they carried him forth beyond the limits of the city. And after they had carried him out they said, "Run for your lives, and do not look back or tarry anywhere within the valley, but flee for the hills, so that you might not be devoured."

Lot said to them, "Oh no, my lords. Recognize, your servant has been looked upon by you with favor, and you have shown great mercy in saving my life. Yet I cannot flee into the hills lest some misfortune come upon me so that I might perish there. See, that far city is close enough to reach, and it is but a little one. Allow me to escape there, it is just a small city, and there my life will be spared!"

And they replied to him, "Know then that I will also grant you this thing, that I will hold my hand from the city that you have mentioned. But make haste, flee there now, for there is no action I might take until you have arrived." After this the city was called Zoar ('small') and the sun rose over the earth when Lot had finally arrived at Zoar.

Then Yahweh rained upon Sodom and Gomorrah fire and brimstone, from Yahweh, out of the sky; and he consumed those cities and every one that was in the valley, every inhabitant of those cities that were spread upon the ground. But Lot's wife looked behind them and immediately she became a pillar of salt.

This is the extent of what we know of Abraham prior to the birth of Isaac. Thus, to summarize, we have six episodes here: first Abram's journey where he constructs altars at the sacred oaks, then where they go down into Egypt during the time of famine, where Lot and Abraham separate, when Abraham receives the gift of fire, where Sarai's Egyptian servant Hagar gives him a son named Ishmael, and finally the story of Sodom and Gomorrah.

Epitheus: Truly.

Thaeo: Thus we might conclude that the second of these and the fifth of these, those in which Sarai appears with him, must go together; and that the third and the sixth, those where Lot appears with him, also go together, so as to maintain a continuous narrative.

Epitheus: That would make sense.

Thaeo: The one piece, however, which does not appear to fit into either of these is the declaration by Yahweh that the lands within Abram's sight to the north, south, east, and west are set aside for his descendants. Although this might be fit into the accounts of his wanderings by himself, the declaration of the land has already been made before.* Also there is no mention here as to what the land is, nor are any limits placed upon it; and clearly Yahweh could not have declared this in front of Abraham when he was in proximity to the Jordan valley, for that land to the east had already gone to his brother Lot.

Epitheus: Clearly.

Thaeo: So we might rather conjecture that the lands that were before him were instead the ranges of the entire earth, which lay before him in every direction; and that after which he set forth with his cattle, gold, and silver, with Yahweh granting to him all the land before him to his many descendants.

Epitheus: That is possible, but have we reason to imagine that Abraham might actually have ridden out the flood?

Thaeo: Admittedly no direct evidence arose from our examination, but then consider another flood story which comes from India, when (the Hindu god) Rama decided to send forth a flood to destroy all life upon the earth. It says,

> A moral man, who washed his clothes in a certain river, met a
> fish who came to him and warned him of a coming deluge like

---

* Genesis 12:7

none that had ever been seen before on earth.[*] The fish told him this because the man had always cared for the fish and fed them, and so encouraged him to construct a large box that he might survive the flood. Thus he constructed the box and entered it with his sister and a rooster. Then after the deluge came Rama sent his messenger to collect the latest news and he heard the rooster crowing and discovered the box. Thus Rama had it brought before him and asked the man how he had come to survive the flood and the man told Rama his story. Rama made him turn to the north, east, and west, and to swear upon these directions that the woman with him was his sister. The man did so, swearing that the woman was in fact his sister, but when he faced to the south the man said instead that the woman was his wife. The man was then instructed by Rama to repopulate the earth with his sister and they together had seven sons and seven daughters.[85†]

So we find here that the man who escaped the flood did so along with his sister, who he admits is also his wife, just as Abraham is to have been married to his sister, which he admits is so both to Pharaoh (Genesis 12) and to King Abimelech (Genesis 20). And when Rama confronts him, he has him swear by the cardinal directions that she is in fact his sister; and notice how closely this resembles what we found of Yahweh directing Abraham's attention to the four cardinal directions, saying that his descendants shall occupy these lands, which is the very episode from the narrative we concluded might be a remnant of the flood story.

Epitheus: Truly, and I think that is astounding, but is there anything more which might also be persuasive.

Thaeo: There is a Polynesian story that bears some resemblance, and might be worth mentioning, where it says,

---

[*] The god Ea, who warns Atrahasis of the coming deluge, appears as part human and part fish. (Frazer 1988: 134)

[†] Abraham also had seven legitimate sons: Isaac, Zimran, Jokshan, Medan, Midian, Ishbak, and Shuah.

Once there was a man who went up into the sky, where the stars were the shining eyes of the gods, and he took one of these and brought it with him back to earth. But the gods were enraged at this and so came down to find the stolen star and punish the one who had taken it from them.* So they put on the disguises of ordinary men and went down to earth seeking alms from door to door, but they were always turned away, but for a single old woman who took them into her cottage and kindly served them food and drink. And when they took their leave of her they gave her a warning that she was to make a raft and lie upon it during the night of the next full moon. She did so and when the full moon appeared she lay out upon the raft that night and a great storm came with lots of rain. And the waters rose high and covered all of the islands and mountains, and washed away the homes of the rest of mankind. They all died in the rising flood waters while the old woman slept on the raft until she became caught on the bough of a tree which was upon the pinnacle of Mount Armlimui. And while the old woman had since died, the spirit of a goddess entered her and she conceived, giving rise to the people of those islands.[86]

Here we find the gods coming down and visiting earth is rather like that of the three visitors who come to Abraham's tent before proceeding on to Sodom and Gamorrah; and like this old woman, Lot is the only one among the inhabitants who treats the gods with hospitality, thus assuring his survival from the destruction in the valley. And I will mention one other which comes from the northern (Hareskin) Indians,

It tells of Kunyan ('Wise Man') who foresaw a great deluge and built for himself a large raft. And he told his sister, who was also his wife, that the coming flood was why he was constructing it. Others merely laughed at his activity, thinking that if there ever were such a mighty flood that they could simply climb into the trees, but Kunyan continued his labors by joining great logs together with ropes. Then there came a tremendous flood the

---

* The theft of this 'star' might well be equivalent to the theft of fire, an act which act brought the gods' wrath upon mankind.

likes of which none had ever seen before, and water came in from every direction. And although the other men did climb into the trees, the water rose up underneath them and over them, so they were all drowned.

Kunyan was safe and sound upon his well-constructed raft and when he was floating upon the surface of the water he gathered out from it two of every sort of animal, and birds, and all beasts. Then the earth was submerged for quite some time and none went looking for it before the muskrat, who tried twice to find it: on one attempt he said he could find no bottom, and on the second he said he could smell the earth but not reach it. Then the beaver went down and he was under for a very long time, finally resurfacing upon his back, but he was unconscious. Yet in his paw he held a small amount of mud which Kunyan took, placed upon the water and breathed upon it and it grew. He breathed more and more and it grew bigger and bigger. And after it had become large enough he had all the animals leave the raft to join the bird and the fox, who had already gone ashore, and then he himself came with his wife and son, and said to his wife, "We must repopulate the earth", and so they did.[87]

This story has certain similarities to the one we mentioned from India, where the man's wife is also his sister; but here too, like Atrahasis, he is known as the 'Wise Man'.[*]

Epitheus: That is so.

Thaeo: But there is yet more we might do than merely speak of tales, for we also find that many people trace their origins back to Abraham; and that he can truly be considered, by an examination of his name, to be the Father ('*ab*' or '*abba*').[†]

Epitheus: That is certainly true.

Thaeo: But still Abraham's name could also take the form of **ABBA-HAM** ('father Ham'), and Ham we know to be one of the sons of

---

[*] There is no reference in the Bible to Noah being a wise man or being married to his sister, thus this could not merely be a late borrowing.
[†] His name is sometimes taken to mean 'father of nations' ('*aber-hamon*')

Noah. And this might permit us to make one further connection. For if we go back to the name of Noah's son Japheth, does he not resemble the Greek god of fire Hephaistos ("Jephaist")?

Epitheus: He does, clearly.

Thaeo: And likewise, the name Japheth is even less distant from Iapetos ("Japet"), which is the name of the father of Prometheus, a fire Titan who as we know is interchangeable with Hephaistos.

Epitheus: Yes.

Thaeo: Thus I am wondering whether this son of Noah might also have been at first a fire god. And if we knew this to be true we might also say that his brother Shem is none other than the equivalent to Shamash, the (Mesopotamian) god of the sun. However, the god of the moon we know to be Sin, which does not match closely to the name of Ham. But we might recognize that 'Ham' is similar to the (Anglo-Saxon) god Hama, who is equivalent to the (Nordic) moon god Heimdall. Thus we have the sons of Noah: Japheth, Shem, and Ham corresponding to gods of fire, the sun, and the moon.

Epitheus: Yes, but is this then our solution?

Thaeo: I believe so, for we know that the name Atrahasis means 'greatly wise', and that likewise the moon is persistently linked to intelligence and wisdom.

Epitheus: True.

Thaeo: Then if we take another name, which is likewise similar to Abraham, which is 'Brahmin', we might take this to be of the form 'Abrah-min' which we could then compare to 'Abrah-ham'. And for which we might then consider the components '*min*' and '*ham*' to be equivalent.

Epitheus: That is so.

142

Thaeo: Thus the god of the moon Min we could compare with the god of the moon Ham. And if we associate them in conjunction, in a way that might anticipate an archaic form, we would produce from it the name of **HAM-MIN**, which we might equate with the Egyptian god Amen or Hammon, and the Elamite god Hamman, where '*mon*' also matches the form of our own word 'moon'.[*]

Epitheus: That is truly incredible.

Thaeo: And we can also see how the name **HAMMIN**, taken as an early name for the moon, might lead to it being called either 'Ham' or 'Min', depending upon which syllable had been stressed.

Epitheus: Yes.

Thaeo: Then we might suggest from this that the god Ammon (Amen) would also be a moon god.[†] And do we not find that Ammon is shown with ram's horns, which is a characteristic also shared with the moon god Heimdall; and of whom it is said has a voice of thunder, making him a god of storms.

Epitheus: Truly.

Thaeo: Then too that Heimdall, the defender of the rainbow-bridge and source of wise counsel, is likewise considered to be the father of mankind, as is the Germanic progenitor god Mannus, who also bears a name similar to Amen. And Mannus himself is also like the Hindu progenitor of man named Manu, whom we know also survived a flood. And like both Noah and Atrahasis, Manu was the first man to perform sacrifices to the immortal gods.

Epitheus: Wonderful.

---

[*] Abraham is also known as Abram, thus 'raham' and 'ram' appear to be interchangeable. Possibly also related to the name 'Rahamim' which means 'benevolent' and thus perhaps a god name and merely the name of the ram and of the moon god. Abraham's name could be taken to mean 'Father Ram' or 'Father Moon'. And the Hindu's word for 'god' is 'ram' (Rama).

[†] Later he became associated with the sun god Ra as Amen-Ra.

Thaeo: And it might be worth adding that Heimdall, under the name of Humbli, was the son of Dan and Grytha, and that his brother was Lother.[88] Their mother was the (Germanic) goddess Brechta ('bright'), while Lother (Lodur) is identical with the (Nordic) fire god Loki. And Humbli is also said to be the father of Dan and Angul, the progenitors of the Danes and Angles.

Likewise, the three gods Brechta, Heimdall, and Lother are the gods of the sun, moon, and fire; and associated with the tale of the Brisings' necklace under the names of Freyia, Heimdall, and Loki.[*] So then it might be worth while to examine this episode further if you would like to hear it?

Epitheus: Please.

Thaeo: In the story of how Freyia comes to acquire the necklace, she is made here the equivalent to Odin's wife Frigg.[†]

> Freyia set out from Asgard and came upon the home of four dwarfs named Alfrigg ('great elf'), Dvalin ('retarded'), Berling ('short shaft'), and Grer ('diminutive') who were skilled workers in gold. The door of their cave had been left open and it was by this manner that she came to learn of the necklace and they came to learn of her. Setting her eyes upon it made her desire it greatly, nearly as much as they lusted for the goddess's own good looks. They were just putting the finishing touches upon it right at that moment. So to prevent anyone else from acquiring the fine treasure, she offered to pay for it there and then. But of gold and silver and treasures abounding, no offer of riches was to their liking. And since each had a hand in its making, each was willing to give it to her in exchange for but one thing: that she would sleep one night with each of them. She hungered as much for its enthralling golden glint, as they salivated for her alluring form, that a compatible bargain was soon reached. Thus she returned to their cave on four successive nights, stealing away from her bed, sneaking away from her lover, knowing with each passing day she was one day closer to having that peerless treasure within her

---

[*] These three deities Brechta, Heimdalli, and Lodur are also mentioned as the only three gods of the Germans in the *Gallic War* of Julius Caesar.

[†] These two goddesses are essentially equivalent.

144

own palms. Then on the fourth night she reached forth her hands and received the gleaming metal-work from them, and now in possession of it quickly went home, as if the new adornment around her neck were all that remained of these ignominious nights.

Loki was known for being full of guile, even from his youth, and thus they came to call him Laeviss ('inveigling as venom'). He kept tabs on the ravishing girl, and knew full well how she had happened upon the necklace and of the price she had paid for it. So he dutifully brought this to the attention of Odin, and he asked Loki to get his hands upon the necklace and bring it to him. But Freyia's chamber was so tightly sealed that none might enter it unless by invitation alone, which was not so rare as one might think, yet only upon her own engagement. But in waiting outside Loki was freezing his limbs, so he transformed himself into a fly to search for an opening. The one he found was so small that even a fly had to squeeze through it, but by this means he made his way inside. He gazed around in the dark chamber, but Freyia and her serving girls were all in a carefree sleep, certain of a maiden's safety. Yet this violator had only one intention in mind and approached Freyia's sleeping place, there seeing the necklace beaming about her neck, but with the clasp hidden underneath. So transforming himself into a flea he flew to her fragrant body, alighted upon her fair cheek, and bit her until she turned herself over. Assuming his former form he unclasped the necklace and worked it free, then unlocking the door he swiftly went and passed it on to great Odin.

When Freyia awoke in the morning she saw her inviolate door ajar, but not broken, and reaching to her breast felt that the dear necklace was missing. Dressing herself in her dainty robe she went at once to almighty Odin to seek that jewel back from his care. Odin answered that she would not get it back, not after what she had done to attain it, unless she would agree to a proposition to his liking; which would be to stir up war between two kings, having twenty vassals each, so as to battle one another with such spells that as soon as they were struck down they would rise up again and resume fighting, unless some god might release them from their struggle. Freyia had made one pact to attain the treasure, and now she made another to get it back.[89]

Epitheus: This, I think, is my favorite one of all.

Thaeo: But I should add to it that Heimdall, who also went by the name of Vindhler ('wind-water'), duels with Loki for possession of this necklace, wherein they both take the form of seals.[*] And it is said that Heimdall, the son of nine-mothers, was able to get his hands upon the prize before Loki was.[90] And that he bore it to his gleaming fortress (*Himinbiorg*), away from the villainy and spite of the Great King (Loki) and thereby became eternally blessed.[91] And one must imagine that Heimdall pursued the miscreant for Freyia's sake in order to return the charm to her neck.

Thus here we have identified Humbli and Lother, who are the same as Heimdall and Loki, as kinsmen and specifically brothers. Thus to facilitate the comparison of their names, we would have to mention that Heimdall also goes by the name of Hama and that Loki went by the name of Lopt ('air').[†] So here we might conclude that the names of the brothers Hama and Lopt are hardly different from those of the brothers Abraham (Ham) and Lot.[‡]

Epitheus: Hardly, indeed.

Thaeo: Also we might wonder too whether Loki's name Laeviss ('inveigling as venom') relates also to something quite different; for did we not conclude before that the Canaanite god of fire went by the name of **LEVI**.[§]

Epitheus: Certainly we did.

---

[*] This necklace when referred to as the 'sea kidney' is perhaps a reference to amber, which washed up on the shore and was traded widely by the Scandinavians.

[†] Loki's name Lopt ('airy') also links him to the Mesopotamian air god Ellil, for fire and air seem to have been thought to hold similar properties.

[‡] The King Abimelech ('father king') who confronts Abraham might be Loki ("Lechi"), since Loki appears to also go by the name of Eormanric ('great king').

[§] See *The Eden Enigma: A Dialogue*

Thaeo: This also forms part of the name of the serpent Leviathan. And I wonder if you recall, Epitheus, the contest that took place between Yahweh and this serpent?

Epitheus: I do indeed: Upon that day Yahweh with his renowned mighty hard-edged blade will execute Leviathan the fleeing serpent; Leviathan the twisting serpent; he shall slay the serpent that dwells within the sea.[92]   And there is yet another mention of this which comes from one of the *psalms*,

How long, O God, will enemies be allowed to scorn?
Will adversaries be able to forever curse your name?
For what reason do you keep still your fighting arm?
Why does your right hand lie beneath your wrappings?
Know God, my divine master, that in ages long ago,
You wrought wonders upon the middle kingdom of earth
You split the sea in two with your strength
You severed the heads of the water serpents
You crushed to meat the many heads of Leviathan,
And served him up as food for the many frenzied denizens
Did you not strike open the source of springs and waters?
Did you not parch the eternally flowing stream?
The day belongs to you and the night is yours too;
Did you not set upon their ways the stars, sun, and moon?
Did you not establish every boundary upon the earth?
Did you not make the seasons of summer and winter?
So do not forget, O Yahweh, the enemies that jeer
And that an ungodly people degrades your holy name
Sacrifice not to savages the blood of your cherished dove
Have a thought, evermore, for the wretches under your care
Remember to honor the covenant that you made,
In the forsaken places of earth dens of cruelty abound
Let not the troubled people be brought to disgrace,
Give reason for the poor and needful to revere your name
Make yourself known to them, O God, defend your claims,
Think of how the ungodly revile and mock you every day!
Do not ignore the roar of rancor arising among your foes
Their incessant slander raises a stench unto the highest clouds![93]

Thaeo: You express it with great felicity, as usual, Epitheus. So we find that this sea was populated by water dragons as well as the beast Leviathan.[94]

Epitheus: Clearly.

Thaeo: And that Yahweh destroyed these water dragons and crushed Leviathan to a pulp.

Epitheus: Evidently so. Likewise, he also defeated the dragon Rahab and cast him into the sea, which occurred upon the third day when he made the dry land appear, as it says,

> The waters were stubborn and refused to settle in the lower regions, thus they thereby endangered the earth with flooding, so God pushed it into the ocean basin and then put a barrier of sand against the sea. So that now when the water might wish to surpass its boundaries, it is turned back by the sand. But the waters were simply copying their king Rahab, the demon of the sea, who entered into a rebellion at the time when the world was made. For God had ordered Rahab to swallow the water, but he refused to do so, saying he had already had enough. Thus he was killed for his disobedience and so his body now rests beneath fathoms of ocean, from where the water disperses a putrid odor.[95*]

Thaeo: And in addition to these we find that there are many other sky gods who have confrontations with serpent adversaries: Thor has Iormungand, Hercules has Ladon and the Hydra, Indra has Vrtra, Baal has Lotan, Apollo has Python, Beowulf has the dragon, Marduk has Tiamat,[†] Zeus has Typhon, Krishna has Kalli Naga, and Tishpak defeats Labbu, as Yahweh crushed Leviathan and defeated Rahab. So there might be something more to be gained if we were to take the time to recollect each of the battles in turn.

Epitheus: That would be very enjoyable.

---

[*] See also Psalm 89:9-10
[†] One of Marduk's symbols was the serpentine dragon.

CHAPTER 12

Thaeo: I will commence by presenting Thor's confrontation with the serpent Iormungand ('great monster'), who was to have inhabited the ocean which surrounded the world, and who was so very long that its mouth bit its own tail. Thor's confrontation with this beast was the most famous of his battles. And it is said that upon travelling he took on the appearance of a young lad and went by the name of Veor.

Going over Midgard's meadows Thor travelled one evening until near nightfall he came to the house of a giant named Hymir. That night Thor remained as his guest and when the dawn came Hymir arose and dressed so that he could go into the sea to fish for their breakfast. Thor himself leapt up and was ready to accompany the giant, asking if he might go with him.

Hymir replied, "I hardly think someone so babyish and small as you would be of any help. And if you're far out to sea for the long time which I'm inured to, you'll surely get cold. And I would not want to make the entire row back just to bring you in."

Thor was angry at the giant because of this, which nearly got the better of him, provoking him to smash the giant's skull there and then; but Thor decided to temper himself, since he knew that he would have much better chances to test his strength in the future. Thor simply said, "Let us not delay then any longer in putting out to sea, for we hardly know yet which of us will be the first who wishes to return." Then he asked Hymir, "What then will we use for bait?"

Hymir said to him, "If you want bait then get it for yourself."

So Thor walked away to where there was a herd of oxen that belonged to Hymir. He took a grip on the largest, fattest ox called Himinhriot ('sky destroyer'), ripped off its head from its hams, and bore it down to the boat by the sea. Hymir had already launched his boat, so Thor waded out and climbed aboard, taking his seat at the stern. He took up two oars himself and rowed along while Hymir, who was rowing from the bow, thought there was some evident thrust from what the boy supplied.

So their progress was rapid until Hymir said, "Stop here, because this is the best fishing place, where I usually sit and catch flat-fish."

Thor replied, "I do not wish to tarry here, let us row out further." So they went on for a while longer, until Hymir's muscles were beginning to ache, but he made no sign of it so as to keep it from the boy.

Then Hymir halted and said, "We should go no further for we would be in danger, since beyond this point are the currents wherein lurks the mighty Midgard Serpent."

But Thor said he wished to row on even further and did so without the help of the giant. And there was little Hymir could do; the boy had not tired in the least from his rowing, but he was not happy about being out this deep, saying, "You foolish boy, you will surely be the death of me."

Then Thor completed his rowing and put up his oars, and took out a great line and also a hook he had which was hardly small and no less formidable. Hymir watched as Thor baited his hook with the ox-head and tossed it over the side. The hook and head went straight to the bottom, to the depths where the Midgard serpent immediately spied it. Reaching forth its mouth and opening its maws wide, it bit down on the morsel of ox meat, which caused the hook to stick out the top of its mouth. When it felt the pain it gave a quick jerk that was so powerful that both of Thor's fists were brought crashing down upon the gunwale. Thor grew mad because of this and, so as to haul the serpent up to the surface, called upon all of his divine strength; pushing down with both feet so hard that the force caused them to break through the bottom of the boat, so that they were now set upon the sea-floor.

He pulled on the line until he had gotten the serpent as high as the gunwale, and anyone who did not see how Thor fixed his gaze upon that beast surely does not know what a frightful look is. However, the serpent merely stared back, spitting poison in his direction. At the sight of this horror Hymir was panic stricken and went white as a sheet, both from the baleful glare the serpent gave and the swelling sea currents that splashed into and out of the boat. So just when Thor had reached for his hammer, grasped its handle, and was lifting it high into the air; the giant dug around for his bait-knife and, stretching it forth, cut Thor's line at the

150

gunwale. The serpent at once descended back into the depths of the sea, but Thor was quick to attack and threw his hammer as it dove, so that it severed off its head just before it dropped beneath the billowing waves. Thor, bitten by wrath, swung his clenched fist at the giant, striking his ear so hard that he fell overboard; and head first so that one could see the bottoms of Hymir's feet sticking up out of the water. Then Thor waded ashore.

So that is the story, although it is also said that the Midgard Serpent survived and that the two of them would meet again to fight at the end of the world (*Ragnarok*). Now let us look again at Beowulf, but during the episode later in his life when he is confronting a treasure-hoarding dragon. Here in his fierce fight the hero briefly falters and his sole remaining companion, a young warrior named Wiglaf, deeply moved by his lord's peril, and in his dire need, spoke encouragement and came to his aid.

"Dear Beowulf, do well by the ideal you intoned in your youth when you affirmed that as long as you lived that you'd not let your lauded glories languish. Now you must do so with fearless fighting, with dignified deeds, draw upon your power to protect your life; I will be standing beside you."

With these words the savage serpent, that baleful beast, was seeking a second attack, with a fearsome furnace of flames to fry foes, the humans he hated. The flood of fire burned at Beowulf's broad-shield to the very boss. Armor availed the scant-aged spear-man (Wiglaf) but little, but when his own shield was engulfed and burned to bits he boldly battled under Beowulf's broad-shield. Then once again that battle-brave (Beowulf) was inspired to bring forth his bountiful strength as before, and with a fierce burst wielded his weapon against the writhing worm, driven downward with such a brutal bent that it embedded itself deep within the serpent's skull. Just then Naegling, his long-wielded warring-wand, that embellished medieval metallic edge, became worthless when it broke. It was not his fate that weapons of iron would avail him in his greatest engagements. For the strength of his arm, it is said, put too severe a stress upon the silvery shaft. Though he might bear a blood-tested blade into battle, he was never the better because of it.

Then that perturbed terror, the furious fire-dragon came forth a third time, with evil intent, unleashing again a foray against the formidable fray-fighter. Given a way, enraged and elevated, the enemy entered through an opening, biting right at Beowulf's neck, seizing it between sharp incisors. And a flood of Beowulf's own blood streamed down his body as he bled in buckets.

Then it is said that when the people's defender was in such dire danger, the daring son beside him, with a strength driven by both bravery and boldness welling within him, advanced against the angry asp. Aided in his aim the battle-thane struck severely below the skull, though the heavenly hero's heated hand became badly burned. The gold glinting blade burrowed, which weakened the blazing breeze.

Once more the old hero rose to his feet, drawing his death-dagger, sleek and sharp, from its strap. That Weder defender sliced the serpent right through the middle. The two courage-clad kinsmen extinguished life from their foe, and were partners in its passing. Such should every man do at the moment of a comrade's critical need.

But for that viceroy it would prove to be the very last victory of his valiant hands in this world of deeds. The wound he had received from that worm began to burn and bloat, soon apprehending that venom had mixed with his blood, poisoning him with pernicious proclivity. That wonder-worker, deep in wisdom, sat upon a seat beside the wall. He gazed around at the work wrought by giants, how the everlasting earthen enclosure was stanchioned with stone arches upon strong pillars. Seeing his clan chieftain covered in battle blood, at once that saintly servant with his own two hands washed his foster-father and friend, the weary Geat, with water, and released his hefty helmet.[96]

And this appears to be very like Thor's final duel with the Midgard Serpent which occurs at Ragnarok, in which neither survives, where it says,

Out of the water the encircler of earth opens its ferocious jaws wide, Thor must confront the Midgard Serpent, to be the death-dealer to that voracious wolf. The famous son of Iord, Thor the son of Odin, will move forward to fight in battle against the serpent. In a great fury earth's protector will attack, but every man must abandon his haven. Nine steps Thor will take with great strain back from the serpent who is seldom scorned, before he falls dead from the poison the serpent slavered.

Thus the final confrontation of Beowulf's life against the fire dragon might merely be that of Thor's final confrontation with the serpent in which both expire at the end, with him being overcome by the beast's poison.

Epitheus: Well done.

Thaeo: So, that is the entire comparison that we might make between the two. But also we could consider too that Wiglaf ("Thiglaf") is merely the same as Thor's squire Thialfi ('great elf').[*]

Epitheus: Indeed.

Thaeo: So when we concluded that the first engagement made by Beowulf ("thunderstorm") against Grendel ("moon bear") was the remnant of a creation myth, then the one between Beowulf and the dragon is a struggle which will take place at the end of the world. And the two are thus equivalent to Thor's duel with Hrungnir and Thor's duel with the Midgard Serpent at Ragnarok.

Epitheus: Truly, it seems so.

Thaeo: Thus as we have equated Thor and Thialfi with Hercules and Hylas, now we have added to these Beowulf and Wiglaf.[†] And we are thus equating Thor, Hercules, and Beowulf; not merely as storm gods but as being the same god. So before, we had equated Thor with Hercules through the name **THER**, while we might now also

---

[*] Wiglaf is the son of Weohstan who is related to Aelfhere, whose name carries a meaning of 'noble elf'.

[†] Thor and Hercules are both known as the 'world's defender', and too Beowulf is referred to as the 'people's defender'.

equate Thor with Beowulf through **BEOR** or 'Veor', a name which Thor uses when visiting the giant Hymir.[*]

Epitheus: Splendid.

Thaeo: Then this would be an appropriate point to bring forth the story of George and the dragon, and just like that of Andromeda this is the story a dragon terrorizing the country of Libya. The people inhabiting the town of Silene, so that it would no longer menace them, agreed to give this swamp monster two sheep to eat every day. But once all their sheep were gone the dragon struck again and attacked their town, so they began to offer instead one cow along with one of their own children, and this they did until at last the princess Saba was chosen. It was this girl in her peril that the young George spotted and he went to gain some comprehension as to the cause for her distress. The dragon then emerged from the waters of the pond and George fought against it, wrestling it to the ground. Then he asked the princess to wrap her girdle about the beast, which she did, and it at once lost its ferocity. They returned to the town where all greeted him as a hero and then he beheaded the dragon before them all.

In a French version of this story an ambitious woman of exceptional beauty proved to be too great a seductress, so that she was transfigured into a basilisk and as a consequence caused great destruction across the countryside.[†] Her son George, however, being both good and pious, recognized that he must face this creature in battle and thus he went forth upon his steed to fight with it and from this contest he emerged victorious. The basilisk's body was then rent beneath the hooves of his horse. But from the guilt he felt from slaying his own mother he sought just punishment for himself, which he found was to be burned and his ashes scattered. Thus this is what George sought, but when his ashes were left they did not scatter and a young girl who happened along collected them up. She spied close

---

[*] Just as the eagle was used as a means to gain access to heaven, the wolf allowed one to traverse the path to the underworld. By possessing characteristics of a bear or wolf, Beowulf would have had the ability to travel between worlds like Hermes and Odin.

[†] The basilisk was a creature that had a deadly look and could be destroyed by its own reflection, which recalls the image upon the moon.

154

by a magic apple which she hungrily ate. Thereby the girl became pregnant and gave birth to a son who upon being born called out, "I am George and this is the second time I have been born upon the earth."[97]

The name George can easily be converted to 'Veorve', which not only is the same name as 'Veor' but is also similar to 'Eorve' or 'Eurve', and thus the same as both **EUROPE** and Cecrops.

Epitheus: That is truly astounding, Thaeo.

Thaeo: And now I could relate to you the slaying by Indra of the dragon Vrtra, leader of the Serpas, who is said to have swallowed up the entire universe.

> I will now sing of the heroic feats of Indra, of the very first ones done by the thunderbolt hurler. It was he who killed the dragon, he who sliced open the way of the waters, he who cut open the stomachs of mountains. He it was who slew the dragon who dwelt upon the mountain with the booming thunderbolts Tvastr had created for him. The waters cascaded directly into the sea with the rumble of lowing cattle.
>
> Indra resembled a wild and raging bull when he took the soma into his hands and drank it–what had been pressed within the three bowls during the soma ceremony, which goes on for three days. Indra, not at all tight-fisted, grabbed his thunderbolt and hurled his weapon to destroy the foremost of serpents.
>
> When you performed this feat, Indra, your magic surpassed even that of the master magicians, and at that instant you released the sun, the sky, and the dawn. After this no adversary has arisen who might challenge you.
>
> With his thunderbolt, his supreme weapon, Indra killed his greatest adversary, who lay upon the ground without shoulders; Vrtra was like a tree with its limbs chopped off.
>
> Vrtra was drunk, which does not befit a fighting man, so that he challenged the mighty hero to combat, him who had defeated the great and had consumed soma greatly. Not able to stand up against the onslaught brought about by his weapons, he found Indra to be an adversary fit to defeat him, and himself stricken with a flattened nose.

In the contest against Indra he battled with neither feet nor hands, until he was hit by a flying thunderbolt upon the nape of his neck. Then Vrtra lay like a steer after slaughter, who had before thought himself equal to the bull bursting with seed (Indra). There he lay like a bent reed as the rising waters washed over him, released for the sake of man, the very waters Vrtra had before bound up were now flowing freely over his carcass.

Then Indra hurled his baleful thunderbolt at Vrtra's mother (Danu), whose life-force was drained away. The mother was above and the son was below, like a cow covering her calf. The body was buried within the middle of the rivers of water that were continuously flowing; the waters obscured Vrtra's resting place, while him who was no match for Indra sank down into the deep dark abyss.

These were the waters whose husband was Dasa (Vrtra), their guardian dragon, waters that were trapped just like the cows that the demonic Panis had imprisoned; for after he had defeated Vrtra, Indra had severed the barrier, slicing open a way for the waters to rush.

When Vrtra tried to strike you (Indra) on the side of your face, you made yourself as thin as the hair on a horse's tail. You, the supreme god, the formidable one, gained the cows, gained the soma, and sliced open the sources of the seven raging streams, making them flow.

When Indra fought the dragon there was nothing that could be used to hold him back, not thunder nor lighting, not fog nor hailstones, which Vrtra had sent in every direction. The unforestalled Indra became champion for all time.

But whom did you see, Indra, who came to avenge the death of that dragon which caused you to run away in panic, after you had defeated him; for you walked over the ninety-nine streams as though you were an anguished eagle, making your way over earth and through air?

Indra, he who wields the thunderbolt in his hands, rules both that which is moving and that which is unmoving, and over both tame animals and wild animals. He rules over the people as a king, and encircles all things like a rim which surrounds the spokes of a wheel.[98]

Here we find Indra defeating the dragon Vrtra with his thunderbolt, fashioned for him by his father Kvasir, by striking the dragon at its neck. Then, like the confrontation between Beowulf and Grendel's mother, Indra goes on to kill the dragon's mother Danu. And also like Beowulf, as his companions abandon him in his confrontation with the dragon, so do the Maruts (weather gods) abandon Indra when he fights against Vrtra; and after his defeat Vrtra's followers are then said to flee into the ocean.

In slaying the dragon Indra frees the sun, the sky, and the dawn; just as we had supposed was the case in the slaying of Grendel's mother. Killing Vrtra also releases the flood waters upon which the progenitor of mankind (Manu) rides until he is brought to safety.[*] Indra then divides the monster into two and uses half of it to create the moon while the rest he stuffs into the abyss to become the foundation of the earth; and from his semen which fell to the earth, shed during the battle, came forth all manner of plants and vegetation.[99] Thus we find here what we might have expected to find; that Indra created the world from out of the dragon's carcass.

Epitheus: Well done.

---

[*] Vrtra also takes the form of a bull, and in the simultaneous act Indra both releases the waters from the mountain as well as the cows that were pent up by the demons of drought.

CHAPTER 13

Thaeo: So now I will briefly mention the confrontation between the Egyptian sun god Ra and his adversary the serpent Hak.   The Egyptian records (Papyrus of Ani) say of him,

> Your serpent adversary has been sent to the flames, the demon serpent Sebau (Hak) has been brought down and his arms bound with chains, and you have hacked off his limbs, and the sons of iniquity will never again rise against you.[100]

We find that this serpent is identical to the one called Apophis (Apep), sometimes identified with Set, who confronts Ra as he descends into the underworld.[*]   Apophis was a large serpent representing darkness who, like Iormungand, was coiled so that he held his own tail within his mouth. This serpent too is chained down on his back, his head is crushed and cut off with a knife, his limbs are chopped off, his stomach is split open, and he is finally destroyed by fiery darts shot by Ra; and all of his demon companions are likewise hacked to pieces and destroyed by flame.[101]   Like Iormungand he then sunk into the sea, just as the Egyptian New Year began.[102]

And so we might associate him too with Typhon, which is the Greek name for Set, a formidable creature said to have an upper half which is human with his arms reaching up to the east and west; and is also said to have a hundred serpent heads, and to be winged, while his lower half was a serpentine coil.[103]

Just as we saw with Gaia and Cronos attacking her husband Ouranos, here we find Gaia using Typhon to attack Zeus, as it is told by Hesiod,

> Once Zeus and the gods had defeated the Titans, great Gaia by Tartaros bore the last of her children named Typhon, whose hands and feet were alive, and there emerged from his shoulders a hundred vile serpent heads, from whose eyes shot glaring fire; and from their throats came the most horrid sounds which echoed

---

[*] Sometimes Set is identified with Apophis attacking Ra, who is defended by Horus, but sometimes Set is the one who defends Ra from Apophis.

throughout the high mountains. And the devastation wrought by him would have been beyond the hope of reversing, and he would have emerged to rule both gods and men, if Zeus had not perspicaciously perceived the threat and produced a strong thunder clap which echoed throughout the sea, earth, and sky, and even down into the deep caverns of earth.

Then even great Olympus shook as he moved, the very ground trembled underfoot. There came a hot conflagration which blazed over the face of the deep sea, both from Zeus's lightning and the fires from the monster's light beams, enflamed by the wind which was his breath, over both earth and sky. And the ocean water boiled, and tall waves wreaked havoc upon the headlands from the wind-storm which the two immortals conjured. Even earthquakes arose and Hades, the lord of the underworld, shook. And those Titans who dwelled beneath Tartaros, beside Cronos, were trembling from the deadly contest and its ever-present racket.

Until Zeus collected together his strength and, taking up his mighty glaring thunderbolt, dove down from Olympus's peak and attacked, so that each of those brilliant heads upon the baleful beast was set alight. And when he was overcome from the onslaught he had sustained, Typhon, now wounded, wobbled and collapsed. The wide earth bellowed beneath him, and this mighty one's flames, beaten by roaring thunder, were extinguished by the attack, along that dark and deep mountainous wood. And there the weary world was set afire and melted from the great fiery wind, and it dissolved in the scorching flames, until Zeus in his battle rage sent Typhon toppling down into misty Tartaros, and from him comes the force of the humid winds.[104]

Epitheus: Well told.

Thaeo: And there is somewhat more to say about Typhon, where we learn of his influence when he creates volcanoes and earthquakes beneath Mount Aetna, when Pindar tells us,

The one who now lies in frightful Tartaros with a hundred heads is Typhon, the gods' adversary, once cared for near the famous Cilician cave, but now feels the weight of the seaside cliffs above

Cumae (by the Tyrrhenian Sea), while the pinnacle of snowy Aetna, striking boldly into the sky, which year-round maintains its freezing white cover, holds him firmly down. And up from the abyss pours an infernal fiery spring, far too dangerous to be approached. In the day flow down torrents of swirling smoke, while at night red flowing lava spews forth rocks, which fall and plunge into the wide-bounded sea. That beast is the source of a fountain of Hephaistos' fire, an amazing sight to see and likewise wondrous to hear, among those who have come to witness it. There the creature is caught between the dark-wood forests of Aetna's sides and the wide plain, and the surface which supports him underneath cuts and scrapes his entire backside.[105]

That is the conclusion of matters concerning Typhon, although we are also told by Callimachus that they identified a giant beneath Mount Aetna named Briares, who is said to create earthquakes whenever he shifts the heavy weight of the mountain from one of his shoulders to the other.[106]

So then next it would be fit to speak about the adversary of glorious Apollo. And Python as you know was born from the earth as a consequence of Deucalion's flood.[*] The confrontation between them is a famous one, as told by Homer,

Once the days and the months had come to completion
And the full expression of the seasons entirely turned
And time had brought about the whole cycle of the year
Then Hera gave birth to one neither mortal nor divine
The fearsome and merciless Typhon, a plague to man
Cow-eyed Hera soon took him and gave him to Python
Bringing evil to evil, and the she-dragon received him
That spelled ruin and wrath for the ideal nations of man
He who went to confront the she-dragon met only death
Before Lord Apollo, striking from afar, let loose an arrow
And then in wretched pain she lay wearily, gasping for air,
A heavy flipping heap fitfully writhing upon the earth

---

[*] Just as Python was born from the earth after Deucalion's flood we also find that Typhon was the son of Hera without a father. Hephaistos was also said to be the son of Hera without a father, which is also like Grendel and the Nemean Lion.

160

The eerie shriek which resounded was no common sound
Without peace, thrashing and struggling through the wood
Here and there she, gasping blood, gave up her ghost[107*]

Epitheus: Splendid.

Thaeo: Another contest which comes from a creation myth is that of
the sky god Marduk, though we can speculate that at some point
every one of them amounted to a divine creation story. The defeat of
the demon Tiamat by Marduk is accomplished rather like that of
Shamash against Humbaba.

Marduk created a bow and this he fashioned to be his weapon
Then fletched the arrow with feathers, and set it onto the string
Raising aloft a mace that he held within his rigid right hand
Slinging the bow over his arm, setting the quiver at his side
With lightning before him, eternal flame burning within him
He also fashioned a net which he could use to encircle Tiamat
He mastered the four winds so that she might have no escape
South Wind, North Wind, East Wind, and West Wind he took
Gifts from his father Anu that were kept at hand with the net
He generated the terror-gust, the tempest, and the whirlwind
Four gales and seven winds, the tornado and the hurricane
Setting forth the seven he had made, they followed behind
The Lord raised his mighty mace called the Flood-weapon
Before mounting his awesome, fear-rearing storm chariot[108]

Tiamat and Marduk, defender of the gods, faced one another
Moving towards each other, preparing for the coming clash
The Lord unleashed his net, and cast it out to entrap Tiamat
He called from behind him the terror-gust to fly in her face
Tiamat figured to open her mouth so as to swallow the wind
But the great force of the terror-gust kept her mouth open
The raging winds bloated her belly, she spread her jaws wide
Marduk released an arrow which struck her distended middle

---

[*] In addition to his slaying of Python, Apollo and his sister were responsible
for killing a creature called Tityus, because he had attempted to rape their
mother. And although we cannot be sure it was to have been used, Apollo
is said to have as weapons a golden sword and a silver bow.

Then he cleaved her into two pieces and cut open her heart,
Having defeated her, thus bringing her hateful life to an end
Tossing her down onto the dirt and setting his feet upon her[109]

Here it speaks of four gales, seven winds, and two more, which are
like the 13 winds used against Humbaba. Marduk bloats her with the
wind before piercing her with an arrow, and then slits up her middle,
just as is done with Humbaba.

Epitheus: Clearly.

Thaeo: And then subsequent to her defeat, like Indra, Marduk uses
her body to create the world.

To Tiamat he now turned his attention, the one he had caught
And the Lord Marduk trod upon the lower parts of her body
Raising his merciless hammer high he pulverized her skull
Then sliced open the arteries that carried her watery blood
He caused the North Wind to take it, to convey good tidings
When his forebears saw it they were jubilant and all sang out,
Then made plans to meet him with presents, gifts of greeting
The Lord took a moment to rest and looked over her corpse
He split the monster's cadaver and made marvelous things
Severing it up the middle, flaying it in half like a drying fish
One of which he thrust up to make the vault of the heavens
He drew a gate in front of it, put into the care of a guardian
Her waters were bounded, so that they might not surge free[110]

He set her head out and heaped up deep mounds of terrain
Severing open bursting springs, from which streams poured
He made the Tigris and Euphrates rivers gush from her eyes
Sealed up her nostrils, so that the baleful river would not flow
He gathered together from her udder the treeless mountains
And drilled out holes so as to drain away the stagnant waters
Spanned her tail across, fixing it fast to tie up the heavens*
And established the waters of the Apsu underneath his feet
Then he placed her thigh so as to bolster up the sky's vault

---

* Here her tail spanning the cosmos is a reference to the Milky Way.

Half of her body was used to make the sky, half the earth
He twirled the creation, so that the insides of Tiamat spun
He spread out his net so that it spanned the entire world
Then fixed its end points to places upon heaven and earth
Binding them with knots after looping them around pillars[111]

We saw the defeat of Leviathan was linked to the act of creation, which is the separation of the waters, and thus we might recognize here too traces of an ancestral form. Tiamat's body is split in two so as to make the heavens and the earth, and by comparison we could view that the body of Leviathan became the material utilized in the creation of the world. Though, in any case, there is no question that Yahweh brought the world into being from out of the primal sea.

Epitheus: None at all.

Thaeo: Then let me bring up one further matter. Since we have associated the name 'Levi' with the fire giant Loki, and by comparison with the name Leviathan, we might take a further look at the father of Moses who we presumed to be **LEVI** and the father of Noah who is Lamech.[*] And when we before compared Noah and Moses we thought them to be born from the flood, as both their names arise from the word for birth ('*nova*' and '*mose*'), though each is represented quite differently in their respective narratives.

Epitheus: Assuredly.

Thaeo: So too we can even see how the name 'Lother' (Loki), is also not far from that of Baal's opponent Lotan, who is also known as the 'twisting serpent', as is Leviathan.

Epitheus: Truly.

Thaeo: While another of Baal's adversaries was Yamm (the sea) whom we must consider also to be comparable to Marduk's opponent Tiamat (the sea).[†]

---

[*] See *The Eden Enigma: A Dialogue*
[†] While Balder and Hod are adversaries Baal and Haddu are different names for the very same god.

Epitheus: Yes.

Thaeo: Then consider that just as we have seen, **YEVI** might also be pronounced '*Levi*',* that Yamm might thus equivalently become '*Lamm*', which is similar to Lammu, another name for Leviathan.

Epitheus: Evidently.

Thaeo: And since we might take the name Levi to mean 'wreath' ('*liwya*'), which leads us to the name for Leviathan ('*liwyatan*'), this also appears to imply a serpent encoiled so that both its head and tail come together to form a circle, as we have seen with Apophis and Iormungand.†

Epitheus: Clearly so.

Thaeo: And consider the (Mesopotamian) Lahamu, who are known to be creatures which are half-man and half-fish, born from the primeval waters of Tiamat, end up guarding the gate of the sea and live in the Apsu as partners to the god of water Ea (Enki).[112]

And here as elsewhere the serpent is often a denizen of the deep as in the case of Iormungand, Leviathan, and Lotan; when it does not act the part of guardian as do Python, Ladon, and Beowulf's fire-breathing adversary.‡

Epitheus: Just so.

Thaeo: And likewise the name of Lamech, Noah's father, could also be equivalent to Lammu, and thus also associated with **LEVI**.§ And

---

* See *The Eden Enigma: A Dialogue*
† Like these other world serpents, the male Leviathan was thought to yet inhabit the deep sea ('Joseph and Aseneth' 12:11, 'Apocalypse of Abraham' 21:4, 'Testaments of the Twelve Patriarchs' 7:3, II Esdras 6:52, and 'Haggadah').
‡ Python defends the Pythian oracle, Ladon the tree of the Hesperides, and Beowulf's dragon a treasure hoard.
§ Lamech is also said to have the sons Jabal and Jubal, a dweller in tents and a player of instruments, also Tubal-Cain, a smith. These first two are

this itself would only lend greater reason to perceive an equivalence between Moses and Noah.

Epitheus: It could be as you say.

Thaeo: Thus, to recapitulate, we have found associations, as we might relate them, of the fire giant Lother (Loki) to Lotan, Lotan to Leviathan, Leviathan to Lammu, and Lammu to Yamm, who is the sea.

Epitheus: Yes.

Thaeo: And we find also that the god Baal defeats Yamm just as Yahweh does Leviathan, and thus we might identify Yamm and Leviathan as similar if not entirely identical, since we know that both of them are water dragons defeated by the storm god.

Epitheus: Truly so.

Thaeo: While we find Yamm, being identified with the west, is also little different from Oceanus, who too is associated with the west; for he and Tethys are said to have reared Hera there during the duration of the war between the gods and the Titans.[*]

Epitheus: True enough.

Thaeo: And Oceanus was also the primordial waters which existed prior to the creation of earth, and it is said that from him and Tethys both the gods and men were born.

Epitheus: Yes.

---

equivalent to the sons of Zeus by Antiope, Zethos and Amphion. (Apollodorus, 3.5 § 5; see Hard 1998: 104)
[*] "Past the populated lands, to the east, lies Paradise of seven parts, each one set aside for the righteous by rank. To the west ('yam') lies the ocean, speckled with numerous islands which serve as the habitat for diverse peoples." ('Haggadah'; see Barnstone 1984: 47)

Thaeo: And also Yamm could well be identical to Ymir, the source of the flood from which Bergelmir escaped.* And we have already seen that there exists an equivalence between Odin and Indra, so we might recognize the close similarity between the killing of Ymir and that of Vrtra, who are both involved in acts of creation.†

Epitheus: Indeed.

Thaeo: Thus if what we have been claiming is indeed correct, this figure we've identified with both the sea (Yamm) as well as fire (Loki).

Epitheus: That is how it appears.

Thaeo: And from Iormungand, Apophis, Leviathan, and Oceanus, this creature who surrounds the world is then the same as the encircled serpent or *Ouroboros*.‡

Epitheus: True enough.

Thaeo: So we might take a moment to consider the appearance of the world as Plato describes it, for we should find it to be a familiar one,

> The creation took its toll on each of the four elements, since the Creator accrued the world out of all the fire, and all the water, and all the air, and all the earth, not leaving out either them or their influences. Firstly, he intended that the creature must be, as far as it would be possible, a perfection of its entirety as well as of its parts; secondly, that it must be united without any remnant which might be used toward the creation of another world; also that it must be without the plight of age and remain uncorrupted by disease. Thinking that heat and cold and other natural forces which bind bodies together might rather encircle and penetrate them from without when they are defenseless, so they would be

---

* Ymir was the first mortal go into the underworld, while Yamm is associated with the west because the setting sun marked the way to the underworld.
† Ymir is both like the Hindu giants Purusa and Yama (Death).
‡ The symbolic circular serpent who bites his own tail

166

made decrepit by them, bringing disease and old age to them so that they would atrophy; for this reason he created the world as a single form, making it as a whole and thus perfect so that it would not be vulnerable to old age or disease.

To the world he gave a shape that was both appropriate and natural to itself. And to the creature that was to incorporate all creatures, the form chosen was that which suitably incorporates within itself the form of all the others. Thus he made the world as a globe, spherical as if formed upon a lathe, which has its surface at every point of equal distance from its center (radius), which is the most perfect and the most symmetrical of all shapes; for he thought that the like was far superior to the unlike. This he completed so as to cause the surface to be entirely smooth everywhere and serve multiple purposes.

Firstly, as there was nothing outside to be seen, the living being required no eyes; and as there was nothing to be heard, the living being required no ears; nor was there any atmosphere surrounding it which could be breathed; nor was there any use for organs that would aid in his consumption of food or to relieve him of waste, since there was nothing as yet that went into him or came out of him, for there was nothing else apart from him. Of form he was created in this manner: that what was a production from his own body also served for his ingestion, so that everything that he did or what he suffered took place only within and was done by himself. For the Creator thought that a being which was self-sufficient was far better than one which was wanting; and, since he had no reason to collect anything nor to defend himself from others, the Creator thought it unnecessary to give him either hands or feet, nor of any appendages required for walking; but the motion which suited a spherical form is that which was given to him, of all the seven ones being that which was most suited to mind and thought; made to move in such a manner upon the same spot, within his defined limits, as revolving in a circle. Each of the six other motions were denied him, and so he was not to move according to their divergences. And since this circular motion required no feet, the universe was thus formed without feet or legs.[113]

Thus we have here the same circular form defined as the first being, the spherical world, biting its own tail and partaking of a rotational motion.

Epitheus: One can hardly deny it.

Thaeo: Then consider this, where Erysikhthon, the son of Triopas or Erechthonios (king of the Thessalians), experiences the wrath of Demeter.

For there among the Pelasgians was a marvelous thickly wooded grove containing many kinds of trees that was very much beloved of the gods, where springs produced water that prodigiously fed the roots of the abundant trees. This wood was a sacred grove dedicated to the goddess Demeter. But Erysikhthon became angry at the gods for bringing bad fortune upon him, and set upon an ill-considered misdeed: he went there with twenty giants armed with two-faced brazen axes and tree-toppling hatchets. They rushed there in a fury and the first tree they set upon was a giant oak, the same beneath which the nymphs danced in its ample shade, hand-locked in a ring around its trunk at the time of the high sun. It had been decorated through countless generations and was permanently decked out in wreaths and garlands, tablets and *papyri*, which made it appear as a tremendous spectacle. Striking with a vengeful bent, determined that its decline would strike into the very heart of the goddess herself, he attacked it without mercy. The tree quaked and paled, and some who saw it even went so far as to claim that his penetration of the bark caused scarlet blood to issue forth, as it would from the sacrifice of the bull at the altar; a rivulet of life pouring onto the ground.

While a priestess there named Nikippe appealed to the vile and shameless men, pleading with them to refrain, lest in anger the goddess of the garden (Demeter) might come to expunge them. Yet with a ferocious leonine look incarnated towards her, Erysikhthon told her to keep back or she too would feel the keen blade of his axe.

He declared, "These trees are to become the timber for a banquet hall large enough to seat my colossal soldiers."

168

But when she attempted to hold back his striking blade, he swung at her in a rage, "Receive this in return for your piety," and with a single axe blow struck off her head.

Moving unperturbed back to the oak he struck it again and again, possessed of a fit to bring it down. When from the tree came the voice of Demeter's nymph to persuade him to refrain from his desecration, but this spirit was extinguished when the giant tree finally and piteously crashed to the ground.

These things engendered anger in Demeter so that she assumed her goddess aspect and rode out upon her serpent-hitched chariot. The men were half-dazed with shock when they saw her approaching and fled with such haste that their bronze axes were left stuck in the trees.

She did not care for the others but only for their leader, answering his prior boast, "You foolish dog, go ahead and build your house where you will feast, for from henceforth you will banquet eternally."

Thus is all she said, because she had already formulated a wretched fate for Erysikhthon. To fulfill her promise she caused him to be beset by a fierce and prodigious hunger named Aethon (god of hunger), one that was so wrenching and relentless that he was plagued by this terrible ailment as if by the worst sort of disease. Thus the poor man was struck so that no matter how much he ate, he only desired that much more again. He had twenty who prepared his food for him and twelve who poured his wine; for just as Demeter was wont to bring a curse of victuals against him so (the god of wine) Dionysos followed suit, for he was bound by the same displeasures as she.

Due to the shame that this brought to his parents they would not send him any longer to the communal feasts, and devised all manner of excuses as to why he was unable to attend. And as this went on they made one after another excuse to put others off, while the one who feasted all day merely ate everything, in a quantity far beyond anyone's ability to measure. His beset belly grumbled ever more so that no matter how much he'd already had, and all the foods that poured into him, fruitlessly and carelessly, were like rivers gushing into the bottomless sea or like fire which never wearies of consuming trees. Just as the snow upon the peaks of Mount Mimas or a wax doll melt in the sun, even more so did his body atrophy so that only skin and bone remained of this wretch. His mother was stricken by aggravated weeping, and his two sisters were given to daily grieving for him; they and the ten handmaidens wept for him time after time.

His father Triopas ran his hands through his hair and pleaded to an unsympathetic Poseidon with words such as these, "Improper father, see what has become of your third generation, as I am your son by Kanake, the daughter of Aiolos, and this hapless boy happens to be mine. It would surely have been better had he been struck down by Apollo (with a plague) well before this calamity came, and he had been buried by my own hands! But look as he sits with this curse of gluttony upon him before my very eyes! If you would but lift this cruel fate from him or take and feed him yourself; for look, my larder is empty, deserted are my folds, and barren are my stalls; already do the kitchen servants refuse to fulfill my orders. They already unhitched the mules from the stately wagon and he even ate the cow that his mother had set aside for the goddess Hestia, along with my race horse and war horse, and even the cat who was but a terror to mice."[114]

Erysikhthon became so desperate to acquire food to keep himself fed that he sold off all of his possessions, and then finally even his daughter Mnestra was sold into slavery where she remained for a time; for this being unbearable to her she sought salvation from the sea, from her lover Poseidon, imploring him, "Deliver me from wretched servitude, you who took my precious virginity!" Poseidon heeded her plea and helped to free her by conferring upon her the gift of shape-shifting. And so she took on the form of a fisherman, by which she was able to slip free from her master. Yet her father sold her again or loaned her out in one or another shape: a mare, or cow, or deer, or bird, merely as an aid to keep himself fed.

As long as there remained any stores of food in Triopas's house then the news of this calamity went no further than his own rooms. But when his devouring teeth had consumed the riches of the house he was forced to sit out by the crossroads, begging for a piece of crust and foraging for leftovers from the feasts. Yet this affliction continued until Erysikhthon, unable to find sufficient sustenance, turned to consuming himself in order to satisfy his relentless hunger.[115]

170

It is sometimes said that it was King Triopas himself, rather than his son Erysikhthon, who in wishing to roof his own house, pulled down the ancient temple of Demeter and for this he suffered an interminable hunger that she cursed him with, so that no matter how much he ate he would never be satisfied. Until near the end of his life a snake was sent to beset him and, after much suffering, he came to death and the vengeful goddess put him amongst the stars where he, as a warning to the unwary, became the constellation of *Ophiuchus*: so that the punishing snake could be seen coiled around him, inflicting upon him his well-deserved and eternal punishment.[116]

And the reason I mention this is that we also find it said that Mot ('death') himself was to have had a ravenous appetite, when he says,

I have an appetite like that of a ravening lioness,
I have a craving as deep as the dolphins of the sea
My pool ensnares wild oxen, my well entraps deer
When my appetite is large, like that of a ravenous ass
Then I stuff my face at once with both of my hands[117]

And also we find it spoken of among the hymns to Shiva, where it says,

Hunger, the great serpent,
Has seized the vitals
And the venom is mounting
From foot to brow
Only he is the true Snake-man
In all the world
Who can feed this Hunger food
And bring the poison down,*
Ramanatha[118]

So let us see if we can make sense of all this, for Lotan is clearly associated with Mot ('death'), though also the snake is generally

---

* In his contest with Tiamat, Marduk holds an herb to protect him from her poison. (see *Enuma Elish: The Babylonian Creation Epic*, Tablet 4)

emblematic of the underworld,[119] and it was believed that deities in serpentine form were its inhabitants and acted as escorts for the descending spirits.[120]

Erishkigal, the queen of the underworld, is also associated with serpents,[121] as is the demoness Tiamat, whose husband is the subterranean fresh water sea, the Apsu.* And many of the earliest gods were represented in serpentine form, as rulers of the underworld and inhabitants of the primal seas.[122]

Epitheus: That is beyond reproach, Thaeo. And I might mention in relation to this the question that Baruch asked of the angel, when he said, "Please allow me to ask one question, gracious lord, about what you mentioned of the serpent, the one who drinks a cubit of water from the sea each day. Tell me then how great is his stomach that he is able to drink so much?"

And the angel replied, "His stomach is truly vast Hades. The distance which three-hundred men could toss a weight, such is the space encompassed by it. But now come with me, for even greater mysteries await you."[123]

---

* The Apsu is the watery underworld, equivalent to the Abyss.

CHAPTER 14

Thaeo: I should add that, according to Plutarch, the Egyptians thought that spirits descended beneath the earth to a place called *Amenthes*, which means 'one who takes and gives',[124] and this resembles to me the pair Shiva and Kali who are said to share the dual qualities of swallowing and birthing.[125]

Epitheus: Surely.

Thaeo: And in Babylonia they believed that two serpents had existed within the primordial ocean: one being the *basmu* ('serpent with a womb') and the other the *mushussu* ('furious serpent').[125]

Epitheus: Yes.

Thaeo: We might also identify the female serpent in the poem of Idunn's fall to the underworld,[127] for one of its characters is referred to as 'the begetter', who is named Ividi, which we could associate with 'ivi' (Eve). And this brings us back to the serpent Tiamat who is also called the 'mother of all', and Eve's name (*Havvah*) which is also a word for 'serpent' ('*heviah*').[128]

Epitheus: Astonishing.

Thaeo: And Eve's name too recalls what was chanted by the *Bacchantes* (worshippers of the Greek wine god Dionysos), for during their processions they carried serpents in their hands and wore them upon their heads shouting 'Evah!' which also means 'serpent'.[129*]

Epitheus: Truly.

Thaeo: And the form '*havvah*', as you before pointed out, is likewise similar to our word 'heaven'.[†] Thus we might recognize here a very ancient conception, for consider too that we have already figured that

---

* This name is also given sometimes as 'Evohe'.
† See *The Eden Enigma: A Dialogue*

173

the goddess of heaven was called **EVEH**; and before we considered that she too was associated with the path of the Milky Way.[*]

Epitheus: I remember well.

Thaeo: Thus we are suggesting here that the name 'Eve' could also be associated with the Milky Way, when it is viewed as a cosmic serpent.[†] But we must also mention the god of fire **LEVI**, whom we might also suggest was a serpent, being the root form of the name 'Leviathan'.

Epitheus: True.

Thaeo: And we suggested before that Eve and **LEVI** were foremost participants in the earliest times of creation,[‡] and thus we would find both **LEVI** and Eve to be originally perceived as serpents themselves.

Epitheus: Yes, but I am having trouble understanding how this could be true, for might we reconcile this if Eve is identified as the first woman?

Thaeo: That is difficult to answer, Epitheus, though we might presume, as Soleos suggested, that there are in fact two stories to consider: one being the creation of woman out of the rib of man, the other being the story of the Garden of Eden. And these do appear to be separable, as we considered before when Soleos suggested that Adam (earth) and Eve (heaven) might well be comparable to the Egyptian gods Geb (earth) and Nut (heaven).[§] For it is also said that Nut was the mother of all living things and was the Milky Way.[130] And as the Orphic hymns tell us, that Heaven was the bounteous parent existing as both the origin and termination of all; and she, also

---

[*] See *The Eden Enigma: A Dialogue*
[†] In India the earth is said to be the Serpent Queen (*Sarpa Rajni*), mother of all living things, who formed out of cosmic dust which took serpentine form. (Howey 1955: 372)
[‡] See *The Eden Enigma: A Dialogue*
[§] See *The Eden Enigma: A Dialogue*

called Nature, was the 'queen of heaven' in addition to appearing as the starry sky.[*]

And since we find that both Geb and Adam represent the earth, and also recognize that Eve and Nut represent the Milky Way, we might presume that Adam's rib is the form of the galaxy itself, who thus also became his wife. And this is similar to the (Hindu) first

---

[*] The relevant Orphic Hymns are as follows:

Great Heaven, whose mighty frame no respite knows,
Father of all, from whom the world arose
Hear, bounteous parent, source and end of all,
Forever whirling round this earthly ball;
Abode of gods, whose guardian power surrounds
The eternal world with ever-during bounds;
Whose ample bosom and encircling folds
The dire necessity of nature holds.
Ethereal, earthly, whose all-various frame
Azure and full of forms, no power can tame.
All-seeing Heaven, progenitor of Time,
Forever blessed, deity sublime,
Propitious on a novel mystic shine,
And crown his wishes with a life divine.
(Hymns of Orpheus, iii 'To Heaven', revised by author; Taylor 2007: 57)

Nature, all parent, ancient, and divine,
O much-mechanic mother, art is thine;
Heavenly, abundant, venerable queen,
In every part of thy dominions seen.
Untamed, all-taming, ever-splendid light,
All ruling, honored, and supremely bright.
Immortal, first-born, ever still the same,
Nocturnal, starry, shining, glorious dame.
Thy feet still trace in a circling course,
By thee are turned, with unremitting force.
Pure ornament of all the powers divine,
Finite and infinite alike you shine;
To all things common and in all things known,
Yet incommunicable and alone.
(Hymns of Orpheus, ix 'To Nature', revised by author; Taylor 2007: 64)

man Manu who we find had a daughter named Parsu ('rib'), who likewise became his wife.

So in this sense the female (Eve) resides in the heavens, being the source of all life, while the male (Adam) lies beneath her as the earth, yet they remain in connection with one another as husband and wife.

Epitheus: That is extraordinary, but it recalls to me something that I would like to mention, from a detail I recall of the creation, which arose out of two incorporeal bodies: one which forms the lower half of the world (earth) and one which forms the upper half (heaven), when God says,

"Before anything perceptible could be seen I, the only one, coursed among the incorporeal objects, just like the sun, traveling from east to west and then from west to east. Yet even the sun has time for rest, yet there was no rest for me, because everything had yet to be created. And I thought to myself and fixed in my thoughts that there must be a support upon which to build a perceptible creation.

"First I called to the highest things, 'One of you incorporeal beings come down here where I can see you!' And Adoil came down, who was quite large. And I looked him over and I could see within his stomach there resided a significant light. So I said to him, 'Adoil, dissolve yourself so that what is born from you might be seen.' And he dissolved himself and there emerged a very significant light. And I stood at the focus of this light, carrying all other light forth from this light. And a significant span emerged and revealed all of the creation which I had in my mind's eye devised, and caused me to look upon it with approval.

"Then I placed there a throne for myself and sat down upon it, and to the light I said, 'Travel up to a higher realm than this throne and solidify yourself in this place which is higher than my throne, and so become the support for all the highest objects!' And nothing surpasses light in height but nothing itself, and I seated myself and looked upwards from my throne.

"Then, second, I called to the lowest things, which were very low indeed, and said, 'One of you incorporeal beings come up here where I can see you!' And Arkhas came up, who was firm

176

and solid, and red like clay. So I said to him, 'Open yourself, Arkhas, so that what will emerge from you might be seen!' And he dissolved himself and there emerged a span, which was expansive and black, carrying the lower created objects; and I looked upon this with favor. I said to him, 'Descend to a low point and solidify yourself, and you will become the support for all the lowest objects!' And so it happened; and he descended and solidified, and became the support for all the lower objects. And nothing is lower than darkness but for nothing itself.

"And I gave the command, 'Let some be taken from the light and some be taken from the darkness.' And I said, 'Condense and be surrounded by light!' which I spread out far and wide and it became water. And I laid it out on top of the darkness and beneath the light, and by so doing produced the deep waters, which is the Abyss. And a support of light was made surrounding the water, and seven great spheres were placed within, and I made them crystalline, both wet and dry—which means that of crystal and that of ice—as the way for water and the other elements. And to each of the seven planets I showed the path that they should traverse, with each occupying its own sphere, so that they would continue to travel in this way, and everything looked very favorable to me.

"Then I separated the light from the darkness, which is to say, in the midst of the waters, putting them to one side and to the other. And I commanded that the light would be called 'day' and that the darkness would be called 'night'. And there was an evening and there was a morning, the first day."[131]

Thaeo: Magnificent. And there is too an Egyptian reference to "one serpent coiled within another: the female serpent bites the male serpent, while the male serpent bites the female serpent".[132] And there is something else which bears this very thing out, for (the Greek gods) Chronus and Ananke are two serpents who surround the earth. Chronus ('time') is a self-born deity who appeared at the very beginning of creation, and one envisaged to be of serpentine form with three heads: one of a man, one of a bull, and one of a lion.[*]

---

[*] Chronus is identified with Cronos, the father of Zeus. (Plutarch, '*Isis and Osiris*' 32 ; see Babbitt 1936: 77)

He and his partner Ananke were encoiled around the cosmic egg before they shattered it; creating the universe and separating it out into earth, sea, and sky. But even after they completed their act of creation they still remained entwined about the universe, causing its motion and so being the creators of time.

Epitheus: Very stirring.

Thaeo: Thus it seems that we have identified two different but related representations of the cosmic serpent: on the one hand the encircled serpent, who stretches about the earth, biting his own tail; and on the other the two entwined serpents, one male and one female and whom we identified as Adam and Eve, Geb and Nut, Tiamat and Apsu, Chronus and Ananke, and the male and female Leviathans.

Epitheus: Yes.

Thaeo: Thus the name '**EVEH**', a reference to the god or goddess of the sky, we might say is of the form '*ea-sve*' meaning 'water-wind', with the one lying about the ocean being associated with water and the one spanning the heavens being associated with the wind.[*]

Epitheus: That certainly seems to be, although might we include here too the (Finnish) god Lemminkainen and his sister Annikki.[†] For is not the name of Lemminkainen similar to that of Lammu and Annikki to that of the spouse of Chronus, Ananke?

Thaeo: Indeed, and we also saw the pairing of Poseidon with Kanake, who are said to be the parents of Triopas?

Epitheus: Quite so.

---

[*] Thus the universe is perceived as both male and female, yet at the same time as united, like the Yin and Yang (Ophiolatreia 2008: 22); in this regard it is similar to the Chinese concept of the male and female Sky Dragon and Water Dragon; the wind is the breath of the sky dragon and the rain pours from his mouth. The Iroquois Indians have a water dragon who they take to be the Milky Way.

[†] Annikki is said to be a girl of the night, dusk, and dawn.

178

Thaeo: And further, Typhon was described as having been male while the serpent Python was female. And we could also include here Enlil and Ninlil, who are both deities of the wind; Ninlil herself, known as the 'lady of birth', who begot the moon god Nanna, the death god Narnar, the god of the underworld Ninazu, and the almighty warrior Ninurta.

Epitheus: Yes.

Thaeo: The Egyptians' Great Opet (Apet) is likewise associated with pregnancy and birth,* often shown as a combination of hippopotamus, crocodile, human, and lion.† And she is identified with the hippopotamus goddess Taurt, or Taweret ('Great One'), who is also a goddess of birth and a devourer of evils; although she was also wife of the god of evil, the dreaded serpent Apophis we mentioned before.

And Taurt is shown with seven stars upon her back, and the identification of these stars can be determined from the position of Taurt upon the Dendera Zodiac, which indicates that she was represented by the combined constellations of *Cepheus* and *Draco*.‡

Epitheus: Truly.

Thaeo: And thus if Taurt is identified with *Draco* and her husband is the serpent Apophis (Set), we might wonder whether this represents the pairing of a good and evil serpent, one who gives birth and one who destroys;[133] for we find among the Persians Ormuzd and Ahrinan, the primeval forces who existed from the very beginning of time, in the form of twin serpents,§ one good and one evil, contesting over the cosmic egg which was the seed of the universe.[134]

---

* In Thebes she was considered to be the mother of Osiris.
† The hieroglyph for this hippopotamus also meant 'heaven' (Staal 1988: 140). The hippopotamus and crocodile were also forms taken by the dragon Typhon, who is Set (Olcott 2004: 187).
‡ There are seven major stars in the constellation of *Draco* and five stars that make up *Cepheus*. Taurt is also known as Kheb-ti which means 'seven'. (St. Clair 1898: 397)
§ According to Eusebius the Persians held the greatest deities to be serpents, and it is they who determined the course of the universe. (Deane 2008: 26)

179

While also among the Egyptians we have the good serpent Kneph (Onuphis) who arises in serpentine form, existing not only from the very beginning, but as one who is said to have neither beginning nor end. As the encircled serpent he is said to represent both the creator and the eternal soul of the universe.[135]   And Kneph is also represented with the cosmic egg within his mouth from which was born the god of truth Aphthah, who is also known as Ptah.[136]

Epitheus: Indeed.

Thaeo: And I might mention one more curious thing, for the god Kneph was represented by the Greek letter *theta* (θ). This letter is a circle with a diameter through it, and we might gather its meaning if we were to take the circle as representing the serpent which encircles the earth; while we might also consider that the word 'diameter' means 'divine mother' (*'thia-meter'*), representing the cross-wise piece as the Milky Way, which bisects the circle of the earth.[*]   And we know that the goddess Nut, the starry sky, was likewise called the 'divine mother'.[†]

Epitheus: Astounding.

Thaeo: And recall that in depicting the universe, Tartaros is shown to bisect the circle of Leviathan, just as the diameter bisects a circle.[137]

Epitheus: Yes, and this might indicate that it carries the same meaning as the two Leviathans.

Thaeo: And we might also mention a Persian goddess of the waters named Anahita (equivalent to Ishtar), the Greek goddess Diana, and the Canaanite goddess Anat, who might all be related to Ananke.
And in the name of the fairy Viviana ('white serpent') we also find the name 'Ana' meaning 'serpent',[138] while the Babylonian

---

[*] The mouth of the devouring serpent is the star *gamma* in *Cassiopeia*, which lies along the Milky Way. (White 2008: 93)
[†] In addition she was, like Inanna, called the 'Queen of Heaven' and 'mother of the gods'.

name for heaven is 'Anna',[139]* and also we should include the Egyptian abode of the blessed which is 'Anu'.†

Epitheus: Well done.

Thaeo: The (Mesopotamian) sky god Anu, which also means 'heaven', is represented by a bull, and the storm god Baal is likewise known as a bull.[140] And in Baal's defeat of Lotan it says, "At the time you killed Lotan, the fleeing serpent, ending the days of the twisting serpent, that seven-headed beast, the heavens slumped and sagged, just as do the folds of your robe."[141] And how, Epitheus, does this compare to what you had said before?

Epitheus: You mean, "Upon that day Yahweh with his renowned hard-edged mighty blade will execute Leviathan the fleeing serpent, Leviathan the twisting serpent; he shall slay the serpent that dwells within the sea"?[142]

Thaeo: Yes, they appear to be explicitly the same.

Epitheus: Without question.

Thaeo: Though we might wonder what is meant here when it says that Lammu being slain by Baal caused the heavens to slump and sag.

Epitheus: It does seem curious.

Thaeo: But then we might bring to mind the Anzu bird (a Mesopotamian deity of storms), for he is also associated with the *Pegasus* constellation.[143] And the Anzu bird is not only the bird that carries people to the underworld, but he also originally controlled the destiny of the roiling rivers and played the role of holding aloft the sky.[144]

Epitheus: Indeed.

---

* We find the name of Anathoth, which is a principle location of the Levite priesthood, is '*Ana-Thoth*' ('serpent Thoth').
† Thus "Anna" being the female form and "Annu" the male form

Thaeo: Then recall too that the constellation of *Aquarius* is also associated with Cecrops, who we know is to be half-man and half-serpent.

Epitheus: Yes.

Thaeo: Then starting with the god '**THEURVE**' ('*Thi-Eurve*') we can derive the god's original name as '**EURVE**'.[*] And when we take this and add to it the ending for 'serpent' ('*ops*') we end up with the name '**EURVOPS**' (Europe).

Epitheus: Extraordinary.

Thaeo: Then we also know that this constellation (*Aquarius*) is likewise associated closely with *Pegasus* and *Andromeda*, which appear together in the sky, and as the figure with upraised arms.[†] Thus when the cosmic serpent Lotan was slain by Baal we can imagine that the outcome of this was that the sky itself drooped; so we find here the figure to be supporting the vault of heaven with his arms.

Epitheus: Indeed it must be.

Thaeo: And this will remind us too of Ophiuchus, whose very name expresses his connection with the serpent ('*ophis*').

Epitheus: Certainly.

Thaeo: And this is also the form of the name 'Triopas' ('*Tri-opas*'), the father of Erysikhthon. For if we examine the name we find that, apart from its prefix ('*tri*'), his name is likewise connected to the serpent ('*ophis*'), and his name would also mean 'divine serpent'.

Epitheus: Undeniably.

---

[*] The name appears to be related to '*eorman*', which means 'great one', and thus may merely be a name for 'divinity'.
[†] See *The Eden Enigma: A Dialogue*

Thaeo: And among the other gods we find that Thor was to have lifted the Midgard Serpent from off of the ground; as well as the (Finnish) Old God, known as the thunderer, who resides at the pole of heaven and is said to hold aloft the sky.[145] And who himself is paired with the Old Woman who is underground.[146]

Epitheus: Yes.

Thaeo: Then too (the Greek god) Ouranos is a personification of the night sky (Milky Way), and is also equivalent to the Hindu god Varuna. And it says of him,

> Beyond the two halves of the world and the space which exists in-between, Varuna emptied his water jar by tipping low its mouth. In this way the emanation of the universe provides water to the land like plentiful rain does the growing grain.
>
> He provides water to the world, and to the land, and to the sky. When Varuna calls for the nourishing milk to fall, the mountains enshroud themselves in clouds and, infused with clout, the champions of the storm release them upon the world.
>
> I do proclaim the divine miracles of Varuna, the auspicious sky god, who raised himself up in the space between and measured the span separating them, using the sun like a measuring bob.
>
> None have yet dared to equal the wondrous feats of Varuna the masterful god, so that the cascading waters he sends falling down never so much as breach the limits of the one vast ocean.[147]

Here the god Varuna causes the sky to separate from the earth,[*] and in addition his having turned the water cask to pour out its waters into the world ocean is like the constellation of *Aquarius* (the water pourer), which as we saw is associated with Cecrops.[†]

---

[*] We find several gods given credit for having separated the Father Sky from the Mother Earth, while also locating the sun: Varuna, Agni, Soma, and Indra. Like Shiva, Indra is credited of being lord over that which is in motion and that which is still, like Marduk and Zeus he set the stars in the heavens, and like Atlas he made the sky his crown.

[†] Varuna is associated with an asterism within *Aquarius*. (Olcott 2004: 35)

Epitheus: Truly.

Thaeo: And it seems to me that Cecrops we might identify with the Egyptian king of the gods named Set Chreps, also known as the 'Aeon' ('time'), and who is said to have swallowed the serpent and generated the motion of both the sun and the moon.[148]   Thus Set Chreps is responsible for both time and the motion of the heavens; and so is equivalent to Ouranos, and as the 'thunderer' is also like Zeus, thus combining the very qualities which Cecrops possesses.

Epitheus: Extraordinary.

Thaeo: We also before associated Shiva with the *Pegasus* constellation,[*] who has four arms with which to lift the cosmic serpent Rahu to form the vault of the sky and likewise cause the motion of the heavens.[149][†]   And it says of Shiva,

> You balanced the globe on the waters
> Like a pot sitting upon a dancer's head
> You made the sky stand without pillar or prop
> O Ramanatha, what other gods could have done this[150]

Epitheus: So it does.

Thaeo: Then the testimony of the Egyptians tells of the creation where Geb (earth) and Nut (sky) are joined together in one another's embrace within the primeval waters of Nu until from these waters emerges Shu, the god of heaven.[‡]   This newly born god pushed himself between the bodies of Geb and Nut and, bracing his hands against Nut, pushed her star-studded body up above his head with his arms raised high.   Yet her feet and hands remained in contact with the earth and these then became the four pillars upon which are held the firmament of heaven.[151]

---

[*] See *The Eden Enigma: A Dialogue*
[†] Mahadeva (Shiva) is shown with serpents around his neck, in his hair, and upon both arms. Mahadeva is 'Maha-Thevah', meaning 'Great Heaven'.
[‡] Nut is also Nuit which is related to the word 'night'. The sun god Ra is also said to be self-born from Nu (Budge 1987: 37).

Epitheus: Yes, and we find too an identical mention of Yahweh, who is known as the one who holds up the heavens; and having himself separated into two the original androgynous form of the progenitors Adam and Eve.[152*]

Thaeo: And we also know Cronos and Rhea defeated the serpents Ophion (Ophioneus), Eurynome, and their children (Ophionidae), casting them down into Tartaros (Ogenos); and by doing so freed the world and came to rule the heavens. Orpheus, leaning upon his lyre, sang a song about this, of the bygone age when earth, sky, and sea were amassed together within a single form; of how after a deadly contest they became separate from one another; of how the stars, the moon, and the sun's path are faithful on their ways; how the mountains came into being; how the Nymphs and their boisterous rivers and all the beasts of earth came to be. And he told how in the earliest age Ophion and Eurynome, daughter of Oceanus, ruled the world from snow-peaked Olympus, and how they were each deposed: Cronos replacing Ophion and Rhea replacing Eurynome; and of their fall into the depths of Oceanus, while their usurpers came to rule over the joyful Titans. This all when father Zeus was but an infant inhabiting the Dictaean cave, still only with the concerns of a newborn; and long before the Cyclopes, born of Gaia, had given him his thunderbolts, the thunder and lightning which were to become his famous weapons.[153]

And Rhea, who is also called Cybele, was known among the Romans as Ops. Ops is likewise associated with the Milky Way and at the time when she brought to Saturn (Cronos) a stone in place of the child she had borne (Jupiter), he doubted her veracity and thus ordered her to offer it her milk. And when she squeezed her breast, the milk which flowed forth became the arc of the Milky Way.[†]

Epitheus: That is truly satisfying.

---

[*] This is like the figure of Meschia in the Persian story of the garden of Heden, who is divided into male and female, Meschia and Meschiana (Howey 1955: 114). Simile is used to compare the support between a male and female with that between the heaven and earth. ('Kabbalah'; see Barnstone 1984: 146)

[†] This story also applies to Hera with Heracles and Mercury (Hermes).

Thaeo: So then too we find it said of Sarasvati, the (Hindu) goddess of the sky's river (Milky Way),

> Sarasvati, your inexhaustible breast flows with the food of life with which you provide anything one might desire. Giving freely treasure, wealth, and rich gifts–bring it within reach that we might suck.[154]

And the sky bull (Dyaus) and the earth cow (Prsni) are also said to provide nourishment to man,[155] as did the Egyptian cow Hathor who was to give the departed their food from the sacred sycamore.[156]

Epitheus: Yes.

Thaeo: Likewise both Nut and Geb were known to be the providers of food for both the living and the dead;[157] and let us not forget there are also Asherah and Anat, who were known as the two 'wet-nurses' of the gods,[*] with Asherah also being called the 'mother of all living'.

Epitheus: Truly.

Thaeo: And we also know that Shiva's wife Parvati was the 'mother of all living' and was also known as Annapurna, the goddess of food, who among the ancient Romans was known as Anna Perenna ('eternal serpent').

And as spirits were known to return to Shiva, they travelled along the course of the Milky Way, known as the 'way of spirits', which was also the river which provided their nourishment.

Epitheus: And this seems rather like the male and female Leviathan who become the food for the pious in the world to come;[†] for is it not also said that, as with Shiva, that the spirit returns to God?[158]

---

[*] As are Isis and Nephthys
[†] The female Leviathan was killed and pickled, while the male Leviathan will be attacked by angels in the final days before Leviathan and Behemoth engage in a contest which claims both their lives. ('Haggadah'; see Barnstone 1984: 22) The role of providing food for the righteous is also

Thaeo: Indeed, it is so. And according to Macrobius the spirit travels in the form of a bird to the Milky Way to then return back to the material world in a never-ending cycle of rebirths.[159]   And the Egyptians, like the Orphics, believed that spirits made their way into heaven to become one among the stars.[160]

Epitheus: Certainly.

Thaeo: And does not the encircled serpent symbolize both the soul of the universe and time without end?[*] And that this coil of eternity is represented in the serpent which is wrapped around the figures of Erechthonios, Serapis, Harpocrates, and Mithras.

Epitheus: Indeed, it would seem to be none other.

Thaeo: So this brings us back to the figure of Ouroboros, which itself is a form representing the never-terminating cycle of ends and beginnings.

Epitheus: Truly so.

---

taken by Leviathan and Behemoth. This is somewhat like Brimir's hall, said to provide plentiful drink after Ragnarok, the end of the world.

[*] This is a Christian Gnostic concept. Celsus records that Leviathan was known among Christians as the 'soul of the universe' which was represented by a single large circle, where ten smaller circles were shown around its circumference, with a line bisecting the diagram which represented Tartarus. (see Hoffman 1987: 96)

CHAPTER 15

Thaeo: So we might suspect that the name of the eternal Knouphis (Kneph) arises from '*knu-ophis*' ('serpent Knu'), which thus makes him equivalent to Nu, the primordial abyss, which is likewise said to be the soul of the universe.[*]

And Ptah ('one who opens') was the self-born creator who arose from the Flood of Nu appearing as the primordial mound ('*ben-ben*').[†] Ptah dreamed the world into form before he uttered it into existence, which first came forth as the Apis, the force of generation, known as the 'repetition of Ptah'.

The Apis as we have seen is equivalent to Serapis, who is taken to be either the son of Phoroneus or the son of Hercules.[161] And we can also recognize the Apis as similarly 'Ophis' ('serpent'), although Apis is known as the sacred bull while '*ophis*' means serpent.

Epitheus: Surely.

Thaeo: Then we might consider that, according to Plutarch, Serapis is the source of winds.[162] And we could also consider Ellil, the Mesopotamian fire god and source of winds, as being related to the fiery serpent; for Ellil is also the lord of time, and we know the perception of time arises from the movement of the heavens.

Epitheus: Just so.

Thaeo: While we know that Apis is also the same as Hapi, god of the Nile River,[‡] which was thought to arise from the cosmic abyss of Nu (Apsu).[§]

Epitheus: Indeed.

---

[*] The Egyptian name of the primordial waters 'Nu' (personified as Nun) might also be equated with 'Noe' or 'Noah'.

[†] The Egyptian 'self-born one' was known as Atum in Heliopolis, Ptah in Memphis, Amen in Thebes, and Ra in Hermopolis.

[‡] Apis was the ancient Greek rendering of the Egyptian Hapi.

[§] The name of the Mesopotamian god Ea, lord of the Apsu, means both 'life' and 'serpent' (Howey 1955: 89). Moreover, '*sar apsi*' is merely a variation on Serapis (Lehmann-Haupt quoted in de Santillana 1977: 314).

Thaeo: And Osiris is called the soul of the Nile,[163] while the Apis bull is an animal sacred to Osiris (Opas); and at the same time the two are said to be joined into one.[*] The Apis and Osiris were likewise the two bulls said to be brought into Egypt by Dionysos.[164] And Serapis is also said by Plutarch to be the visible representation of the soul of Osiris,[†] who creates the motion of the heavens and has dominion over baleful demons.[165]

Epitheus: That is so.

Thaeo: And the Hindu serpent Asootee, upon whose head rests the world, is the dragon who is said to swallow the moon or sun during an eclipse.[166] This makes him rather like the great serpent (of Egypt) Apophis, who lives within the celestial ocean, and from whom Horus protects the sun each day as it descends into Oceanus.

Epitheus: Yes.

Thaeo: It is also said that in Egypt they conceived of each of the four elements as being a different form of the serpent: that of the earth being a horned one, that of water being an undulating one, that of air being an erect and hissing one, while that of fire was a serpent rising upon its tail with a globe resting upon its head.[167]

Epitheus: Formidable.

Thaeo: And like the Egyptian god Kneph ('Nu'), for whom the good serpent spread himself out as a canopy above his boat, we find the Hindu god Vishnu ('Vish-Nu') to be found asleep upon the serpent goddess Isi (or Devi), who carried him over the waters of the deluge.[168] Likewise, Sesha is a seven-headed (or thousand-headed) god whom the lord Vishnu is said to be lying upon, and is also

---

[*] The soul of the sacrificed bull Hapi (Apis) joined then with Osiris (Asar) to become Osiris-Hapi or Asar-Apis (Serapis).

[†] Plutarch says, "It remains preferable to identify Osiris as being Dionysus and Serapis as being Osiris, for he acquired this name when his nature changed. This makes Serapis the god of everyone, just as Osiris truly is, but those who have been initiated into the sacred rites would already know this." (Plutarch, '*Isis and Osiris*' 28; see Babbitt 1936: 69)

known as Ananta-Sesha ('eternal Sesha'), who floats serenely upon the cosmic ocean. Whenever the serpent uncoils there follows a new creation, but it is said that he destroys his creation each time he coils up again.[*]

There is a story of Sesha, who was the eldest-born son of Kashyapa and Kadru, which says that his brothers were very cruel to him, so that he left them to become an ascetic, so much so that he was able to exist by consuming only air. After he lost every last bit of his physical bulk, Brahma was so impressed by his dedication that he asked him to name his reward. Sesha only requested that he be able to be possessed of a tranquil mind so that he might continue his ascetic life. Brahma granted this request gladly but also made an appeal to Sesha that he descend beneath the earth to support it so as to keep it steady. Sesha agreed and went to spend eternity down in the underworld, where he continues to hold up the earth upon his unwavering head.

Like Sesha it is the buffalo serpent Naga Padoha, who resides coiled beneath the tree of life, who when becoming weary tipped his head, upon which the world was sitting; and thus he was responsible for submerging the entire earth, and bringing about the Great Flood. And it is said that in shaking his head from time to time he is likewise responsible for causing earthquakes.[†]

Epitheus: Tremendous.

Thaeo: And there is yet another story to tell, when the lord of the universe wished to save the pious king Satyavrata, he said to him, "You, defeater of armies, know that seven days hence the three worlds will be inundated by a depth of doom, but you will find for yourself a great ark floating before you upon the savage seas, which I have sent to you. You will then collect every kind of medicinal plant, and every kind of seed, with a pair of every sort of beast, along with the Seven Sages, and you will enter the great ark and remain within; thereby you will be protected from the treacherous deluge.

---

[*] The stars are said to be held within Sesha's hood.
[†] The Nagas are seven-headed serpents who are shown with the body of an encoiled dragon with the head of an ox (Howey 1955: 374). The Nagas live in the ocean with Naga as their king, and they are said to be responsible for controlling the weather (Howey 1955: 261).

And you will find yourself upon a single large ocean without a glimmer of light, but for the holy radiance of the seven great sages. Then when the ark is buffeted by cantankerous winds, you will tie your boat with a long sea serpent onto my horn, for I will be there in the guise of an enormous golden fish."[169]

Epitheus: Wonderful.

Thaeo: And almighty Zeus, as you know, also carries the name of *cerastes*, which means the 'horned serpent'. And as you recall it was Zeus who sent the deluge of destruction upon the island of Atlantis, manifested in earthquakes and a great flood. And it is Poseidon, the stentorian roarer who encircles the earth, who is said to be responsible for the movements of both earth (earthquakes) and sea (tides), and is likewise known to take the form of a bull.

Epitheus: True enough.

Thaeo: Further, we might add that the (supreme Canaanite) god of the heavens El, was not only the 'father of time' but was likewise associated with the bull; and his abode was said to be at the source of the twin rivers, between the waters of the two seas.[170] Thus El in this way is similar to Shiva known as the 'lord of the meeting rivers'.*

Dilmun, where Utnapishtim lived eternally, is the place where there were rivers that ran into the sea. And this mouth of rivers is equivalent to the Greek 'springs of Oceanus' where the Elysian Fields were located, where we find the red-haired Rhadamanthus (son of Zeus by Europa), as Homer says,

'Concerning you, Menelaus, whose foster-father is Zeus,
It was not destined that you must resignedly face your fate
And to come to your end in Argos, city of many horses,
Instead, the gods decreed that you go to the Elysian Fields,
To the furthest reaches of the earth

---

* Utnapishtim is said to live at the 'mouth of the rivers' which is very like the 'sources of the springs' mentioned by Hesiod as existing in misty Tartaros (Hesiod, '*Theogony*' 738; see Lattimore 1991: 167), just as Yama was said to live at the place of the 'young waters' (Rig Veda 9.113; see O'Flaherty 1981: 133).

For that land is where red-haired Rhadamanthus resides
And where the lives of mortal men are of great ease
There comes no snow, nor tempests, nor rain to spoil it
And where Oceanus blows in a perpetual sea breeze,
The West Wind gusting in calms and refreshes men
It is because Helen is your wife, the reason they do this,
They know you as him who wed the daughter of Zeus.'[171]

Shiva, who is known as Ramanatha ('Lord of Rama'), is also red-haired like Rhadamanthus; and he rides upon the back of his white bull (Nandi) while holding aloft the heavens, which as we saw is the cosmic serpent Rahu, whom we take to be the Milky Way.

Epitheus: Assuredly.

Thaeo: Shiva is also the god of truth while his bull is the lord of *dharma* ('rightness'), and we find that Aphthah (Egyptian god of truth) is Ptah, who is equivalent to the Greek fire god Hephaistos (Roman Vulcan), a god of the underworld.

Epitheus: Indeed.

Thaeo: And the Egyptian (moon) god Thoth, like Ptah, is both a god of truth and known as the founder of the world, and (the sun god) Ra is said to himself stand upon 'truth' ('*maat*').[172] It also says of Osiris,

> Lord of Abydos, you rest yourself upon both Right and Truth, your limbs imbue the underworld throughout. You are the one for whom deceit and guile are unbearable.[173]

And it is said among the Hindus that 'truth' supports the earth just as the sun supports the sky.[174*]

Epitheus: Very true. Judgment

---

* Yahweh is said to establish the earth upon nothing, through his judgement alone. (Hellenistic Synagogal Prayers; see Charlesworth 2009, Vol. 2: 691; also Job 26:7)

Thaeo: So then let us consider that we have here a triumphant god of truth, and also a figure of serpentine form in the underworld. And from this we must assume that Shiva as god of truth was given the dual role of both balancing the circle of the earth and of supporting the vault of heaven.

Epitheus: From what has been said, it would be difficult to say otherwise.

Thaeo: And then at the same time, from the various contests between the sky god and serpent, we might identify that the vanquished serpent became the foundation of the world. And hence the term 'dead dragon' is used as an expression for the earth.[175*]

Epitheus: Truly.

Thaeo: We might then equate the bull and the serpent by assuming that the bull-serpent was envisaged to exist beneath the earth, with horns upon which he supported the pan of the world, while the female cow-serpent was the heavenly begetter spanning the sky.[†]

Epitheus: That would make perfect sense.

Thaeo: So now let us consider the Gaulic god Hu (Pridain), the 'ruler of the world', who was represented as a serpent, a horned serpent, or a dragon.[176] The form of this god's name (*'khu'*) we had determined before would lead to the names of both the gods Cronos and Uranus,[‡] and thus in initial form might have been something like **KHURAN** ('divine sky').[§]

---

[*] The word Iormungrund ('mighty ground'), similar to Iormungand, was a word used for 'earth'. (Simek 1993: 179-180)

[†] Shiva thus stands upon a bull and raises a serpent aloft, and is himself closely associated with them both at the same time. The Chumash Indians believed that two great serpents supported the earth from beneath (Krupp 1991: 278).

[‡] See *The Eden Enigma: A Dialogue*

[§] *'Khu'* is the Egyptian god of light and word for the everlasting spirit, and in Hebrew 'Hu' meaning 'I am' is how Yahweh addresses himself. The derivation of the name "Khuran" would thus be *'khur'* meaning 'spiritual'

Epitheus: Yes we did, I well recall.

Thaeo: Then we have the Phoenician name for the firmament, which is Ilus (El); and as we know this is also a name for Cronos.[177] And Cronos (**KHURAN**) we might also liken to 'crown' ('*corona*'), meaning the crown of the sky ('*stephanos*'), being the Milky Way.[*]

Epitheus: Without doubt.

Thaeo: So not only are the adversaries of the gods of serpentine form, but the sky gods themselves are as well,[†] as we conceived them to be in the name of the god of heaven, **EAVEH**.[‡] And likewise we find nearly every Greek god and goddess is associated with the serpent, as are many of the Egyptian and Hindu gods.[178]

Epitheus: Without question.

Thaeo: And the serpent also represents the cosmic sea, and there is reason to believe that serpentine gods were to have been the original inhabitants of that sea; for the earliest representations of divinity are represented in serpentine form, while the serpent itself, we already know, symbolizes 'eternity'.

Epitheus: Indeed.

Thaeo: The serpent was likewise seen to be a symbol of creative energy and birth, and of divine wisdom ('*hagia sophia*'). And '*hagia*' itself contains the word '*hag*' which is likewise the name of the serpent ('*hak*'); while the word 'divine' itself contains the name of the Milky Way and goddess of birth within it ('*ivi*').

---

or 'divine' and '*anu*' meaning 'heaven' or 'serpent', thus perhaps corresponding best to 'eternal serpent'.

[*] Cronos, like his father Ouranos, appears to be a god of the sky, the moon, and the tides; thus to the universal motion and the keeping of time ('*chronos*'), as Saturn is god of time and at times of serpentine form.

[†] Zeus, Cronos (Saturn), Apollo (Ophel), Hercules, and Osiris are associated with serpents. Add to this Hera, Rhea (Ops), Athena, Cybele (Demeter), Diana, Faunus, Cecrops, Ceres, Ea, Kneph, Opet, Ptah, Set, and Isis.

[‡] See *The Eden Enigma: A Dialogue*

Epitheus: Assuredly.

Thaeo: Then let us return again to our discourse concerning Medusa, for we also find that Medusa's head was held to be a token of divine wisdom,[179] which also associates her, more so, with Metis ('wisdom'), the mother of Athena.[*]

Epitheus: True.

Thaeo: And Athena is sometimes said to be the daughter of the winged Titan Pallas,[†] who after giving birth to the ravishing goddess attempted to rape her, and thus she fought against him and killed him. Then, similar to the slaying of the Gorgon, the flayed skin of Pallas became her protective *aegis* ('goat-skin').[‡] And so through this we might again consider the Gorgon to be the mother of Athena. And we learn too that Athena (Minerva) was even known to have actually been the slayer of the Gorgon.[180]

Epitheus: So I have heard.

Thaeo: The Gorgon's head, which was affixed to Athena's shield, was also used as an icon, with its benign face and frightful serpents symbolizing both healing and ruin.[181] And we might ask whether or not creation and destruction are to be viewed as separate forces or whether, as with the entwined serpents, they are merely both components of the same entity of existence.

Epitheus: We might well ask.

---

[*] Athena herself is said to be 'bright eyed' ('*glaukopis*') which is a quality also attributed to serpents.
[†] Selene is also given as the daughter of Pallas, son of Megamedes ('Great Medes'), suggesting that the two goddesses were identified with one another.
[‡] There is a close connection between the Gorgon and Athena, and Athena was actually known under the name of Gorgo on the island of Cerne, while the Attic Gorgon was born of the earth and slain by Athena. (Howey 1955: 164)

Thaeo: And this then I imagine could be the meaning of the serpent-bodied Cecrops and Ophiuchus (Triopas), who are locked in a perpetual combat with the serpent who we find is truly the other half of his own self, as Set is said to be the other half of Horus.[*]

Epitheus: Yes.

Thaeo: Then the serpent who is slain we must see as one-half of the being who performs the slaying; and taken together as the one who brings death and birth upon itself, the self-born one, representing the manifestation of eternity.

Epitheus: Incredible.

Thaeo: We also find Cecrops appearing as the progenitor of the Athenian race, who was said to have originally been a serpent but who later metamorphosed into a man.[182] Strabo tells us that the race called the Ophiogenae descended from a serpent who then transformed himself into a man,[183] and according to Aelian this was a serpent within Diana's sacred grove that mated with a woman who had accidently found her way inside.[184]

Epitheus: As you say.

Thaeo: And apart from the Athenians, many other peoples have imagined that their communal ancestor was either a serpent or a half-human half-serpent being,[†] while in Ceylon it was believed that the race of serpents had once been human, but had been reduced to their present state as a consequence of their own wickedness.[185]

Epitheus: But why then did these people believe that they had descended from serpents?

---

[*] See the discussion of the serpentine sitting gods in White (2008), p. 191.
[†] The first Europeans were said to be descended from a being who was half-woman and half-serpent (Ophiolatreia 2008: 110). Kings in Central American claimed descent from serpents (Howey 1955: 299), while the Aztec mother-goddess serpent is said to have given birth to twins, the progenitors of humankind (Howey 1955: 301).

Thaeo: A fine question, Epitheus. But that would be difficult to fathom, though it is said that sometime before the 'fall of man' that serpents were thought to have possessed arms and legs like humans, and this is suggested even in the garden of Eden, when it is said that from then on the serpent would go about on his belly.[*]

Epitheus: Indeed it does.

Thaeo: And this also recalls the ancestral king Erechthonios who is described as being half-human and half-serpent; and because he was born lame he was to have invented the chariot, upon which he then travelled through his realm, and thus is identified with the constellation of 'the charioteer' (*Auriga*). So in this way he is not unlike his father, the fire god Hephaistos, who was banished from heaven and is at times said to have been lamed by his fall to earth.

Epitheus: Just so.

Thaeo: And Hephaistos we must remember would be equivalent to **LEVI**, and we found that Moses was a child of **LEVI**, who was also to have been born out of the Nile.[†]

Epitheus: Yes.

Thaeo: Yet we might also consider how Athena could have been born out of the head of Zeus and from the River Triton at the same time.[‡] And how could Pegasus have been born both from the neck of Medusa and from a roiling spring, unless the two were viewed to be one and the same?

Epitheus: But what do you mean?

Thaeo: In other words, the idea was either that the wound became the source of the river or that the river was the deity itself; just as we find the Milky Way representing both a serpent as well as a river.

---

[*] This is also like Ahriman, a speaking serpent with legs in the Persian garden of Heden.
[†] See *The Eden Enigma: A Dialogue*
[‡] A Triton is described as being half-fish and half-man. (Budge 1988: 160)

Epitheus: Yes.

Thaeo: And recall that the birth of Zeus from Rhea was not only the event which caused the many springs of Ida to arise, but that she herself caused the cleansing flood-waters to be released from Mount Lycaon in Arcadia, which was the river Neda. And it was the Neda that flowed near the city of Lepreion, and combining with Nereus (the sea) gave rise to the primordial waters from which drank the sons of Arcas. Arcas (*Ursa Minor*) being the son of Callisto (*Ursa Major*), and Callisto being the daughter of King Lycaon of Arcadia, who himself is said to have been responsible for motivating Deucalion's great flood. And subsequent to infuriating Zeus we find Lycaon was turned into a wolf, while another wolf we know (Fenrir) is said to have been the source of the river Van ('hope').

Epitheus: Truly.

Thaeo: And just as in the case of Bergelmir, it was the killing of the primordial giant which released a surging river that first flooded the world. But we find this to also be an act of birth, if we think of Bergelmir as born from the flood as we saw in the release of Pegasus and Chrysaor; but also from the birth of Moses in the Nile and Noah in the flood, when we considered their names both arose from the word for 'birth'. And, in the case of Noah, he is remembered as the one man who survives; as in the case of Manu, who became the progenitor of all humanity; as indeed did Heimdall and Abraham, whose descendants, he is told, will outnumber the sands of the seashore and the stars in the sky.

Epitheus: Surely.

Thaeo: Thus we are speaking here of a cosmic event, a creation that also leads to the origin of mankind.

Epitheus: I could not agree more.

Thaeo: And recall that it is Metis and Zeus who give birth to Athena, which suggests that these two were likewise also the two cosmic serpents. Hephaistos, who was born first, freed his sister and thus

198

released the flood waters, creating the River Triton, though there is no specific mention of a flood in this story of Athena.

Epitheus: No, indeed.

Thaeo: And the severing of the Gorgon's head was also to have produced a spring, and we know the blood that came from the Gorgon could be used for healing and raising of the dead. Thus we might not be faulted for believing that the act of killing the Gorgon had likewise created the source of the well of immortality. And that Pegasus, sprung from the source of Oceanus or the blood of Medusa when she was beheaded, was at the same time the spring (*'pegai'*) which gave rise to his name. While it is also said of Pegasus that he himself stamped out a fissure with his hoof which gave rise to a fount of poetic inspiration (Hippocrene).[*]

Epitheus: Truly, he did.

Thaeo: And we might well accept that the River Triton became the source of the flood waters which inundated the entire earth as the Milky Way, while the source and spring of eternity was itself the constellation of *Pegasus*.

Epitheus: One hardly need say more.

Thaeo: This suggests to me that the Gorgon Medusa was held to represent the divine unity, and the point at which all things came together. And perhaps this is why we find the Gorgon's head used with such frequency as an important icon, and an emblem representing rebirth, from the view that out of destruction comes rejuvenation.[†] The simple message symbolized by the encircled serpent, that the end is also the beginning.

Epitheus: Yes, it is deeply fathomable.

---

[*] Poseidon formed the Erechthean spring with a blow from his trident, but it is also said he released a fierce horse. Thus we can presume that the horse and the spring were one and the same.

[†] Like Medusa and Shiva, Pegasus is sometimes thought of as a 'rejuvenator' and as a 'destroyer'. (Olcott 2004: 302)

Thaeo: And many gods closely associated with serpents likewise fill the role of healing, as do Thoth, Aesculepius, Serapis, Kneph, Shiva, and Isis; Isis herself being an Egyptian goddess of life and healing, though she is also known for her vengeful aspect in which she wore a holy diadem of serpents upon her head. From Plutarch we know that one of the names of the goddess of life (Isis) was Muth, meaning 'mother', the one who gives birth to death.[*] And this is rather like Eve, who was both recognized as being the 'mother of all' and also as the 'bringer of death'.[†] So again we have the serpent representing the cycle of regeneration.

Epitheus: Assuredly.

Thaeo: And do you recall that when Set was brought in chains before Isis that she set him free, causing Horus to remove the holy diadem from her head, which Thoth then replaces with a helmet in the form of a cow's head?[186]

Epitheus: Indeed, I do.

Thaeo: Then can we presume that these two pieces of wearing apparel truly represent dual aspects of the goddess herself, as the one who gives birth and replenishes (cow) and the one who swallows and destroys (serpent)?[‡]

Epitheus: Clearly, they must.

Thaeo: Thus the time the goddess assumes the aspect of the cow would clearly have occurred during the wet season (starting in the spring when *Taurus* rules); while when she takes the aspect of the

---

[*] Eusebius tells us that Muth was the son of Saturn and Rhea (Ops), who was Death.

[†] Isis is the same as the Hindu Isi, whose consort is Isa, and equivalent to Adam (Ish) and Eve (Ishah). (Deane 2008: 163)

[‡] Isis was compared to Pasht in her benevolent aspect and Sekhet in her vengeful aspect (St. Clair 1898: 281). Hera is also described and shown as a cow as well as a serpent, as is the Egyptian goddess Hathor who is often identical with Isis. Hera is even said to drive the sun (*The Iliad* xviii, 276; Fagles 1990: 475).

serpent, that this would occur during the dry season (starting in the autumn when *Scorpius* rules).[*] And Plutarch mentions that the death of Osiris occurred when the sun was in *Scorpius* (autumnal equinox), and thus during this time Isis assumed her inglorious phase; but after the restoration of Osiris and the defeat of Set by Horus, she regains the aspect of the cow with the aid of divine Thoth.[†]

And Horus and Set were to have battled first as men and then in the form of bears, and because Isis came to the aid of Set, Horus in anger beheaded her.[187] And just as we find Horus beheading Isis when she represents the serpent, where Horus is represented by the hunter *Orion*, she then takes on the appearance of a heifer. Horus was known as the Great Bull, and we know that the centaur Chiron was known by the title of the 'Bull Killer'[188] and represented by the bowman *Sagittarius*, who would then be his uncle Set.[‡]

This corresponds with the notion that the summer is ruled by the sun (serpent) while the winter is ruled by the moon (cow), with the life-giving rain (milk) alternating with the parching dry heat (poison). And this associates too with the commonplace symbolism where the serpent is often emblematic of the sun as the cow is of the moon.

Epitheus: Precisely so.

---

[*] There are three serpents along the radial axis of *Scorpius*, the other two being *Draco* and *Serpens Caput*, the head of *Draco* being called 'Isis' (Olcott 2004: 190). The constellation *Scorpius* is associated with the goddess of war Ishara, which is also a name for the goddess Venus (White 2008: 179). Nephthys, the sister and other half of Isis, was also called Venus (Plutarch, '*Isis and Osiris*' 12; see Babbitt 1936: 33).

[†] One form of Isis associates her with the goddess Serq (Selk) the Egyptian goddess of protection, who wears a scorpion upon her head. Isis is also said to be accompanied by seven scorpions, which could be because the *vernal equinox* occurs within the seventh month following the *autumnal equinox*. Likewise there were seven Hathors. This would be as Plutarch mentions, which is that the *summer solstice* occurs in the seventh month following the *winter solstice*. This is so because the year divided in half is about 182 days, thus with months 28 days long the seventh month would be between 168 and 196 days after the winter solstice.

[‡] The constellations of *Taurus* and *Sagittarius* and likewise *Scorpius* and *Orion* are opposite each other in the sky.

201

Thaeo: Then there is something more, for we might also relate this to the mother goddess Demeter, known sometimes as Demeter Erinys ('Demeter Fury').[*] Since the Furies are known too to have had serpents for hair; and Demeter Erinys is likewise shown with the appearance of a Gorgon.[†] And just as Poseidon pursued the beautiful Medusa, so too he is said to have chased fleet Demeter, who took the form of a mare and hid in the pastures among King Onkios' herd. Yet Poseidon, taking the shape of a stallion, sought her out and because of this tryst Demeter bore a daughter named Despoina and the horse Arion. And this rape incensed the goddess so very greatly that she is hid within a cave in the mountains of Arcadia; though washing herself in the River Ladon assuaged her fury and thus she became Demeter Lousia ('Demeter Cleansed'). And here too we see the dual aspect of the goddess, the mild and the savage: kind Medusa and the dreaded Gorgon, serpent Isis and cow Isis, and Demeter Lousia and Demeter Erinys. Thus both represent the tranquil, attractive and alternately the irate, fearsome sides of the goddess.[‡]

Epitheus: Clearly, they do.

Thaeo: This makes the dual aspects of the goddess Isis equivalent to the duel between Horus (hawk) and Set (serpent), which reflects the continuing conflict whereby Set is never fully defeated and escapes to return again, as indeed happens in the conflict between Balder and Hod. And here we find that although Balder is able to return when the entire world weeps for him, he cannot remain and must soon return again into Hel's domain.

---

[*] The Erinys (Furies) and Muses were also beings of dual aspects.

[†] In one Orphic Hymn to the Furies (lxix) they are described as appearing with both snakes for hair and flashing death-dealing eyes (see Taylor 2007: 134). Isis also possesses such a deadly stare in her vengeful aspect, and she was known in Hermopolis as the foremost of Muses (Plutarch, '*Isis and Osiris*' 3; see Babbitt 1936: 11).

[‡] Because of Demeter's obvious link with agriculture, it is possible that the beheading of the Gorgon, with the emerging 'spring' (Pegasus) and 'golden blade' (Chrysaor), were interpreted at some point to relate to the transition into the growing season. Thus explaining why the battle against Grendel and other beasts occurs at the time of the winter solstice.

Epitheus: Just so.

Thaeo: And Isis' move to free Set would then merely arise from her recognition that Set and Horus are truly one and the same,[189] and that one cannot be destroyed without destroying the other. For they were engaged in the perpetual battle of light and darkness, and at the same time were conceived as two heads joined to a single body.[190]* Thus Isis knew it a necessary to maintain the balance of the universe.†

Epitheus: This again makes perfect sense.

Thaeo: Then it occurs to me that this also gives meaning to the phrase "the bull begot a serpent and the serpent begot a bull".‡ For does this not also represent the alternating constellations of *Taurus* and *Scorpius*, as both are at opposite ends of the Milky Way, so that when one of them sets the other rises?

Epitheus: It does appear so.

Thaeo: And this alternation would explain why the same generative principles alternate or combine in the serpent (*serpas*) and the bull (*apis*), in the figure of Serapis.§

Epitheus: Good heavens.

Thaeo: So thus encapsulated in the image of the Apis, who holds the dual quality of both bull and serpent, whichever one resides beneath the earth also takes on the role of supporting it upon its horns.

Epitheus: Everything falls neatly into place.

---

* They are shown with Set having either the head of an ass or vulture and Horus with his usual hawk's head. (St. Clair 1898: 383)
† This might relate to the *Pegasus* constellation, which is often identified with a bird and clearly has a bird's head, but beneath he is assumed to be within the water. This also recalls the image of Abraxas who is shown to have the head of a rooster but legs as twin serpents.
‡ This is from Clement of Alexandria's '*Protrepikos Pros Hallenas*' (2.16)
§ The river god Achelous turned himself into a serpent and then a bull in his contest with Hercules.

Thaeo: What is not clear to me though is precisely why this is of significance; unless it is perhaps because the bull represented generation and the serpent regeneration. And thus we might presume that it was taken merely as a metaphor for life; the cycle of mortal to immortal and then back to mortal again.

Epitheus: That is entirely satisfactory to me.

Thaeo: Then it seems we have fulfilled the fullness of our inquiry, Epitheus, and we also find that the dawn will soon be upon us. For the discussion has wrought within us, though keeping us away from sleep, enough stimulation to keep us fully awake for the entire night. Though before we retire I am inclined to provide just one further story, as it seems to me that everything we have said might be tied together within it. And this is the (Chippewa) tribal story of Manobozho, if you are prepared to hear it, in the manner perhaps of a bedtime story.

Epitheus: By all means, Thaeo, let us finish off with a bang.

Thaeo: Good then, so it begins,

When Manobozho was returning home from a long journey he could not find his young cousin and shouted for him, but it was of no use. So he went out searching and gazed over the sand for footprints, but there he found the tell-tale trail of the serpent Meshekenabek, and now knew that his cousin had been taken by his vile adversary. So he took his bow and arrows and followed after the trail, and went through the river and over the mountain until he came to the Devils Lake (Manitou Lake) where the trail came to an end as it entered the water. This was the lair of Meshekenabek along with a host of his servants and companions, who assumed serpentine form. They could be seen deep within the waters, and there in the center of the many slithering shapes was his hated foe, coiled about his fearful cousin. He could see the creature's blood-red head and fiery eyes, with armor-hard scales which glinted every hue and shade. Manobozho could not contain his anger and pledged to vanquish his adversary, commanding the clouds to leave the heavens and the winds to calm, and the sun to burn down with great heat upon the waters of the lake. In doing so he thought Meshekenabek might relocate himself into the shade of the trees which lined the bank.

And he hid himself in the form of a stump of an old tree, right where he expected them to take shelter from the sun's heat. This happened and Meshekenabek moved out of the waters with his company of evil serpents, and they suspected that the old trunk, which they had not seen before, might be their enemy Manobozho in disguise. So one of them encoiled it with his tail and attempted to pull it free, but it held firm; and they continued on into the shade of the trees behind their king.

But while they were all sleeping, there in the coolness of the shade, Manobozho took out his bow, set an arrow into it, and let it fly straight into the heart of Meshekenabek. He bawled out in agony so that the mountains trembled. He quickly made his escape back into the lake followed by his many companions, and there they rent Manobozho's cousin into countless pieces. But once Meshekenabek knew that his wound was fatal he became ten times more savage, and he and his companions caused the lake waters to rise from their infernal depths.

It began to spread out and surged with the roar of a tempest, pushing forward rocks and trees with relentless force. The injured and bleeding Great Serpent was travelling upon the foremost wave, his red eyes terrible to see, with the poisonous exhalations of his companions hissing within the wave as it swelled up behind the fleeing Manobozho. He ran and thought of warning his village to save both them and his children; so as he ran by he called to them to flee at once into the mountains, for the Great Serpent was causing a flood to spread over the earth in his dying fury, which would not spare a single one.

He eventually found refuge upon a tall mountain that was beyond Lake Superior, where there were also many people and animals who had come there to escape the rising flood waters, which had already come to submerge the highest hills. Yet the waters rose evermore so that even the other mountains were overwhelmed by it, all but for the tallest one which Manobozho had escaped to.

Thinking even then they might still be threatened, he began to gather logs together and made for them a raft, and all of the people and animals climbed aboard. And just in time too because then the rising deluge climbed over the last visible mountain top, the one they had taken refuge upon. Then they were alone on the wild foaming sea, and for many days they rode the waters and many of them died, some grew despondent, and others asked Manobozho if he might cause the flood to subside so that they might be saved.

The dreaded foe Meshekenabek was now dead but Manobozho could not bring the land back until he first had a piece of earth from which to build it. So the beaver stepped forward and offered to dive down into the depths to find the earth he needed. He did so with great mettle but was drowned by the vicious currents. Next the otter came forward, but he too shared the same fate. Then the muskrat went beneath the waters to make the attempt, but he was below the surface for such a long time that all had given him up for dead; when in an instant he broke the surface and weakly made his way back to the raft. He was too weary to speak and as soon as he made it back upon the raft he was dead, but within his claws they found a few pieces of mud.

Manobozho took these pieces from the muskrat's paws and blew them over the flood waters. As soon as he had done so they began to lower and retreat until they were finally gone, with nothing left but the thick mud which Manobozho had blown upon the sea. Meshekenabek's evil clan was no longer heartened, knowing their master was no more, and so they fled in fear into the depths of Devils Lake and did not dare venture forth from there again. And to the beaver, the otter, and the muskrat the tribe of Indians from henceforth held them to be sacred creatures, and considered them as their brothers, so that they never would dare to kill or harm any one of them.

So what do we have here but the killing of the demon serpent, the arising of the flood, and the saving of both man and animal upon a raft. And we find the name Manobozho is similar to that of (the Hindu) Manu, the man who escapes the flood which arises after Indra slays the dragon Vrtra.

While Manobozho's dreaded foe here is none other than Meshekenabek who shares a similar name with Melchizedek, the King of Salem, who encounters Abraham after his defeat of King

Chedorlaomer ('hand of sheafs'),[*] in an episode wherein Abraham's nephew (Lot) has been captured.[†]

And Manobozho (Minabozho) sometimes takes the form of the rabbit, which could associate him with the moon, which shows upon it a rabbit mixing the drink of immortality. And this drink was to have been formed from the blood of a dragon,[191] just as we know the blood of the Gorgon was capable of restoring life.

This encounter of Manobozho, finding his adversary in the middle of a lake, likewise closely resembles the story of Grendel, wherein the confrontation takes place within a swamp which held its own serpentine swarm. And as we saw Vrtra's followers flee into the ocean after his defeat, we find just the same happens here among the followers of Meshekenabek.[‡]

So if you are satisfied that we have come to a sensible conclusion, Epitheus, then at this early hour we have found a suitable place to refrain for now.

Epitheus: I am.

---

[*] Genesis 14

[†] The 'Book of Jubilees' associates the capture of Lot with Abraham looking to the north, south, east, and west. (12:19; see Charlesworth 2009, Vol. 2: 83) The 'Sky Spirit' of the Choctaw Indians, equivalent to Manobozho, is named Aba.

[‡] The ocean was also the dwelling place of the Nagas.

Read other books from the Paleoastronomy Series:

Volume 1: The Eden Enigma

Volume 2: Roar of the Tempests

Volume 3: The Death of King David

Volume 4: The Zodiac Mysteries

Volume 5: Blood & Incest

Visit: www.timothyjstephany.com

Bibliography

Ananikian, Mardiros H. <u>Armenian Mythology</u>. 1922. Los Angeles: Indo-European, 2010.

Anonymous. <u>Ophiolatreia: Serpent Worship, Rites & Mysteries</u>. 1889. n.l.: Forgotten Books, 2008.

Apollodorus. <u>The Library of Greek Mythology</u>. 1997. Trans. Robin Hard. New York: Oxford, 1998.

Apollonius of Rhodes. <u>The Voyage of Argo</u>. 1959. Trans. E. V. Rieu. London: Penguin, 1971.

Barnstone, Willis, ed. <u>The Other Bible</u>. San Francisco: Harper, 1984.

Bonfante, Larissa and. Judith Swaddling. <u>Etruscan Myths</u>. Austin: University of Texas, 2006.

Boyce, Mary, trans. ed. <u>Textual Sources for the Study of Zoroastrianism</u>. 1984. Chicago: University of Chicago, 1990.

Budge, E. A. Wallis. <u>Egyptian Religion: Egyptian Ideas of the Future Life</u>. 1899. London: Arkana, 1987.

Budge, E. A. Wallis. <u>Egyptian Magic.</u> 1899. London: Arkana, 1988.

Byock, Jesse L., trans. <u>The Saga of King Hrolf Kraki</u>. London: Penguin, 1998.

Caesar, Julius. <u>The Gallic War and Other Writings</u>. Trans. Moses Hadas. New York: Modern Library, 1957.

Celsus. <u>On the True Doctrine: A Discourse Against the Christians</u>. Trans. R. Joseph Hoffman. Oxford: Oxford University, 1987.

Charlesworth, James H., ed. <u>The Old Testament Pseudepigrapha</u> <u>Vol. 1: Apocalyptic Literature and Testaments</u>. 1983. Peabody, Mass: Hendrickson, 2009.

Charlesworth, James H., ed. <u>The Old Testament Pseudepigrapha</u> <u>Vol. 2: Expansions of the "Old Testament" and Legends, Wisdom</u> <u>and Philosophical Literature, Prayers, Psalms, and Odes, Fragments</u> <u>of Lost Judeo-Hellenistic Works</u>. 1983. Peabody, Mass: Hendrickson, 2009.

Condos, Theony. <u>Star Myths of the Greeks and Romans: A</u> <u>Sourcebook</u>. Grand Rapids: Phanes, 1997.

Coogan, Michael David. <u>Stories from Ancient Canaan</u>. Louisville: Westminster, 1978.

Dalley, Stephanie, trans. <u>Myths from Mesopotamia</u>. 1989. New York: Oxford, 2000.

Deane, John Bathurst. <u>Worship of the Serpent: Traced Throughout</u> <u>the World</u>. 1833. n.l.: Forgotten Books, 2008.

de Santillana, Giorgio and. Hertha von Dechend. <u>Hamlet's Mill: An</u> <u>Essay Investigating the Origins of Human Knowledge and its</u> <u>Transmission through Myth</u>. 1969. Boston: Godine, 1977.

Frazer, James George. <u>Folklore in the Old Testament: Studies in</u> <u>Comparative Religion, Legend, and Law (Abridged Edition)</u>. New York: Avenel, 1988.

Friedman, Richard Elliott. <u>The Bible with Sources Revealed: A New</u> <u>View into the Five Books of Moses</u>. New York: HarperCollins. 2003.

Grammaticus, Saxo. <u>The History of the Danes: Books I-IX</u>. Trans. Peter Fisher. Ed. Hilda Ellis Davidson. Cambridge: D. S. Brewer, 1979 and 1980.

Grigsby, John. <u>Beowulf & Grendel: The Truth Behind England's Oldest Legend</u>. London: Watkins, 2005.

Grimm, Jacob. <u>Teutonic Mythology</u>. 1883, 1888. Trans. Ed. James Steven Stallybrass. 4 vols. New York: Dover, 2004.

Harley, Timothy. <u>Moon Lore</u>. 1885. Tokyo: Charles E. Tuttle, 1970.

Heaney, Seamus, trans. <u>Beowulf</u>. New York: Farrar, Straus & Giroux, 2000.

Hesiod. <u>The Works and Days, Theogony, The Shield of Herakles</u>. 1959. Trans. Richmond Lattimore. Ann Arbor: University of Michigan, 1991.

Homer. <u>The Iliad</u>. Trans. Robert Fagles. New York: Viking, 1990.

Howey, M. Oldfield. <u>The Encircled Serpent: A Study of Serpent Symbolism in All Countries and Ages</u>. New York: Arthur Richmond, 1955.

Josephus. <u>Josephus: The Complete Works</u>. 1737. Trans. William Whiston. Nashville: Thomas Nelson. 1998.

Keith, A. Berriedale and. Albert J. Carnoy. <u>Mythology of All Races</u>. Vol. VI (Indian, Iranian). New York: Cooper Square Publishers, 1964.

Krupp, E. C. <u>Beyond the Blue Horizon: Myths and Legends of the Sun, Moon, Stars, and Planets</u>. New York: HarperCollins, 1991.

Larrington, Carolyne, trans. <u>The Poetic Edda</u>. 1996. New York: Oxford, 1999.

Lonnrot, Elias. <u>The Kalevala</u>. Trans. Keith Bosley. New York: Oxford, 1989.

Mair, A. W. and. G. R. Mair, trans. Callimachus, Lycophron, Aratus. 1921. Cambridge: Harvard, 2006.

McCulloch, J. A. Mythology of All Races. Vol. II (Eddic). New York : Cooper Square Publishers, 1964.

Ovid. The Metamorphoses of Ovid. Trans. Allen Mandelbaum. San Diego: Harcourt, 1993.

O'Flaherty, Wendy Doniger, trans. Rig Veda. London: Penguin, 1981.

Olcott, William Tyler. Star Lore: Myths, Legends, and Facts. 1911. New York: Dover, 2004.

Pausanias. Guide to Greece: Vol. 1 Central Greece. Trans. Peter Levi. 1971. London, Penguin, 1979.

Pausanias. Guide to Greece: Vol. 2 Southern Greece. Trans. Peter Levi. 1971. London, Penguin, 1979.

Pindar. The Complete Odes. Trans. Anthony Verity. New York: Oxford, 2007.

Plutarch. Moralia, Vol. V. Trans. Frank Cole Babbitt. Cambridge: Harvard, 1936.

Ramanujan, A. K. Speaking of Siva. London: Penguin, 1973.

Simek, Rudolf. Dictionary of Northern Mythology. 1984. Trans. Angela Hall. Cambridge: D. S. Brewer, 1993.

Smith, Mark S. The Early History of God: Yahweh and the Other Deities in Ancient Israel. 1990. Grand Rapids: Eerdmans. 2002.

St. Clair, George. Creation Records Discovered in Egypt. London: Strand, 1898.

Staal, Julius D. W. The New Patterns in the Sky: Myths and Legends of the Stars. Blacksburg, Virginia: McDonald & Woodward, 1988.

Sturluson, Snorri. Edda. Trans. Ed. Anthony Faulkes. London: Everyman, 1987.

Orpheus. The Hymns of Orpheus: With the Life and Theology of Orpheus. 1792. Trans. Thomas Tyler. n.l.: Forgotten Books, 2008.

White, Gavin. Babylonian Star-Lore. London: Solaria, 2008.

Notes

[1] 'Enki and Ninhursag'

[2] Weidner or Esagila Chronicle

[3] The Gilgamesh Cycle (2014), p. 3; also 'Gilgamesh' 1.1, (see Dalley, 2000, p. 50)

[4] The Gilgamesh Cycle (2014), p. 4; also 'Gilgamesh' 1.1, (see Dalley, 2000, p. 51)

[5] The Gilgamesh Cycle (2014), pp. 25-28; also 'Gilgamesh' 2.6-3.1, (see Dalley, 2000, pp. 62-64)

[6] The Gilgamesh Cycle (2014), pp. 39-40; also 'Gilgamesh' 4.1, (see Dalley, 2000, pp. 67-68)

[7] The Gilgamesh Cycle (2014), pp. 49-51; also 'Gilgamesh' 4.5, (see Dalley, 2000, pp. 70-71)

[8] The Gilgamesh Cycle (2014), p. 54; also 'Gilgamesh' 5.1, (see Dalley, 2000, pp. 71-72)

[9] The Gilgamesh Cycle (2014), p. 59; also 'Gilgamesh' 5.3, (see Dalley, 2000, p. 75)

[10] The Gilgamesh Cycle (2014), p. 61; also 'Gilgamesh' 5.5, (see Dalley, 2000, p. 76)

[11] The Gilgamesh Cycle (2014), p. 62; also 'Gilgamesh' 5.6, (see Dalley, 2000, pp. 76-77)

[12] From Dr. Santiago Uceda Castillo, Director, Huaca de la Luna Archaeological Project; rendered by author

[13] Compare to Apollodorus, Library ii, 'Argive Mythology' (see Hard, 1998, pp. 58-67)

[14] White (2008), p. 185.

[15] White (2008), p. 185.

[16] White (2008), pp. 185-188.

[17] theoi.com, 'Khrysaor'

[18] Pseudo-Hyginus, Astronomica 2.29 (see Condos, 1997, p. 30)

[19] Paraphrase of Beowulf, lines 1-85.

[20] Beowulf, lines 99-104.

[21] Beowulf, lines 115-178.

[22] Beowulf, lines 710-765.

[23] Beowulf, lines 781-851.

[24] Beowulf, lines 1251-1259.

[25] Beowulf, lines 1279-1309.

[26] Beowulf, lines 1399-1464.

[27] Beowulf, lines 1494-1553.

[28] Beowulf, lines 1556-1607.

[29] Beowulf, lines 1612-1643.

[30] Apollodorus 2.5 (see Hard ,1998, p. 76)

[31] Apollodorus 2.5 (see Hard, 1998, p. 73)

[32] 'Saga of Hrolf Kraki' (see Byock, 1998, pp. 47-52)

[33] Sturluson, Edda, 'Skaldskaparmal' 16-17 (see Faulkes, 1987, pp. 77-80)

[34] See Apollodorus 2.7 (Hard, 1998, p. 91)

[35] Grammaticus, History of the Danes 51, (see Davidson, 1979, Vol. 1, p. 55)

[36] Grammaticus, History of the Danes 77, (see Davidson, 1979, Vol. 1, p. 83)

[37] Beowulf, lines 1365-1366 (see Heaney, 2000, p. 95)

[38] Brothers Grimm (1998), p. 249.

[39] Beowulf, lines 1570-1572 (see Heaney, 2000, p. 109)

[40] Olcott (2004), p. 127.

[41] Grigsby (2005), p. 186.

[42] White (2008), p. 231.

[43] Sturluson, Edda, 'Gylfaginning' 34 (see Faulkes, 1987, pp. 28-29)

[44] Sturluson, Edda, 'Gylfaginning' 51 (see Faulkes, 1987, p. 54) and Poetic Edda, 'Voluspa' 58 (see Larrington, 1999, p. 12)

[45] Sturluson, Edda, 'Gylfaginning' 14-15 (see Faulkes, 1987, p. 17)

[46] Poetic Edda, 'Grimnismal' 50 (see Larrington, 1999, p. 59)

[47] Poetic Edda, 'Vafthrudnismal' 6 f. (see Larrington, 1999, pp. 40-41)

[48] Poetic Edda, 'Sigdrifurmal' 13-14, 18 (see Larrington, 1999, p. 169)

[49] Poetic Edda, 'Voluspa' 37 (see Larrington, 1999, p. 9)

[50] Rig Veda 10.135 (see O'Flaherty, 1981, p. 55 'The Boy and the Chariot')

[51] See Pindar, 'Olympian Ode 3' (Verity, 2008, pp. 12)

[52] See Simek, 1993, p. 216 ('Mimameidr')

[53] See Simek, 1993, p. 109 ('Ginnungagap')

[54] See Boyce (1990), p. 71.

[55] Hesiod, Theogony 126-138 (see Lattimore, 1991, pp. 130-131)

[56] Hesiod, Theogony 161-187 (see Lattimore, 1991, pp. 132-134)

[57] Callimachus, I 'Hymn to Zeus' (see Loeb 129, p. 41)

[58] Apollodorus 1.5-2.1 (see Hard, 1998, pp. 27-28)

[59] Orphic Hymn, fragment

[60] Genesis 9:20-27

[61] Genesis 6:1-9:19

[62] Enuma Elish: The Babylonian Creation Epic (2013), pp. 96-97; also 'Atrahasis' 3.1, (see Dalley, 2000, pp. 29-30)

[63] Enuma Elish: The Babylonian Creation Epic (2013), pp. 97-98; also 'The Epic of Gilgamesh' 11.1, (see Dalley, 2000, p. 110)

[64] Enuma Elish: The Babylonian Creation Epic (2013), p. 98; also 'Atrahasis' 3.2, (see Dalley, 2000, p. 30)

[65] Enuma Elish: The Babylonian Creation Epic (2013), p. 98; also 'The Epic of Gilgamesh' 11.2, (see Dalley, 2000, p. 111)

[66] Enuma Elish: The Babylonian Creation Epic (2013), pp. 98-99; also 'Atrahasis' 3.2, (see Dalley, 2000, p. 31)

[67] Enuma Elish: The Babylonian Creation Epic (2013), pp. 99-100; also 'Atrahasis' 3.3, (see Dalley, 2000, p. 31)

[68] Enuma Elish: The Babylonian Creation Epic (2013), p. 100; also 'The Epic of Gilgamesh' 11.3, (see Dalley, 2000, p. 113)

[69] Enuma Elish: The Babylonian Creation Epic (2013), pp. 100-101; also 'Atrahasis' 3.4, (see Dalley, 2000, p. 32-33)

[70] Enuma Elish: The Babylonian Creation Epic (2013), p. 102; also 'The Epic of Gilgamesh' 11.3, (see Dalley, 2000, pp. 113-114)

[71] Enuma Elish: The Babylonian Creation Epic (2013), p. 103; also 'Atrahasis' 3.5-6, (see Dalley, 2000, pp. 33-34)

[72] Genesis 7:11

[73] Genesis 8:4

[74] Genesis 8:5

[75] Genesis 8:13

[76] Genesis 8:14

[77] Poetic Edda, 'Vafthrudnismal' 35 (see Larrington, 1999, p. 45)

[78] See Josephus, The Antiquities of the Jews 2.9.4 § 221.

[79] Josephus, The Antiquities of the Jews 2.9.2 §§ 205-206.

[80] Josephus, The Antiquities of the Jews 1.7.1 § 157; 'Book of Jubilees' 13:4, 13:9, 16:20 ff.

[81] 'Gilgamesh' 11.2, (see Dalley, 2000, pp. 111-112)

[82] Genesis 13:2

[83] Genesis 13:13

[84] Genesis 13:14-17

[85] Frazer (1988), p. 79, (Bhils, Central India)

[86] Frazer (1988), p. 96, (Micronesian)

[87] Frazer (1988) p. 121, (Tinneh, Hareskin Indians)

[88] Grammaticus, History of the Danes 10, (see Davidson, 1979, Vol. 1, p. 14)

[89] From 'Sorla Thattr'

[90] Sturluson, Edda, 'Skaldskaparmal' 16 (see Faulkes, 1987, p. 77)

[91] Beowulf, lines 1197-1201.

[92] Isaiah 27:1

[93] Psalm 74: 10-23

[94] Job 38:16-17 and Esdras 4:7-8. (the underworld is water)

[95] 'Haggadah', (see Barnstone, 1984, p. 19)

[96] Beowulf, lines 2663-2723.

[97] Howey (1955), pp. 182-83.

[98] Rig Veda 1.32 (see O'Flaherty, 1981, p. 149-151 'The Killing of Vrtra')

[99] Howey (1955), p. 372.

[100] Budge (1987), p. 30.

[101] Budge (1987), pp. 100, 151; Budge (1988), pp. 78-79.

[102] Maspero quoted in St. Clair (1898), p. 426

[103] pseudo-Apollodorus, Bibliotheke

[104] Hesiod, Theogony 820-869 (see Lattimore, 1991, pp. 172-175)

[105] Pindar, 'Pythian Ode 1' 16-28 (see Verity, 2008, pp. 41-42)

[106] Callimachus, IV 'Hymn to Delos' (Loeb 129, p. 97)

[107] Homeric Hymns, 'Hymn to Apollo' 349-362 (see Cashford, p. 46)

[108] Enuma Elish: The Babylonian Creation Epic (2013), pp. 25-26; also 'Epic of Creation' 4, (see Dalley, 2000, p. 251)

[109] Enuma Elish: The Babylonian Creation Epic (2013), pp. 27-28; also 'Epic of Creation' 4, (see Dalley, 2000, p. 253)

[110] Enuma Elish: The Babylonian Creation Epic (2013), p. 29; also 'Epic of Creation' 4, (see Dalley, 2000, p. 254)

[111] Enuma Elish: The Babylonian Creation Epic (2013), p. 33; also 'Epic of Creation' 5, (see Dalley, 2000, p. 257)

[112] White (2008), p. 83.

[113] Plato, 'Timaeus' 32-34

[114] Callimachus, VI 'Hymn to Demeter' (see Loeb 129, pp. 127-133) and Ovid, Metamorphoses 8.739 ff. (see Mandelbaum, 1993, p. 277), see theoi.com, 'Demeter Wrath: Erysikhthon, Triopas, or Aithon'.

[115] Ovid, Metamorphoses 8.843 ff. (see Mandelbaum, 1993, p. 281), see theoi.com, 'Demeter Wrath: Erysikhthon, Triopas, or Aithon'.

[116] Pseudo-Hyginus, Astronomica 2.14 (see Condos, 1997, pp. 142-143)

[117] 'Baal', (see Coogan ,1978, p. 107)

[118] Devara Dasimayya 25 (see Ramanujan, 1973, p. 98)

[119] White (2008), p. 183.

[120] White (2008), p. 192.

[121] White (2008), p. 184.

[122] White (2008), p. 175.

[123] 3 Baruch 5:1-3, (see Charlesworth, 2009, Vol. 1, pp. 668, 669); also 'Haggadah', (see Barnstone, 1984, p. 22)

[124] Plutarch, 'Isis and Osiris', Moralia V 362D (Loeb 306, p. 73)

[125] Howey (1955), pp. 67-68.

[126] White (2008), pp. 183-184.

[127] Poetic Edda, 'Song of Odin's Ravens' (see northvegr.org)

[128] See Friedman (2003), p. 36 footnote.

[129] Ophiolatreia (2008), p. 3.

[130] Budge (1987), p. 94.

[131] 2 Enoch (J) 24:4-27:4 (see Charlesworth, 2009, Vol. 1, pp. 142-146)

[132] Pyramid of Unas hieroglyphs, circa 2350 BC
[133] Howey (1955), p. 229.
[134] Deane (2008), p. 26.
[135] Howey (1955), p. 21 and Deane (2008), pp. 62-63.
[136] Howey (1955), p. 17.
[137] See Hoffman (1987), p. 96.
[138] Howey (1955), p. 227.
[139] White (2008), p. 165.
[140] White (2008), pp. 88-89.
[141] 'Baal', (see Coogan ,1978, p. 106)
[142] Isaiah 27:1
[143] White (2008), p. 50.
[144] White (2008), pp. 91, 51.
[145] Lonnrot, Kalevala 17:301-302, (see Bosley, 1989, p. 207)
[146] Lonnrot, Kalevala 2:301-322, (see Bosley, 1989, p. 19)
[147] Rig Veda 5.85 (see O'Flaherty, 1981, p. 211 'The Deeds of Varuna')
[148] Budge (1988), p. 217.
[149] Allama Prabhu 277 (see Ramanujan, 1973, p. 154)
[150] Devara Dasimayya 4 (see Ramanujan, 1973, p. 97)
[151] Maspero quoted in Howey (1955), pp. 376-77.
[152] 'Apocalypse of Adam' 1:4, (see Charlesworth, 2009, Vol. 1, p. 712)
[153] Apollonius of Rhodes, Argonautica 1.495 f. (see Rieu, 1971, pp. 49-50)
[154] Rig Veda 1.164 (see O'Flaherty, 1981, p. 81 'The Riddle of the Sacrifice')
[155] Rig Veda 6.70 (see O'Flaherty, 1981, pp. 206-207 'The Two Full of Butter')
[156] Budge (1987), pp. 108, 184.
[157] Budge (1987), p. 94.
[158] Ecclesiastes 12:5-7
[159] White (2008), pp. 11, 92.
[160] Budge (1987), p. 196.
[161] Apollodorus *supra*; Plutarch, ' Isis and Osiris' 29, Moralia V 362B (Loeb 306, p. 71)
[162] Plutarch, 'Isis and Osiris' 61, Moralia V 375F (Loeb 306, pp. 145, 147)
[163] Howey (1955), p. 24.
[164] Plutarch, 'Isis and Osiris' 56, Moralia V 362C (Loeb 306, p. 71), Plutarch considered this information unreliable.
[165] Plutarch, 'Isis and Osiris' 29, Moralia V 362D (Loeb 306, p. 71); Deane (2008), p. 65.
[166] Deane (2008), p. 40.
[167] Kircher given in Ophiolatreia (2008), p. 104
[168] Deane (2008), p. 35.

[169] Howey (1955), pp. 389-90.
[170] 'Aqhat', (see Coogan ,1978, p. 38) and 'Baal' (see Coogan ,1978, p. 95)
[171] Homer, Odyssey iv, 564
[172] Budge (1987), p. 34.
[173] Budge (1987), pp. 67-68.
[174] Rig Veda 10.85 (see O'Flaherty, 1981, p. 267 'The Marriage of Surya')
[175] de Santillana (1977), p. 228.
[176] Deane (2008), p. 129 and Howey (1955), p. 186.
[177] Ophiolatreia (2008), p. 46.
[178] Deane (2008), p. 219.
[179] Howey (1955), p. 161.
[180] Pseudo-Hyginus, Astronomica 2.12 (Condos, 1997, p. 158)
[181] Ophiolatreia (2008), p. 112.
[182] Deane (2008), p. 95.
[183] Strabo, lib. 13, given in Deane (2008), p. 55
[184] De Animal. lib. xii. c. 39, given in Deane (2008), p. 55
[185] Deane (2008), p. 38.
[186] Plutarch, 'Isis and Osiris' 19, Moralia V 358D (Loeb 306, p. 49)
[187] Budge (1988), p. 226.
[188] Olcott (2004), p. 318.
[189] Howey (1955), p. 26.
[190] Budge (1987), p. 97.
[191] Howey (1955), p. 272.